NTC's
Dictionary
of
COMMONPLACE
WORDS
in
REAL-LIFE CONTEXTS

NTC's
Dictionary
of
COMMONPLACE
WORDS
in
REAL-LIFE CONTEXTS

Anne Bertram

Printed on recyclable paper

NTC Publishing Group
Lincolnwood, Illinois USA

Library of Congress Cataloging-in-Publication Data

Bertram, Anne.
    NTC's dictionary of commonplace words in real-life contexts / Anne
Bertram.
        p. cm.
    Includes index.
    ISBN 0-8442-0845-0 (hardcove. -- ISBN 0-8442-0846-9 (pbk.)
    1. English language--United States--Terms and phrases. 2. Home
economics--Dictionaries. 3. Americanisms--Dictionaries. I. Title.
PE2389.B37 1997
423'.1--dc20   96-26183
                                                                    CIP

6 7 8 9 0 BC 9 8 7 6 S 9 8 7 6 5 4 3 2 1

Contents

Introduction

This is a dictionary about the commonplace things and activities associated with getting along in modern American society. Gadgets and machines in the home and workplace, as well as the vehicles that take us from home to work, present hundreds of special terms necessary for survival in the modern world. This dictionary includes terms commonly encountered in instructions for practical, everyday tasks, such as home maintenance, yard work, TV, VCR, and stereo operation, car repair, cooking, and computer use. The up-to-date word list deals with sewing, communications, plumbing, gardening, sports, hair care, construction, tools, kitchen appliances, travel, safety, and electronics, among other topics.

Going beyond the simple linking of a word and an object, the goal is to help users make these commonplace words a part of their everyday vocabulary.

The dictionary also provides a category index that lists all of the terms in a particular subject area. The dictionary is a boon to the new-to-English citizen as well as native speakers of English who are new to domestic matters or to the details of home maintenance.

A

18-wheeler a truck with eighteen wheels on five axles. (Informal.) □ *Jim drives an 18-wheeler for a living.* □ *I hate having to pass those 18-wheelers on a two-lane road.*

35 mm **1.** [of photographic film] 35 millimeters wide. □ *I need some 35-mm film.* □ *I got a 35-mm print of the movie.* **2.** [of a camera] using film that is 35 millimeters wide. □ *I use a 35-mm SLR.* □ *I have a disc camera and a 35 mm.*

45 an audio disc that plays at 45 revolutions per minute. (Informal. A 45 usually contains only one song per side.) □ *She has a collection of 45s of great hits of the 1960s.* □ *Will this turntable play a 45?*

78 a phonograph disc designed to be played at 78 revolutions per minute. (78s were popular in the first half of the 20th century but are no longer made.) □ *I have a set of 78s of John Phillip Sousa marches.* □ *This is a tape recording of an old 78.*

800 number a telephone number with an area code of 800. (There is no charge for calling an 800 NUMBER. Compare with 900 NUMBER.) □ *If you have any questions about our product, please call our 800 number.* □ *Is there an 800 number for that airline?*

900 number a telephone number with an area code of 900. (900 NUMBERS are services that charge a fee, usually some amount of money per minute. Compare with 800 NUMBER.) □ *The time and temperature service is not a free call. It's a 900 number.* □ *The fortune-teller had a 900 number.*

a/b switch a switch that allows one of two devices to operate. □ *Flip that a/b switch to "b" if you want to use the television antenna instead of cable.* □ *The two antennas are on an a/b switch. You can only use one of them at a time.*

A/C See AIR (CONDITIONING).

à la mode   served with ice cream. (Usually describes pie.) □ *Dessert was apple pie à la mode.* □ CUSTOMER: *I'll have some of that cherry pie, please.* WAITER: *Would you like it à la mode?*

absorbent   able to soak up liquid easily. □ *Which paper towel is the most absorbent?* □ *The absorbent mop made it easy to clean up the spill on the floor.*

abutment   a place where something rests on the thing that supports it. □ *There is a crack here in the concrete abutment.* □ *We sheltered under the bridge abutment, waiting for the rain to stop.*

AC   See ALTERNATING CURRENT.

accelerator (pedal)   a pedal that controls the speed of a vehicle. (See also BRAKE (PEDAL).) □ *She slammed her foot down on the accelerator pedal, and the car zoomed ahead.* □ *The pedal on the right is the accelerator. The one on the left is the brake. Don't get them confused!*

accessory   something added on. □ *This dress will have a whole new look with different accessories. Try it with a bright scarf and these dramatic earrings.* □ *The price of the computer includes accessories such as a mouse and a built-in modem.*

access road   a road leading to a specific place, such as a highway or a building. (See also FRONTAGE ROAD.) □ *To get to the mall, take the access road from the highway.* □ *There is an access road that leads to the park headquarters.*

Ace™ bandage   an elastic bandage used to support injured joints. □ *"Keep that sprained ankle wrapped in an Ace bandage," the doctor said.* □ *"There's an Ace bandage in the first-aid kit," Bill told me.*

acetaminophen   a drug which relieves pain. □ *Aspirin gives me a stomachache, so I use acetaminophen when I need a pain reliever.* □ *Joe took some acetaminophen for his headache.*

acetate   1. a plastic. □ *The technician printed the X-ray on a thin film of acetate.* □ *The architect traced the floor plan onto a sheet of acetate.* 2. a synthetic fabric. □ *The satin blouse looked like silk, but it was really acetate.* □ *The fabric is 40% rayon and 60% acetate.*

acetone   a chemical often used as a solvent. □ *I used acetone to clean the bearings on my bicycle.* □ *Acetone is the main ingredient in nail polish remover.*

acid   containing a high level of acid, as used to describe soil. (See also ALKALINE.) □ *Gardenias grow best in acid soil.* □ *The soil here is too acid to grow good hot peppers.*

acorn nut AND **cap nut**   a NUT with a dome that covers the end of a BOLT. □ *Loosen the acorn nut that holds the mechanism to the bicycle frame.* □ *Use an open-end wrench to tighten the cap nut.*

adapter   1. a device that allows things to work together even though they were not designed to do so. □ *The plug on the printer cable doesn't fit the plug on your computer. You'll need an adapter to get the printer hooked up.* □ *I have an adapter that lets me play my cassette tapes on an 8-track tape machine.* 2. a device that converts electric power into the form used by a particular machine. □ *You can run the tape player on batteries, or you can run it off an electrical outlet with this AC adapter.* □ *This adapter plugs into your car's cigarette lighter.*

additive   something, usually a chemical, added to something, such as food. □ *The cereal contains additives to keep it from spoiling.* □ *Our brand of lunch meat contains no additives whatsoever.*

adhesive   a substance that sticks things together. □ *What kind of adhesive should I use to fix this plastic cup?* □ *Epoxy is a powerful adhesive.*

aerator   a device which puts air bubbles into water. □ *The faucet on the kitchen sink has an aerator attached.* □ *You will need an aerator in the fish tank to give the fish enough oxygen.*

aerial a metal device used to pick up radio or television signals. (See also ANTENNA.) □ *The car's aerial automatically retracts when you turn off the motor.* □ *Jim has a big TV aerial up on the roof of his house.*

aerogram a piece of thin writing paper that folds up to form its own envelope, used for airmail letters. □ *I got an aerogram from my aunt in Australia.* □ *He bought a package of aerograms so he could send letters to his friend overseas.*

aerosol **1.** a very fine mist. □ *The antiseptic is available both as an aerosol and as an ointment.* □ *This asthma medicine must be dispensed as an aerosol.* **2.** a container which dispenses a very fine mist under pressure. □ *Some studies have shown that the chemicals used in aerosols are harmful to the environment.* □ *Aerosols can explode at high temperatures.*

afghan a crocheted or knitted blanket. □ *Grandma made an afghan to match my new rug.* □ *He wrapped an afghan around his shoulders to keep off the chill.*

aftershave a preparation, usually scented, to put on the skin after shaving. □ *This bracing aftershave tones your skin.* □ *I liked the smell of his aftershave.*

agitator the part of a WASHING MACHINE that makes clothes move around in the wash water. □ *Something's wrong with the washing machine. The agitator's not moving.* □ *A pair of pants got tangled around the agitator and fouled everything up.*

airbag a car safety device that inflates during a crash to keep passengers from hitting the DASH(BOARD) or the window. □ *This model has a driver's side airbag.* □ *All our cars have automatic seat belts and airbags.*

air (conditioning) AND **A/C** a device for cooling the air. (The abbreviation A/C is often used in advertising.) □ *The air conditioning in our building broke down. Boy, was it hot!* □ *It was hot in the car, so I turned on the air.* □ *For rent: 2 bedroom apartment, A/C, no pets.*

air duct   a pipe that carries hot or cold air through a building. ☐ *The air ducts run from the furnace in the basement to the warm-air registers in each room.* ☐ *We put a thick layer of insulation around the air duct.*

air filter   a device that traps dirt while letting air flow through. ☐ *The car's air filter cleans the air before it enters the carburetor.* ☐ *I put a new air filter in the air conditioner.*

(air) ionizer   a device that cleans indoor air. ☐ *When Joe heard that I have allergies, he recommended using an air ionizer.* ☐ *Have you noticed any difference in the air since you installed the ionizer?*

air pump   a device for pumping air into tires, balls, and other inflatable objects. ☐ *I always carry a hand-operated air pump with me on my bicycle in case I get a flat tire.* ☐ *The electric air pump filled the inflatable mattress in no time.*

airsickness bag   a bag you can use to vomit into if you get motion sickness on an airplane. (A euphemism.) ☐ *You will find an airsickness bag in the seat pocket in front of you.* ☐ *I felt sick, but I didn't have to use the airsickness bag.*

alarm clock   a clock that can be set to make a noise at a certain time. (ALARM CLOCKS are usually used to wake people up in the morning.) ☐ *I set my alarm clock for 7:15 AM.* ☐ *The alarm clock went off in the middle of the night.*

align   to put something in line with something else. ☐ *Align the red mark on the jar lid with the red mark on the rim of the jar.* ☐ *When did you last have your tires aligned?*

alkaline   having a high level of alkali (lime). (See also ACID.) ☐ *You can adjust the pH level of alkaline soil by adding wood chips or peat moss.* ☐ *The alkaline soil in New Mexico is perfect for growing really hot peppers.*

alkaline battery   a battery that lasts longer and gives more power than a carbon cell battery. ☐ *I bought an alkaline battery for my smoke detector.* ☐ *Alkaline batteries are expensive, but they last a long time.*

Allen™ wrench AND **hex wrench; hex key** a wrench which is hexagonal in cross-section and fits into a hexagonal hole in the head of a screw. □ *"You can't use a screwdriver on that kind of screw," Jill said. "You have to use an Allen wrench."* □ *I have a good set of hex wrenches.* □ *The hex key was hard to use because it had such a short handle.*

alligator pear an avocado. □ *For an appetizer, we had slices of nice, ripe alligator pear.* □ *To find out if an alligator pear is ripe, press lightly on the stem end. It should feel a little soft.*

allspice a spice, the berry of the allspice tree. □ *The pumpkin pie recipe calls for a quarter teaspoon of allspice.* □ *Allspice is the secret ingredient in Mary's salad dressing.*

alternate key AND **Alt key** a key, labeled "Alt," on a computer keyboard. □ *Hit "Alt-D." That is, hold down the Alt key and press D.* □ *The alternate key has a different function than the control key.*

alternating current AND **AC** an electrical current that reverses direction repeatedly, at a particular frequency. (The electrical current from most WALL SOCKETS is ALTERNATING CURRENT. Compare with DIRECT CURRENT.) □ *The CD player won't operate on AC. You need a DC adapter for it.* □ *Simply plug the toaster into any alternating current outlet.*

alternator a part of a car engine which produces electrical current. □ *As you drive the car around, the alternator will recharge the battery.* □ *The mechanic said that the alternator would need to be replaced.*

Alt key See ALTERNATE KEY.

aluminum foil AND **tin foil** a thin sheet of aluminum, usually used to wrap food. □ *We wrapped the leftover chicken in aluminum foil and put it in the refrigerator.* □ *Cover the top of the jar with tin foil.*

AM/FM See AMPLITUDE MODULATION and FREQUENCY MODULATION.

AM See AMPLITUDE MODULATION.

ambulance a vehicle used to take sick or injured people to the hospital. □ *The ambulance sped down the street, its siren wailing.* □ *I think she's choking! Call an ambulance!*

American Standard Code for Information Interchange AND **ASCII** a way of storing letters and numbers in a computer file so that many different programs can read them. (See also PLAIN TEXT.) □ *What is the ASCII code for a capital G?* □ *The American Standard Code for Information Interchange allows you to save the document in a form that can be transferred from one computer to another.*

ammo See AMMUNITION.

ammonia a chemical often used for cleaning. □ *He cleaned the windows with ammonia.* □ *This fertilizer contains ammonia.*

ammunition AND **ammo** material used in firing a gun; cartridges. (AMMO is slang.) □ *The clip contains six rounds of ammunition.* □ *The hunters stopped at a convenience store to pick up some ammo.*

amp See AMPLIFIER.

amplifier AND **amp** an electronic device which amplifies sound. □ *I hooked the CD player up to the amplifier and turned it on.* □ *She brought her electric guitar and her amp.*

amplitude modulation AND **AM** a kind of radio signal. (Compare with FREQUENCY MODULATION.) □ *My little transistor only gets amplitude modulation stations.* □ *Tune in to all-news radio, AM 760.*

analgesic AND **pain killer; pain reliever** a drug that relieves pain. (PAIN KILLER is informal.) □ *Aspirin is an analgesic.* □ *Do you have any pain killers? I have a terrible headache.* □ *This capsule contains two different kinds of pain reliever.*

analog   using a continuous scale rather than a discrete one. (ANALOG watches have hands and a dial rather than a digital display. ANALOG radio tuners have a pointer that moves smoothly along a scale rather than a digital readout.) □ *Jane thinks I'm old-fashioned for preferring analog watches to digital ones.* □ *Do they make analog radio tuners anymore?*

andiron   one of a pair of metal stands used to support firewood in a fireplace. □ *He bought a pair of brass andirons.* □ *They heaped the firewood on the andirons.*

anemometer   a device that measures wind speed. □ *The weather forecaster checked the anemometer. The wind was blowing at 12 miles per hour.* □ *Airplanes are equipped with anemometers.*

angel food cake   a light cake made with whipped egg whites. □ *Dessert was angel food cake and strawberries.* □ *Angel food cake is my favorite.*

annual   [of plants] lasting only one year. (Compare with PERENNIAL.) □ *Marigolds are a popular annual.* □ *Most vegetables are annuals, so you have to replant them every year.*

(answering) machine   a machine that answers a telephone, plays a message to the caller, and records a message from the caller. □ *This answering machine has a special feature. It can screen out callers you don't want to talk to.* □ *When I got home, there were four messages on the machine.*

antacid   a drug that reduces the amount of acid in the stomach. □ *My stomach felt upset, so I took an antacid.* □ *This antacid also gives upset stomach relief.*

antenna   a device that picks up radio or television signals. (See also AERIAL.) □ *Try moving the radio antenna around to see if you can get a clearer signal.* □ *The ham radio operator had a giant antenna in his backyard.*

antibiotic   a drug that kills germs or bacteria. □ *She is taking an antibiotic to prevent an infection.* □ *Apply this topical antibiotic to the wound.*

antifreeze a substance that keeps an engine from freezing in cold temperatures. □ *When autumn comes around, I always check the antifreeze in my car.* □ *Add a mixture of half antifreeze, half water to the radiator.*

antihistamine a drug that relieves a stuffy nose. □ *I take an antihistamine for my allergies.* □ *Mary has a cold, so she's taking antihistamines.*

antioxidant a chemical that prevents oxidization. (Some vitamins are ANTIOXIDANTS.) □ *I read an article that says antioxidants have great health benefits.* □ *This vitamin supplement contains antioxidants.*

antiperspirant a preparation that reduces the amount you perspire. (See also DEODORANT.) □ *After his shower, Bill applied antiperspirant.* □ *This new antiperspirant has a pleasant scent.*

antiseptic a preparation that kills germs and bacteria, especially one applied to the skin. □ *She cleaned the cut on her arm with antiseptic.* □ *You should have some antiseptic in your first-aid kit.*

appetizer a dish served before the main course of a meal. (See also CANAPÉ, HORS D'OEUVRE.) □ *The menu lists several different appetizers.* □ *I had shrimp cocktail for an appetizer.*

apple corer a device that removes the core of an apple. □ *Making apple pie is easy if you have an apple corer.* □ *This apple corer also peels the apple as it cuts out the core.*

appliance a machine, especially one used in the house or office. □ *The store sells kitchen appliances, such as refrigerators, freezers, stoves, and microwave ovens.* □ *Joe has a handy little appliance for pressing his clothes.*

appliqué **1.** a cutout shape of fabric sewed onto another piece of fabric as a decoration. □ *The quilt had lovely flower appliqués in every panel.* □ *The shirt was decorated with multicolored appliqués.* **2.** the method of decorating fabric with APPLIQUÉS. □ *I took a class in appliqué.* □ *Just look at the exquisite appliqué work on that vest.*

apron **1.** a garment worn to protect clothing from spills or dirt. □ *Nancy put on her apron and got to work in the kitchen.* □ *Bill wears an apron when he cleans the house.* **2.** a wide, paved area, especially the widest part of a driveway, or the paved area around an airport. □ *There are several cracks in the cement of the driveway apron. I'll have to patch them.* □ *The plane came to a stop on the apron and workers came hurrying to unload it.* **3.** the part of the trim around a window that is under the windowsill. □ *She chose a nice, plain molding for the window apron.* □ *He carefully cut the apron a little shorter than the sill.*

area rug a rug or carpet that covers a large area. □ *They bought drapes to match the area rug.* □ *I need an area rug big enough for my living room.*

armature a framework. (Often used for the framework of a sculpture.) □ *The shelf was supported on an armature made of wood.* □ *The sculptor built a metal armature for her clay figure.*

arrow key a key on a computer keyboard, labeled with an arrow pointing up, down, left, or right. □ *Use the arrow keys to move the cursor.* □ *Push the "up"-arrow key.*

artificial sweetener a substance that tastes sweet but is low in calories. □ *I'm trying to lose weight, so I use an artificial sweetener instead of sugar.* □ *The diet soda is low in calories because it is made with artificial sweetener.*

ascending order [of numbers] from smallest to largest; of letters, from A to Z. (Compare with DESCENDING ORDER.) □ *The database sorted the list in ascending order.* □ *Please file these receipts in ascending order according to their serial numbers.*

ASCII See AMERICAN STANDARD CODE FOR INFORMATION INTERCHANGE.

ashtray   a tray or dish for the ashes of cigarettes, pipes, cigars, etc. □ *I don't have an ashtray, but you can use this saucer.* □ *Since there is an ashtray on the table, I assume that this restaurant permits smoking.*

aspic   a gelatin dish that is savory, not sweet. □ *I have a good recipe for tomato aspic.* □ *You can add peppers, celery, and chopped meats to aspic.*

aspirin   a drug that relieves pain and reduces fever. □ *There is a bottle of aspirin in the medicine chest.* □ *The doctor prescribed aspirin for my arthritis pain.*

AstroTurf™   a brand of synthetic grass. □ *"I'm thinking of putting AstroTurf in my front yard," Mark said. "Grass is too hard to take care of."* □ *"The soccer field is AstroTurf. It won't get muddy in the rain," said the sports commentator.*

athletic shoes   See TENNIS SHOES.

ATM   See AUTOMATIC TELLER MACHINE.

attic   the story of a house just below the roof. □ *We keep our holiday decorations in the attic.* □ *She went up into the attic to look for some things.*

auto focus   a device that focuses a camera automatically. (See also POINT AND SHOOT.) □ *Does this camera have auto focus?* □ *The more expensive model has electronic flash and auto focus.*

automatic   **1.** operating by itself. □ *I set the automatic oven timer to turn the oven on at 5:30.* □ *The toilet has an automatic flush mechanism.* **2.** [of a car transmission that] shifts gears automatically. (Contrasts with STANDARD or MANUAL.) □ *The has power steering, power brakes, A/C, and automatic transmission.* □ *JANE: Is your car standard or automatic?* BILL: *Automatic.*

automatic feed   a device that draws something into a machine automatically. □ *The copier is easy to use. It has* *automatic feed.* □ *You can use the automatic feed, or you can feed the paper in by hand.*

automatic (pistol)   a pistol that reloads automatically. □ *She kept an automatic pistol in the drawer of her bedside table.* □ *He bought an eight-round clip for his automatic.*

automatic shut-off   a device that turns something off automatically. □ *The iron has automatic shut-off. That way, if you accidentally leave it on, it won't burn anything.* □ *The headlights are on an automatic shut-off.*

automatic teller machine AND **ATM; cash machine**   a machine that performs bank transactions automatically. (CASH MACHINE is informal.) □ *Is there an ATM near the grocery store?* □ *This automatic teller machine does not accept deposits.* □ *I need to get to a cash machine before we go to the movie.*

automatic weapon   a rifle or machine gun that fires automatically. □ *Some people think that automatic weapons should be illegal.* □ *Each soldier was issued an automatic weapon.*

auto reverse   a device that automatically plays the other side of an audio cassette when the end of the first side is reached. □ *The tape player in my car has auto reverse.* □ *No need to turn the tape over. That machine has auto reverse.*

auto timer AND **self-timer**   a device that turns something else on and off at set times. □ *The rear-window defroster is on an auto timer. It will shut off by itself.* □ *The oven has a self-timer. You can set it in the morning, and it will have your casserole baked and ready for you when you get home at night.*

awl   a tool for making holes. □ *Use an awl to poke several holes in the jar lid.* □ *Where's the awl? I need to punch a new hole in my belt.*

awning   a piece of cloth stretched out to form a shelter, usually from the front of a building over the sidewalk. (See also CANOPY.) □ *All the shops on State Street have brightly colored awnings.* □ *The main entrance to the building has a red awning with the street address printed on it.*

axe a tool with a wide blade, used for chopping. (See also HATCHET.) □ *You'll find the axe out by the wood pile.* □ *The firefighters took their axes and chopped through the door of the burning building.*

axle the shaft on which a wheel or pair of wheels revolves. □ *The front axle on my bike is bent.* □ *The hub is the end of the axle.*

B

(baby) bottle   a bottle with a rubber tip, used for feeding a baby. □ *He warmed the milk in the baby bottle.* □ *She gave her son some orange juice in his bottle.*

baby food   soft, mashed, or ground-up food prepared for babies. □ *She opened several jars of baby food for the baby's lunch.* □ *Cooked cereal is a popular baby food.*

(baby) formula   a milk mixture or milk substitute fed to babies. □ *To make baby formula, use one part of this powder to two parts water.* □ *There's plenty of formula in the refrigerator if you need to feed the baby while I'm gone.*

baby oil   a light mineral oil usually used to prevent rashes on a baby's skin. □ *I put some baby oil on the baby after her bath.* □ *She used baby oil to take her make-up off.*

baby powder   talcum powder, often used to prevent rashes on a baby's skin. □ *Put a little baby powder on baby's bottom before you put on the diaper.* □ *Baby powder keeps my skin dry in the summer.*

babysitter   someone who is paid to take care of children while the parents are away. □ *I told the babysitter we'd be back at eleven o'clock.* □ *Give the babysitter the phone number of the restaurant where we'll be.*

backhoe   a construction machine for digging large holes. □ *The construction workers brought in a backhoe to dig the hole for our new swimming pool.* □ *The driver shifted a lever, and the backhoe bit into the ground.*

backpack   a sack carried on the back with straps over each shoulder. □ *The students carried their books in backpacks.* □ *We packed our camping gear into our backpacks.*

backspace (key)   a key on a typewriter or computer keyboard that moves the carriage or the cursor one space back.

(The BACKSPACE (KEY) is usually marked with either "back space" or a "left" pointing arrow.) □ *Use the backspace key to move back to the beginning of the word.* □ *I can't find the backspace on this keyboard.*

backsplash AND **splashboard**   a molding on the wall behind a sink that protects the wall from splashes. □ *The backsplash behind the sink is too short to protect the wall very much.* □ *She installed a splashboard that matched the countertop.*

backstitch   to stitch in the opposite direction. □ *Backstitch at the end of the seam to keep it from unraveling.* □ *Just flip this lever to get the sewing machine to backstitch.*

backup   an extra item, especially an extra copy of a computer file, for use in case something goes wrong with the original. □ *I keep my old typewriter around as a backup in case my computer breaks down.* □ *I made a backup of each document on the disk.*

backup disk   a copy of a computer disk for use in case something goes wrong with the original. □ *TOM: This program disk isn't working. JANE: Try the backup disk.* □ *I made a set of backup disks for the operating system.*

backup light   a white light on the rear of a car, which turns on when the car is in reverse gear. □ *The backup light illuminated the car behind me.* □ *The backup lights on the car ahead of me warned me that the car was in reverse.*

bacon bits   pieces of crumbled bacon, usually used as a GARNISH. □ *There are bacon bits in the salad dressing.* □ *The salad bar had bacon bits, croutons, grated cheese, and other tasty things to put on top of a salad.*

baffle   a device for keeping back the flow of a liquid or gas. □ *We set up the wind baffle to keep the camp stove sheltered.* □ *The baffle in the septic tank keeps the sewage from splashing.*

bagel   a round bread roll with a chewy crust and a hole in the middle. □ *We had bagels and cream cheese for breakfast.*

☐ *The shop sells twelve different kinds of bagels, including sesame, poppy seed, and garlic.*

bagel chips crisped, fried, or baked slices of BAGELS. ☐ *Bagel chips are Bill's favorite snack.* ☐ *They served bagel chips and dip for an appetizer.*

baggage claim the area in an airport where travelers collect the baggage they checked on the airplane. ☐ *Passengers from flight 459 can collect their bags at baggage claim area number six.* ☐ *Shall I meet you at the gate or at the baggage claim?*

baggage compartment a compartment for transporting luggage in a bus, train, or airplane. ☐ *The passengers lined up outside the bus to put their luggage in the baggage compartment.* ☐ *That suitcase is too large for you to bring it onto the plane. It will have to go in the baggage compartment.*

Baggies™ a brand of plastic bags. (You may hear BAGGIE used to refer to a single plastic bag.) ☐ *"Remember to get a box of Baggies when you go to the store," Jim reminded me.* ☐ *"Baggies are just the right size for a sandwich," Linda said as she packed her lunch.*

bake to cook something in an oven, with dry heat. ☐ *I got up early and baked muffins for breakfast.* ☐ *Jim likes to bake bread.*

bake cups See BAKING CUPS.

Baker's Chocolate™ unsweetened chocolate used in baking and candy making. ☐ *The brownie recipe calls for six ounces of Baker's Chocolate.* ☐ *Melt the Baker's Chocolate in the top of a double boiler.*

baking cups AND **bake cups; cupcake liners** paper or foil cups used to line the compartments in a muffin pan. ☐ *Grease your muffin tin, or use baking cups.* ☐ *Grandma used special bake cups printed with Christmas designs when she made cupcakes at Christmas time.* ☐ *Each child got a cupcake liner full of candy as a party favor.*

baking mix   a mix of flour, salt, and baking powder, used to make biscuits, pancakes, and other baked goods. (See also BISQUICK™.) □ *Add milk to the baking mix and knead lightly.* □ *These muffins are easy to make if you start with baking mix.*

baking pan   a square or rectangular pan, usually an inch or two deep. □ *Spread the batter into an 8 × 8 baking pan.* □ *Grease and flour a 13 × 9 inch baking pan.*

baking powder   a mixture of cream of tartar, bicarbonate of soda, and salt, used to make dough and batter rise. □ *Add half a teaspoon of baking powder.* □ *The baking powder in these biscuits is what makes them so wonderfully light.*

baking sheet AND **cookie sheet**   a flat pan, with short sides, for baking. □ *Spread the frozen French fries onto a greased baking sheet and bake at 400 degrees.* □ *How many cookies will fit on this cookie sheet?*

baking soda   bicarbonate of soda, often used as LEAVEN-ING. (See also BICARB(ONATE OF SODA).) □ *Sift the flour with one teaspoon baking soda.* □ *Baking soda is a popular ingredient in toothpaste.*

balcony   an enclosed platform attached to an upper story of a building. (See also GALLERY, PORCH, VERANDA.) □ *The balcony had a beautiful wrought-iron railing around it.* □ *Juliet stood on the balcony and dreamed of her Romeo.*

ball-peen hammer   a hammer with a round knob on the end of the head, opposite from the striking surface. (See also CLAW HAMMER, HAMMER.) □ *I have both a ball-peen hammer and a claw hammer.* □ *She hammered the metal into shape with a ball-peen hammer.*

ballpoint (pen)   a pen that writes with ink flowing around a small ball in the tip. □ *This was written with a ballpoint pen.* □ *This ballpoint's out of ink.*

balustrade   a stair rail and its supports. (See also BANIS-TER.) □ *The stairway had a fancy carved balustrade.* □ *The balustrade was unstable and had to be replaced.*

band   a range of radio frequencies or wavelengths. (AM, FM, and SHORT WAVE RADIO are BANDS.) □ *Tune in to 101.3 on your FM band.* □ *I'm picking up a weak signal on the SW3 band.*

Band Aid™   a brand of ADHESIVE bandages. □ *"That's a nasty blister," Jim said, taking a look at my injured hand. "Let me put a Band Aid on it."* □ *"Does anyone have a Band Aid?" Carol asked. "I cut myself."*

banister AND **handrail**   a rail at one side of a staircase that people can hold for support. (See also BALUSTRADE.) □ *She gripped the banister and limped up the stairs.* □ *The handrail was worn smooth with generations of use.*

barbecue   **1.** to cook something, usually meat, at a high temperature and with a spicy sauce. □ *We barbecued some ribs on the outdoor grill.* □ *She has a special way of barbecuing chicken.* **2.** an occasion on which food is barbecued or cooked outdoors. □ *They're having a big barbecue to celebrate Mary's graduation.* □ *Did you go to the company barbecue?*

(barbecue) grill AND **outdoor grill**   a gas, charcoal, or electric grill for cooking food outdoors. (See also GRILL, HIBACHI.) □ *Set up the barbecue grill. Let's have a picnic.* □ *Jim has some steaks going on the grill, and I'm making a big batch of potato salad.* □ *This outdoor grill is easy to clean.*

barbed wire   wire with barbs or little spikes along it. □ *They strung barbed wire along the top of the fence.* □ *The barbed wire keeps cattle in and people out.*

bar code   a machine-readable black-and-white-striped code. (See also UNIVERSAL PRODUCT CODE.) □ *If you have a complaint about this product, simply mail in the bar code from the bottom of the box to the following address.* □ *The clerk aimed the laser wand at the bar code on my library card.*

bar (cookie)   a cookie made by pressing dough into a flat pan before baking and then cutting it into rectangles or squares. (See also DROP COOKIE, PRESSED COOKIE.) □ *These chocolate chip bar cookies are delicious and easy to make.* □ *Jim jealously guards his recipe for lemon custard bars.*

barometer   a device that measures atmospheric pressure. □ *The barometer is rising. We'll have clear weather today.* □ *The barometer is holding steady at 29.25 inches of mercury.*

barrel   **1.** the hollow, cylindrical part of a gun out of which the bullet is fired. □ *He had a two-barrel shotgun.* □ *She cleaned out the barrel of her gun.* **2.** the hollow, cylindrical part of a pen. □ *The barrel of this pen is just the right size for me to grip it comfortably.* □ *The fountain pen has a plastic barrel and a steel nib.*

barrette   a clip for holding hair back. □ *She parted her hair on the side and held it back with a gold barrette.* □ *The little girl wore barrettes shaped like pink bows.*

baseboard   a molding attached where a wall meets the floor. □ *I painted the baseboard to match the rest of the wall.* □ *He fastened the baseboard in place with nails and glue.*

baseboard heat   a heating system that uses hot water, electricity, or steam to produce heat along the bottom of the walls. □ *This apartment has baseboard heat.* □ *Does this house have forced air or baseboard heat?*

base coat   the first coat of paint or varnish. □ *Let the base coat dry before you put on the second coat.* □ *Sand the wood before you apply the base coat.*

basement   an underground story of a building. □ *When we heard the tornado alarm, we went down into the basement.* □ *The basement sprang a leak during the last big storm.*

basin   a sink. □ *Try this powerful new basin, tub, and tile cleaner.* □ *He plugged the basin and filled it with warm water.*

basket   the part of a WASHING MACHINE that holds the clothes. □ *When I opened the lid of the washing machine,* *the basket was full of water and soap bubbles.* □ *Don't over-load the basket.*

baste **1.** to sew something temporarily, with large stitches. □ *She basted the dress together to check the fit before sewing it.* □ *Baste the gathers in place, then sew the seam.* **2.** to brush or drip a liquid, usually fat, over something as it is cooking. □ *He basted the turkey.* □ *Baste the potatoes with some of the drippings from the roast.*

bath mat a small rug placed outside a tub or shower. □ *She stepped out of the shower onto the soft bath mat.* □ *The bath mat caught the drips as he got out of the tub.*

bathroom fixtures the sink, toilet, bathtub, shower, or any other permanent appliances in a bathroom. □ *The bath-room fixtures in this house are very old-fashioned.* □ *We asked for an estimate to have the bathroom fixtures replaced.*

bathroom tissue See TOILET PAPER.

bath towel a large towel used to dry oneself after a bath or shower. □ *I will get you a nice, clean bath towel.* □ *The warm, fluffy bath towel felt good after the hot shower.*

(bath)tub a tub that holds water for a bath. □ *He scrubbed out the bathtub with cleanser and a sponge.* □ *After a long, hard day, I like to sit and soak in the tub.*

batter a thin mixture of flour, liquid, and other ingredi-ents. □ *Pour the batter into a cake pan.* □ *He dipped the vegetables in batter before frying them.*

battery a device that stores and delivers electric power. □ *I left the lights on in my car, and the battery died.* □ *What size batteries does your tape recorder use?*

baud rate the speed at which a computer or a modem can send or receive information. □ *What's the baud rate on this fax modem?* □ *The terminal can receive at a baud rate of 2400.*

bay window AND **bow window**   a window or a set of windows that projects outward from the outside wall. □ *The old-fashioned house had a charming bay window in the parlor.* □ *She stood in the bow window, looking out at the storm.*

BB   a small pellet for shooting from an air rifle. (See also BB GUN.) □ *He peppered the tree with BBs, but failed to hit the bird.* □ *The vet found a BB in the dog's leg.*

BB gun   an air rifle that shoots small pellets called BBs. (See also BB.) □ *When I was 10 years old, I wanted a BB gun for my birthday.* □ *My father explained that the BB gun was not a toy.*

beach towel   a very large towel, used for lying down on while sunbathing and drying off after swimming. □ *He spread out his beach towel and lay down in the sun.* □ *After a day at the beach, my beach towel was covered with sand.*

beacon   a signal, usually a light, used to attract attention. □ *The control tower could barely see the tiny airplane's flashing beacon.* □ *The traffic beacon warned that the road was closed.*

beat   to stir something vigorously. □ *Beat the cake batter until it is smooth and light.* □ *He beat the eggs with a wire whisk.*

beater   a rotating metal whisk that is part of an electric mixer. □ *You can remove the beaters from the mixer to wash them.* □ *Whenever my mother made cake batter, I always wanted to lick the beaters.*

beater bar   the part of a vacuum cleaner that rotates to move dust and dirt up into the vacuum. □ *Something's wrong with the vacuum. The beater bar's not moving.* □ *A long string got tangled around the beater bar.*

bedclothes   sheets, pillow cases, blankets, and (bed)spreads. (See also BED LINEN.) □ *She tossed and turned all night. The bedclothes were in a tangle.* □ *Wash all the bedclothes, even the spread.*

bed linen   sheets and pillow cases. (See also BEDCLOTHES.) □ *The bed linen in the hotel room was clean and crisp.* □ *The bride and groom received some lovely bed linen as a wedding gift.*

bedpost   an upright post at the corner of a bed frame. □ *He pulled off his necktie, wrapped it around the bedpost, and fell exhausted into bed.* □ *The bedposts were carved with a pretty pattern.*

bed rail AND **side rail**   the horizontal bar along the sides of a bed frame. □ *The old-fashioned bed had a high, carved bed rail.* □ *The mattress was too wide for the bed frame. It stuck out over the side rails.*

(bed)spread   a blanket spread out on top of a bed to protect the sheets and blankets underneath from dust and dirt. (See also COUNTERPANE.) □ *I bought a new bedspread and curtains to match.* □ *He tucked in the spread at the foot of the bed.*

bedstead   the part of the bed frame at the head of the bed. □ *They had an antique brass bedstead.* □ *I woke up suddenly in the middle of the night and bumped my head on the bedstead.*

beeper   a device that beeps in order to signal someone. (See also PAGER.) □ *The doctor carried a beeper so that she could be notified in case of emergency.* □ *Bill's beeper went off in the middle of dinner.*

beeswax   wax produced by bees. □ *The tailor coated the thread with beeswax to make it stiff and strong.* □ *She polished the wood with beeswax.*

belt sander   a device that makes wood smooth by moving an abrasive belt across it. □ *Using the belt sander, I got the door sanded in no time.* □ *The belt on the belt sander is looking worn out. I'd better replace it.*

bench seat   a car seat with a low, straight back, like a bench. □ *The truck has a bench seat.* □ *It's a bench seat, so* *if the driver wants to move forward, the whole thing moves forward.*

berm a large, long pile of dirt. □ *They constructed a berm between the backs of the houses and the highway, to muffle the traffic noise.* □ *She hoped that the berm at the bottom of the hill would keep the water out of her backyard.*

bevel an edge cut at an angle. □ *Cut carefully, so you get a nice smooth bevel.* □ *The sun sparkled in the bevel at the edge of the windowpane.*

beverage a drink. □ *The menu listed appetizers, entrees, and beverages.* □ *Would you like a beverage with your meal?*

bias a line diagonal to the threads of a fabric. (See also BIAS TAPE.) □ *The designer created the beautiful lines of the dress by cutting the fabric on the bias.* □ *Fabric tends to stretch along the bias.*

bias tape a thin strip of fabric cut diagonal to the direction of the threads of a cloth. (See also BIAS.) □ *Bind the edges of the quilt with bias tape.* □ *The hem was decorated with bias tape.*

bicarb(onate of soda) a substance (sodium bicarbonate) used as a LEAVENING, a cleaner, and an ANTACID. (See also BAKING SODA. BICARB is informal.) □ *I scrubbed the face-plate of the iron with a little bicarbonate of soda.* □ *Do you have some bicarb? I've got an upset stomach.*

bicycle chain a chain that runs between the pedals and the rear wheel of a bicycle, and transfers power from the pedals to the rear wheel. □ *He soaked the bicycle chain in solvent to clean it.* □ *That bicycle chain is too loose. No wonder you're having trouble pedaling it.*

bifocals eyeglasses that have two different lens areas, one for seeing distant objects and one for seeing things close up. □ *I feel like an old man now that I have to wear bifocals.* □ *She tilted her head up to read through her bifocals.*

big screen TV   a television with a very large screen. (See also PROJECTION TV.) ☐ *They invited all their friends over to watch the game on their big screen TV.* ☐ *He has a videodisc player and a big screen TV.*

binder   **1.** a set of cardboard or plastic covers with a clip to hold loose pages inside. (See also THREE-RING BINDER.) ☐ *I kept my class notes in a binder.* ☐ *Please submit your final project in a binder.* **2.** a rubber band. (Regional.) ☐ *She wrapped a binder around the stack of index cards.* ☐ *He shut the bag with a binder.*

birth control   See FAMILY PLANNING.

biscuit   a small round of baked dough, usually LEAVENED with baking powder. ☐ *This is a nice recipe for buttermilk biscuits.* ☐ *How do you get your biscuits so nice and flaky?*

biscuit cutter   a device for cutting a round shape out of dough. ☐ *It's easy to make rolled biscuits when you have a biscuit cutter.* ☐ *Instead of a biscuit cutter, she used the rim of a drinking glass.*

bisque   a cream soup, often containing shellfish. ☐ *We had an excellent lobster bisque.* ☐ *I bought some fresh shrimp. I'll make shrimp bisque tonight.*

Bisquick™   a brand of biscuit mix. (See also BAKING MIX.) ☐ *"This shortcake is really easy. You start with two cups of Bisquick," said Grandma.* ☐ *"You can make pancakes and waffles with Bisquick," George told me.*

bit   the smallest unit of the DIGITAL code used by computers. ☐ *There are usually 8 bits in a byte.* ☐ *Bits are coded either 0 or 1.*

black and white   showing a picture in shades of gray, black, and white. (Contrasts with COLOR.) ☐ *Are you using color film or black and white?* ☐ *I love those old black-and-white movies.* ☐ *I bought a black-and-white TV set.*

blade a flat piece of metal or plastic, used to cut, chop, or mix. □ *Careful. That knife has a sharp blade.* □ *Which blade should I use in the food processor?*

blanch to put something into boiling water for a very short time, usually in order to make the peel easier to remove. □ *Blanch the tomatoes and peel them.* □ *She blanched two cups of almonds.*

blazer a tailored jacket. □ *She wore a navy blue wool blazer.* □ *This gray blazer will go with anything.*

bleed valve a VALVE that lets out excess gas or liquid. □ *She opened the bleed valve and a stream of air came out.* □ *I found the bleed valve for the brake system.*

blend to mix things together. □ *Blend the chocolate evenly into the batter.* □ *He blended the two colors of paint.*

blender a device that uses rotating blades in a tall jar to mix things, usually liquids. □ *This blender has twelve speeds.* □ *He uses his blender to chop nuts.*

blender jar a tall glass or plastic jar, part of a BLENDER. □ *My blender jar broke. I'm going to the hardware store to get a new one.* □ *She poured the mixed drinks from the blender jar into the glasses.*

blinker See (TURN) SIGNAL.

blister pack a package with the contents displayed in a plastic bubble or bubbles. □ *The racks were filled with toys in blister packs.* □ *The cold remedy came in a blister pack.*

blouse a loose-fitting shirt, especially a woman's loose-fitting, buttoned shirt. □ *This blouse has dainty lace accents on the collar.* □ *I spilled red wine all over my new silk blouse.*

blow [for a FUSE] to overload and burn out. (Slang.) □ *Lightning struck nearby, and all the fuses blew.* □ *If you try to run six appliances off that circuit, the fuse will blow.*

blower a fan that moves air through a heating or cooling system. □ *Something's wrong with the air conditioning. The blower runs, but the air that comes out is warm.* □ *Turn on the blower. Let's get a breeze going through here.*

bluing a blue substance used in washing white clothes or white hair, in order to keep the white from looking yellow. □ *Put a little bluing in the wash water when you do those sheets.* □ *She used so much bluing in her hair, her hair turned blue!*

boat neck a shirt neck that goes straight across from shoulder to shoulder. (See also CREW NECK, V-NECK, SCOOP NECK.) □ *This boat neck sweater is 100% cotton.* □ *He wore a boat neck jersey over a turtleneck sweater.*

bobbin a small spool, especially one used under the needle of a sewing machine. □ *I looked for a bobbin of the same color as the spool of blue thread.* □ *He wound the yarn onto a bobbin.*

bobby pin a small hair pin made of flat wire. (See also HAIR PIN.) □ *She held her chignon in place with bobby pins.* □ *She used bobby pins to keep her hair from getting in her face.*

Bobcat™ the brand name of a compact earth mover that can move through narrow openings and operate in a residential yard. □ *"I would like to rent a Bobcat for the weekend," Tom told the rental agent.* □ *"I need a Bobcat to dig a hole for my swimming pool," said Bill.*

bobèche a small dish at the base of a candle, used to catch dripping wax. (Pronounced bo-BESH.) □ *The silver candlestick was molded with a fluted bobèche at the top.* □ *Use these plastic bobèches when you put those candles out on the table.*

bodice the part of a dress that fits over the torso. □ *The bodice is ornamented with sequins and seed pearls.* □ *The dress has a tight-fitting bodice and a flared skirt.*

boil **1.** to heat a liquid until it bubbles. □ *The water is boiling. Shall I put the spaghetti in?* □ *Boil the maple sap until it thickens into syrup.* **2.** to cook something in a boiling liquid, usually water. □ *Boil the potatoes.* □ *Boil the sweet corn for just two or three minutes.*

boiler the part of a hot water heating system that heats the water. □ *The pilot light on the boiler went out, and the building got very cold.* □ *The water in the boiler is at very high pressure.*

boldface heavy type, used to draw attention to a word or words. □ *The important names in the article are in boldface.* □ *The entries in this dictionary are in boldface.*

bolt a metal shaft used to fasten two things together and usually held in place with a NUT. □ *The bed frame is held together with bolts.* □ *The hole you drilled is too small for this bolt.*

bolt action [of a rifle that is] loaded by pulling back on a bolt. □ *Bolt action rifles are popular because they are quick to reload.* □ CUSTOMER: *Is this a machine gun?* GUNSELLER: *No, it's bolt action.*

bolt cutters a device that can cut a metal rod. □ *I had to use a pair of bolt cutters to remove that rusty old bolt.* □ *The thief cut the lock off with bolt cutters.*

boombox a large radio or tape player with powerful speakers. (Slang.) □ *We brought our boombox to the beach.* □ *You could hear his boombox coming a block away.*

booster seat a small seat placed on top of a chair to make it possible for a child to reach the table. □ *We asked the waitress for a booster seat for Bobby.* □ *You're getting so tall, you almost don't need a booster seat!*

boot (up) to start up a computer. (See also REBOOT.) □ *Boot up the computer.* □ *The computer should perform a memory check when you boot it.*

bore the cylindrical hole in the barrel of a gun. □ *Muskets, the earliest guns, had smooth bores.* □ *She used a wire brush to clean the bore.*

bottle brush a long, cylindrical brush used to clean the insides of bottles. □ *He washed the vase with a bottle brush.* □ *You'll need a bottle brush to get through the narrow neck of that bottle.*

bottom an article of clothing worn from the waist down, such as a skirt or a pair of pants, especially one that is part of an outfit. (Informal. Contrasts with TOP.) □ *Do you have any bottoms that will match this top?* □ *Where are my pajama bottoms?*

bouillon a clear soup made by boiling and straining meat or vegetables. (See also BROTH, STOCK.) □ *Chicken bouillon is good for an upset stomach.* □ *I like to use beef bouillon as a soup base.*

bouillon cube concentrated BOUILLON packaged in cubes. □ *Dissolve one bouillon cube in two cups of hot water.* □ *Add a bouillon cube or two to give your soups extra flavor.*

bow window See BAY WINDOW.

box-end wrench a wrench with enclosed ends that can surround a nut or a tube. (Contrasts with OPEN-END WRENCH.) □ *He used a box-end wrench to loosen the nut.* □ *The box-end wrench got a good grip.*

box spring a rigid, rectangular frame containing a set of springs, used to support a mattress. □ *The low price includes both mattress and box spring.* □ *The box spring is too big for the bed frame.*

brace and bit a drill for wood that is cranked by hand. (See also EGG-BEATER DRILL.) □ *He used a brace and bit for his carpentry work.* □ *She thought electric drills were unreliable. She preferred to work with a brace and bit.*

bracket   a structure that holds something in place. ☐ *I attached the shelf bracket to the wall, then fixed the shelf in place on the bracket. ☐ The table legs are held in place by a folding bracket.*

brad   **1.** a thin nail. ☐ *She tacked the molding in place with brads. ☐ You can barely see the tiny brads that hold the carving in place.* **2.** a pin with a flat head and two prongs that bend outwards to hold papers together. ☐ *The script was held together with brads. ☐ She put a brad through the top hole of her papers.*

braise   to cook something slowly in a covered pot. ☐ *Larry braised the pot roast. ☐ Braise the leeks, then serve them as a side dish.*

brake caliper   a metal arm that moves a brake shoe onto or away from a rotating wheel or disc. ☐ *The brake calipers were stuck, so the brake shoes were dragging against the wheel. ☐ This cable moves the brake calipers on the front wheel of the bicycle.*

brake fluid   a fluid used to regulate the pressure in a car's hydraulic brake system. ☐ *I really have to push hard on the brake pedal to get the brakes to work. I wonder if the brake fluid is leaking. ☐ Use the bleed valve to bleed the air out of the system. Add more brake fluid if necessary.*

brake light   a set of red lights on the rear of a car that signal that the driver has applied the brakes. ☐ *He's slowing down. His brake lights are on. ☐ I saw the brake lights of the car ahead of me and immediately stepped on my brakes.*

brake line   a pipe that carries brake fluid through a car's brake system. ☐ *If your brake line springs a leak, you're really in trouble. The brakes won't work. ☐ The mechanic checked the brake lines.*

brake pad   a pad that rubs against a wheel or disc to slow it down. ☐ *When I step on the brakes, I hear a terrible shrieking noise. Sounds like the brake pads are worn* *through.* □ *The brake pad on my bike is rubbing against the tire instead of against the wheel rim. I'd better fix it.*

brake (pedal) a pedal that, when pressed, makes a vehicle slow down. (See also ACCELERATOR (PEDAL).) □ *He applied gradual pressure to the brake pedal, and the car came to a stop.* □ *She had one foot on the accelerator and one foot on the brake.*

brake shoe a device that is attached to a brake caliper and that rubs against a wheel or disc to slow it down. □ *The bicycle's brake shoes are worn out. They need to be replaced.* □ *The brake shoes came in contact with the brake disc.*

bran the outer layer of a grain. □ *Bran is good for your digestion.* □ *This cereal contains oat and wheat bran.*

brand a kind of product manufactured by a particular company. □ *JILL: What brand of detergent do you usually buy? BILL: Blix with Bleach.* □ *Try Johnson's Homemade Jam. It's a locally-made brand and very tasty.*

brand-name made by a well-known company and having a well-known name. □ *Jane uses only brand-name cleaning products.* □ *These generic potato chips taste just as good as the brand-name kind.*

(brandy) snifter a wide-mouthed glass with a flat bottom and a short stem, usually used for serving brandy. □ *Don't serve that fine brandy in a wine glass! Use a brandy snifter.* □ *After dinner, I enjoyed a snifter of excellent brandy.*

bra(ssiere) an undergarment that supports the breasts. (BRA is the more common term.) □ *What size bra do you take?* □ *Will you look at all the lace on that fancy brassiere!*

bread to cover something in bread crumbs or meal. □ *I breaded the shrimp and fried them.* □ *She breaded the okra in cornmeal.*

bread basket a basket used for serving bread at a meal. □ *The bread basket was heaped with warm muffins.* □ *The bread was served in a fancy silver bread basket.*

bread bin See BREAD BOX.

bread board a board on which bread is kneaded. □ *Turn the dough out onto a lightly-floured bread board and knead for ten minutes.* □ *He rolled the dough out on the bread board.*

bread bowl **1.** a large bowl used for mixing and kneading bread dough. □ *The cook kneaded the dough in the bread bowl.* □ *He measured the flour into the bread bowl.* **2.** a bowl made of bread. □ *The Caesar salad is served in a tasty bread bowl.* □ *You'll enjoy our salads in their fresh-baked bread bowls.*

bread box AND **bread bin** a box for storing bread. □ *Get me the sourdough bread out of the bread box.* □ *Just throw the leftover rolls in the bread bin.*

bread knife a knife with a wavy blade for slicing bread. □ *Use the bread knife with a gentle sawing motion.* □ *The bread knife sliced cleanly through the loaf.*

bread machine See BREAD MAKER.

bread maker AND **bread machine** a machine that mixes and bakes bread automatically. □ *I put the ingredients into the bread maker at night, and when I get up in the morning, there's a fresh, hot loaf waiting for me.* □ *Our new bread machine makes two loaves at a time.*

breakfast nook an area in a house, usually near the kitchen, designed as a place to eat breakfast and other informal meals. □ *Come on into the breakfast nook and have a cup of tea.* □ *The family eats most of our meals in the breakfast nook, but when we entertain, we use the dining room.*

breakfront a cabinet in which dishes and glassware can be stored and displayed. (See also CHINA CUPBOARD, HUTCH.) □ *I inherited this breakfront, and most of my china, from my grandmother.* □ *She had a set of German crystal displayed in her breakfront.*

breast   a cut of meat from the front of a fowl, including the breastbone. □ *JILL: Would you like white meat or dark? JANE: I'll have a breast, thank you.* □ *I bought a package of chicken breasts.*

breath mint   a usually mint-flavored candy that is supposed to make breath smell better. □ *I ate a breath mint before the job interview.* □ *Anxious to make a good impression, Jim had a breath mint before meeting his date.*

breech   the rear part of a gun barrel. □ *The next cartridge slid into place in the breech.* □ *The firing pin is located in the breech of the weapon.*

breezeway   a covered outdoor passageway. □ *A breezeway connected the two buildings.* □ *There's a leak in the roof of the breezeway.*

briefs   close-fitting underpants. □ *I don't need to pack much for the weekend. Just my toothbrush and a couple pairs of clean briefs.* □ *The department store is having a sale on women's cotton briefs.*

Brillo™ pad   a brand of steel SCOURING PAD that contains soap. □ *Max sighed, "I'll need a Brillo pad to get all this junk off the frying pan."* □ *"Scour your copper-bottomed pots with a Brillo pad to keep them nice and bright," Cathy advised.*

brine   salt water. □ *The olives were packed in brine.* □ *Pickle the meat in brine.*

bring something to a boil   to heat something until it starts to boil. □ *Bring the soup stock to a boil, then add the cut-up vegetables.* □ *Bring six cups of water to a boil.*

brisket   a cut of beef from behind the animal's front leg. □ *Brisket was cheap at the butcher's today.* □ *Corned beef is usually made from brisket.*

bristle   a fine, stiff fiber, especially those on a brush or broom. □ *The hairbrush had plastic bristles.* □ *She scrubbed the concrete floor with a scrub brush that had wire bristles.*

British thermal unit AND **BTU** an English (not metric) unit for measuring energy. (One BTU is the amount of energy needed to raise the temperature of one pound of water by one degree Fahrenheit. Air conditioners are often rated in BTUs.) □ *This air-conditioning unit has a capacity of 12,000 BTUs.* □ *How many British thermal units will it take to cool a 120-square-foot room?*

broadcloth a tightly woven fabric. □ *These Oxford shirts are made of 100% cotton broadcloth.* □ *Broadcloth is a good material for pants.*

broil to cook something with high heat applied to one side at a time. □ *She broiled the lamb chops.* □ *The chef broiled the lobster and basted it with butter.*

broiler a device, often part of an oven, that BROILS food. □ *I put the cheese sandwiches in the broiler to brown.* □ *Allow the broiler to preheat before you put the meat in.*

broom a tool with a handle and a set of long bristles, used for sweeping. □ *He got the broom and swept the kitchen floor.* □ *The plastic bristles on this broom are easy to clean.*

broom closet a closet where cleaning equipment is stored. □ *The janitor got a bucket from the broom closet.* □ *JANE: Where's the mop? MARY: In the broom closet.*

broth a clear liquid made by boiling meat or vegetables. (See also BOUILLON, STOCK.) □ *The vegetable soup is made with a chicken broth.* □ *Simmer the beans in beef broth.*

brown to cook something until it turns brown. □ *He browned the potatoes in pork fat.* □ *Bake the muffins until they are nicely browned on top.*

brown sugar unrefined sugar, containing some amount of molasses. □ *Use half a cup of brown sugar, packed.* □ *For chocolate chip cookies, you'll need both white sugar and brown sugar.*

brunch   a meal eaten in the late morning, between the usual times for breakfast and lunch. (The word BRUNCH is a combination of the words *breakfast and lunch*.) □ *The Harrisons have invited us for brunch on Saturday.* □ *We had a nice brunch of waffles, omelets, and fruit salad.*

BTU   See BRITISH THERMAL UNIT.

bucket seat   a high-backed car seat that is separated from the seat next to it. □ *The sports car had a leather interior and bucket seats.* □ *The bucket seats are individually adjustable.*

buckwheat   a kind of grain. □ *Jim makes good buckwheat pancakes.* □ *Jill likes to eat kasha, which is hulled buckwheat.*

buff   to rub something gently in order to polish it. □ *The jeweler buffed the silver bracelet with a soft cloth.* □ *She waxed her car and then buffed it.*

buffet   **1.** a meal at which each person serves himself or herself from a number of dishes all set out together. □ *That restaurant has an excellent lunch buffet.* □ *Dinner will be a buffet. Help yourselves!* **2.** a piece of furniture in which silverware and dishes can be stored, and on which dishes of food can be placed to make room on the table. (See also SIDEBOARD.) □ *This lovely old buffet has a special tarnish-proof drawer for silver.* □ *They passed each dish around the table and then set it on the buffet until someone wanted seconds.*

bug spray   See INSECT REPELLENT.

buildup   an unwanted accumulation of some substance. (See also DEPOSITS.) □ *If you use wax furniture polish, you'll get an ugly wax buildup.* □ *The lime in the water leaves a white buildup on the tiles in the shower.*

built-in   built permanently in place, included as part of the structure. □ *I just love the built-in bookcases in this room.* □ *The tape recorder has a built-in microphone.*

bulb   the round, fleshy structure from which some plants grow. (Onions, tulips, and irises all grow from BULBS.) □ *When is the best time to plant bulbs?* □ *I ordered some tulip bulbs from the seed catalog.*

(bulb) baster   a hollow syringe with a bulb at one end, used for dripping fat or other liquid onto meat as it cooks. □ *She filled the bulb baster with soup stock and basted the chicken with it.* □ *I used the baster to draw up some of the fat from the bottom of the pan.*

bulk   a large quantity. (Usually with *in*.) □ *I buy toilet paper in bulk, a case at a time.* □ *The restaurant buys flour and sugar in bulk.*

bulk section   the part of a grocery store that offers un-packaged foodstuffs for sale. □ *If you don't want to buy a whole one-pound bag of cornmeal, you go to the bulk section and measure out just the amount of cornmeal you want.* □ *The bulk section in this store has flours, sugars, spices, mixes, candies, and pet food.*

bulldozer   a machine that pushes earth in front of it with a wide blade. □ *Bulldozers came and flattened out the vacant lot.* □ *The bulldozer knocked over the flimsy old shed.*

bullet   a piece of lead shot from a gun. □ *It was a bullet from a .45 caliber gun.* □ *The bullet had gone clean through the quail's head.*

bullhorn   a hand-held device that amplifies sound. (See also HAILER.) □ *The police officer called through the bull-horn, "Come out with your hands up!"* □ *The coach used a bullhorn to shout instructions to the team.*

bumper   a structure that protects someone or something in case of a collision. □ *The front bumper was completely smashed, but nobody in the car was hurt.* □ *The skating rink has a rubber bumper around the wall.*

Bundt™ **pan**   a ring-shaped, fluted cake pan. □ *The next step in the recipe says, "Pour the batter into a Bundt pan."*

□ *"This recipe calls for a Bundt pan," said Linda. "Do we have one?"*

bureau   a piece of furniture with several drawers, used for storing clothes. (See also CHEST OF DRAWERS.) □ *I keep my socks in the top drawer of my bureau.* □ *He kept a picture of his wife in a silver frame on top of his bureau.*

burglar alarm   a device that makes a loud noise or alerts the police if someone enters the building or the area. □ *My neighbor's burglar alarm went off in the middle of the night.* □ *I have to type in a special code to turn on the burglar alarm.*

burlap   a rough, woven fabric. □ *The sturdy sack was made of burlap.* □ *The walls were covered in orange burlap.*

burner   the element of a stove that heats up. □ *Put this pot on the back burner while you put the frying pan on the front.* □ *What's the matter with this gas burner? It doesn't light.*

burr   a tiny spur of metal. □ *The machinist carefully filed the burrs off the edge of the metal plate.* □ *I cut my hand on a burr on the lid of the can.*

bus   a major wire that collects current or signal from and delivers it to several different locations. □ *When you add a new board to the computer, you have to hook it up to the bus.* □ *There's no power coming to any of the devices on this bus.*

bushel   32 quarts. □ *I bought a half bushel of apples.* □ *We got a couple of bushels of potatoes out of the garden this year.*

business (class)   a travel class lower than first class, but higher than coach or economy class. (A class of airplane travel.) □ *I travel business class when I can afford it.* □ *Business and first-class passengers may have beverages at any time during the flight.*

bus stop   a location where a bus stops to pick up and un-load passengers. □ *There's a bus stop up at the corner.* □ *I'll wait for you at the bus stop.*

butcher block   a table with a thick wooden top that can be used as a cutting surface. □ *I chopped up the vegetables on the butcher block.* □ *The butcher block is handy for tender-izing meat.*

butcher knife   a long knife with a curved tip, used for sec-tioning meat. □ *She cut the turkey apart with a butcher knife.* □ *He used a butcher knife to cut a leg of lamb for me.*

butt   the grip of a pistol, or the flat end of a rifle. □ *He brought the butt of the gun crashing down on his enemy's head.* □ *She settled the butt of the rifle against her shoul-der and took careful aim.*

butter   **1.** fat derived from milk. □ *Would you like some butter for your toast?* □ *Use half a cup of butter.* **2.** to put a thin coat of BUTTER on something. (See also GREASE.) □ *But-ter a 13 × 9 inch baking pan.* □ *Butter your hands before you handle the dough.*

butter compartment AND **dairy compartment**   a com-partment in a refrigerator for keeping BUTTER and cheese. □ *Put the butter in the butter compartment.* □ *You'll find some Swiss cheese in the dairy compartment.*

butter dish   a rectangular dish with a lid, used to hold a stick of BUTTER. □ *I unwrapped a stick of butter and put it in the butter dish.* □ *He gave her a silver butter dish engraved with her initials.*

butterfly nut   See WING NUT.

butter knife   a flat, dull, rounded knife, used for spreading BUTTER. □ *Her set of silver includes a pearl-handled butter knife.* □ *He tried to cut his meat with the butter knife, with-out much success.*

buttermilk   thick, sour-tasting milk, formed by adding a bacterial culture to skim milk. ☐ *I'll have a glass of butter-milk, please.* ☐ *The pancake recipe calls for two cups of but-termilk.*

butter plate   a small plate for bread and BUTTER; part of a formal table setting. ☐ *The butter plate goes to the left of the dinner plate.* ☐ *She took a bite of her roll and then set it down on her butter plate.*

button   **1.** a small, usually round clothing fastener that passes through a corresponding buttonhole. ☐ *My shirt but-tons were in the wrong buttonholes.* ☐ *One of the buttons fell off my coat.* **2.** a small device which is pressed to turn some-thing on or off. (See also KEY, KNOB, SWITCH.) ☐ *She pressed the black button to ring the doorbell.* ☐ *He got on the eleva-tor and pushed the button for the fourth floor.*

button-down collar   a shirt collar with buttonholes on the pointed ends which fasten onto BUTTONS on the front of the shirt. (Compare with TAB COLLAR.) ☐ *He wanted a blue shirt with a button-down collar.* ☐ *I find that a button-down col-lar helps keep my tie in place.*

buttonholer   a device that makes buttonholes, usually at-tached to a sewing machine. ☐ *CUSTOMER: Does this sewing machine have any special attachments? SALES CLERK: Yes, it comes with a buttonholer.* ☐ *With this buttonholer, I can make a shirt placket in no time.*

buzz   to mix or chop something in a BLENDER. (Informal. See also WHIZ.) ☐ *Buzz the yogurt and the banana in the blender until they form a smooth mixture.* ☐ *To chop the nuts, just buzz them in the blender.*

byte   a unit of 8 bits of information. (Computer files and memory capacities are measured in BYTES.) ☐ *It's a very small file, only two or three hundred bytes.* ☐ *How many bytes can be stored on this disk?*

C

C/A See CENTRAL AIR.

cable ready able to be hooked up to CABLE (TELEVISION). □ *This looks like an old TV. It may not be cable ready.* □ *All the VCRs we sell are cable ready.*

cable release a cable that attaches to a camera shutter, allowing you to release the shutter by pressing a button at the end of the cable. □ *He used a cable release to take that picture of himself.* □ *The photographer fitted the cable release onto the shutter mechanism.*

cable (television) a system of television programming brought into the home over a wire. □ *Tom has cable and will be able to watch the big game.* □ *Cable television offers many channels.*

CAD/CAM See COMPUTER-AIDED DESIGN and COMPUTER-AIDED MANUFACTURE.

CAD See COMPUTER-AIDED DESIGN.

caddy a rack or other device designed to hold things. □ *This convenient caddy holds both pens and notepaper.* □ *She took the pancake turner from her kitchen caddy.*

Caesar salad a salad of romaine lettuce with a dressing of olive oil, garlic, vinegar, anchovies, raw egg, and Parmesan cheese. □ *The waiter came to our table and made the dressing for the Caesar salad while we watched.* □ *I had a Caesar salad for lunch.*

café curtains curtains that hang from rings on a round rod. (See also CAFÉ ROD.) □ *Café curtains are easy to hang.* □ *The café curtains gave an informal look to the room.*

café rod a round rod for hanging CAFÉ CURTAINS. (See also CAFÉ CURTAINS.) □ *The dark curtains look good with* *that brass café rod.* □ *The drapes hung from a heavy, wooden café rod.*

cake **1.** a sweet, spongy, baked dessert. □ *He baked us the most delicious chocolate cake.* □ *Do you prefer pie or cake?* **2.** a small, usually round, portion of food. □ *See if you can get Jill to give you her recipe for salmon cakes.* □ *He fried up some corn cakes on the griddle.* **3.** a molded piece of soap. □ *The package contained three cakes of soap.* □ *He gave me a cake of scented soap.*

cake decorator **1.** a device for putting patterns of colored frosting on a CAKE. □ *She has a fancy cake decorator with half a dozen different attachments.* □ *He used a cake decorator to write "Happy Birthday Sue" on the top of the cake.* **2.** someone who decorates CAKES. □ *That bakery has an excellent cake decorator.* □ *Cake decorators will find many uses for these special sugar roses.*

cake flour a fine-ground wheat flour low in gluten, used for baking CAKES and pastries. □ *Use two and a half cups of cake flour.* □ *For best results, use cake flour rather than all-purpose flour.*

cake knife a knife with a flat, triangular, serrated blade, used for cutting and serving CAKE. □ *She expertly cut and served the cake with the cake knife.* □ *Here's the cake knife. You can cut yourself a piece.*

cake mix a dry mixture of ingredients, to which liquid (usually water, oil, and eggs) can be added to make CAKE batter. □ *JILL: This cake is delicious! Can I have the recipe? JANE: I made it from a cake mix.* □ *I bought a cake mix at the store, so we can have cake for dessert tonight.*

cake pan a pan in which a CAKE is baked. □ *Pour the batter into a greased cake pan.* □ *I found a cake pan shaped like a duck. I thought it would be cute to make a duck-shaped cake for the baby's birthday.*

cake rack See COOLING RACK.

cake server AND **pie server**   a tool with a handle and a flat, triangular blade for lifting pieces of CAKE or pie. □ *He cut the cake, then used the cake server to give everybody a piece.* □ *The pie was stuck to the bottom of the pan. Even using the pie server, I couldn't get it out.*

cake stand   a plate on a small pedestal, used to serve or display CAKES. □ *She brought in the cake on a lovely crystal cake stand.* □ *The bakery window displayed several decorated cakes on cake stands.*

cake tester   a wire or thin piece of wood or plastic inserted into a CAKE as it is baking, to test if it is done. □ *If the cake tester comes out clean, the cake is done.* □ *I use a toothpick as a cake tester.*

cake tin   a metal container for storing CAKE. □ *She put the cake in a fancy cake tin and gave it to her friend as a gift.* □ *The leftover cake is in a cake tin on top of the refrigerator.*

calculator   an electronic device that makes calculations with numbers. □ *Does your calculator have a square root function?* □ *Students may not use their calculators during the test.*

caller ID   See CALLER IDENTIFICATION.

caller identification AND **caller ID**   a service that tells the person receiving a telephone call the identity of the person making the call. (See also IDENTIFICATION.) □ *I got caller ID to see if I could find out who's been making those obscene phone calls.* □ *This answering machine has caller identification.*

calorie   a unit of energy, used to measure the energy available from food. (Technically, the correct name for this unit is a *kilocalorie*. It is one thousand times the amount of energy needed to raise the temperature of one gram of water by one degree centigrade.) □ *There are two hundred and fifty calories in this candy bar.* □ *If you want to lose weight, you will have to limit the number of calories you consume.*

CAM See COMPUTER-AIDED MANUFACTURE.

cambric a thin, finely-woven fabric made of linen or cotton. □ *She carried a pretty cambric handkerchief.* □ *The cambric blouse had a lacy collar.*

camcorder a device that records picture and sound on videotape. □ *They bought a camcorder when they were expecting their first baby.* □ *This camcorder uses VHS cassettes.*

camisole a woman's thin, sleeveless shirt, often worn under other garments. □ *She wore a cotton camisole beneath her blouse.* □ *This pretty camisole is great for layering.*

camper a portable place to live, especially one attached to or pulled by a vehicle. (See also MOTOR HOME.) □ *We bought a camper that has its own stove and sink inside.* □ *They hauled their pop-up camper behind their pickup truck.*

canapé a very small sandwich or savory pastry, usually served with drinks. (Formal. See also APPETIZER, HORS D'OEUVRE.) □ *The caterers handed around tea, coffee, and canapés.* □ *She served miniature quiches as canapés.*

candelabrum an object that holds a number of CANDLES. □ *In the center of the table, she placed a silver candelabrum.* □ *The candelabrum held eight long, white tapers.*

candle a wax shape molded around a wick, burned to give light. □ *She put long white candles in the candleholder.* □ *The little round candles go in the wrought iron candelabrum.*

candleholder a device that holds a CANDLE. □ *This candleholder is designed to be hung on the wall.* □ *The candleholder was shaped like a fish.*

candle snuffer a tool with a long handle and a bell-shaped end which is placed over a CANDLE flame to put it out. □ *After the meal was over, she put out the candles with a silver candle snuffer.* □ *They used a pair of long candle snuffers to douse the candles after the church service.*

candlestick   a tall, cylindrical holder for a CANDLE. (CAN-DLESTICKS usually come in pairs.) □ *The bride and groom received a pair of crystal candlesticks as a gift.* □ *She placed a candlestick at either end of the buffet.*

candlewick   embroidered with thick, soft cotton thread. □ *What a pretty candlewick bedspread!* □ *The sofa was piled with candlewick pillows.*

caning   strips of rattan woven together. (Some chairs have backs or seats made of CANING.) □ *I need to replace the caning in the seat of that chair.* □ *The caning in that rocking chair is very strong.*

canister   a cylindrical container. □ *He stored the flour in a canister.* □ *She had a little canister of pepper spray in her pocket.*

canister vacuum   a vacuum cleaner with a long, flexible tube connecting the brush to a CANISTER containing the vacuum bag. □ *This canister vacuum is great for cleaning those hard-to-reach places.* □ *Will this vacuum bag fit my canister vacuum?*

can opener   a device that opens tin or aluminum cans by cutting one end out. □ *I need a can opener to open this can of beans.* □ *My pocketknife has a can opener on one of its blades.*

canopy   a piece of cloth suspended over something. (See also AWNING.) □ *A canopy covered the four-poster bed.* □ *A canopy in the backyard provided some shade.*

cap   **1.** a close-fitting hat. □ *She wore a baseball cap.* □ *The brim of his cap shaded his eyes from the sun.* **2.** a tight-fitting lid or top for a cylindrical object. □ *I can't get the bottle cap off the bottle.* □ *Put the cap back on the pen.*

caplet   an oval-shaped pill. (An advertising term. See also CAPSULE, GELCAP, TABLET.) □ *The cold remedy comes in a box of forty caplets.* □ *Take two caplets every four hours while symptoms persist.*

cap nut See ACORN NUT.

cap sleeve a very short sleeve that covers just the top of the shoulder. □ *This elegant silk blouse has a jewel neck and cap sleeves. It's just right for wearing with a summer suit.* □ *She wore a tailored linen dress with princess seams and cap sleeves.*

capstan a spindle that helps to move audio or videotape through a machine. □ *I figured out what was wrong with the VCR. The tape got tangled around the capstan.* □ *The capstan in the tape player isn't turning.*

capsule a small, hollow, oval shell containing powdered medicine. (See also CAPLET, GELCAP, TABLET.) □ *The pain medication came in little pink capsules.* □ *The bottle contains a hundred and fifty capsules.*

carafe a glass container with a narrow neck, used for serving liquids. (Wine is often sold by the CARAFE in restaurants. See also DECANTER.) □ *He ordered a carafe of red wine.* □ *She brought out a carafe of iced tea.*

carbon dioxide extinguisher AND **CO$_2$ extinguisher** a device that puts out fire by spraying it with CARBON DIOXIDE. (See also FIRE EXTINGUISHER.) □ *He bought a carbon dioxide extinguisher for the computer room.* □ *A CO$_2$ extinguisher can extinguish not only burning wood and trash, but burning oil and gas as well.*

carbon monoxide detector AND **CO detector** a device that sounds an alarm if there is too much carbon monoxide in the air. (CARBON MONOXIDE is a poisonous gas.) □ *The city council passed a new law that says every house and apartment must be equipped with a carbon monoxide detector.* □ *He let the car idle in the garage so long that the CO detector in the house went off.*

carbon steel a strong, hard steel that contains a high level of carbon. □ *The knives made of carbon steel hold an edge better than the ones made of stainless steel.* □ *This cleaver is made of carbon steel.*

carburetor a device that mixes fuel and air and passes the mixture into the intake manifold of an engine. □ *A blockage in the carburetor prevented the fuel from getting to the engine.* □ *The car accelerates very sluggishly. I wonder if there's a problem with the carburetor.*

cardigan a sweater that opens all the way down the front. (Compare with PULLOVER.) □ *It's a little chilly today. I'll put on a cardigan over my blouse.* □ *What kind of sweater would you like, a pullover or a cardigan?*

card reader a device that reads the code on a magnetic or bar coded stripe on a plastic card. □ *There's a card reader on the door to the fifth floor. You'll need a card to get in.* □ *The clerk passed my credit card through the card reader.*

card table a square-shaped folding table. □ *Let's get out the card table! It's time to play bridge!* □ *They were poor when they first started out. The only furniture they had was a mattress, a card table, and two folding chairs.*

(carpenter's) level a tool that indicates whether or not a horizontal surface is perfectly level. □ *She used a carpenter's level to check that the shelves were not tilted.* □ *He placed a level along the top of the picture frame.*

carpenter's square a tool that indicates whether two things meet at a right angle. □ *He held up a carpenter's square to the corner of the door frame.* □ *She used a carpenter's square to get the sides of the box aligned before she nailed them together.*

carpet cleaner a machine or a chemical that washes carpets. (See also STEAM CLEANER.) □ *We rented a carpet cleaner and spent the weekend getting all the carpets cleaned.* □ *This new carpet cleaner is great for cleaning stains and spills.*

carpet sweeper a hand-operated device that brushes up and removes dirt from a carpet. □ *He pushed the carpet sweeper up and down the room.* □ *I like to use the carpet sweeper because it's quieter than the vacuum.*

carriage   the part of a typewriter that moves either the paper or the typing element back and forth across a line of type. □ *The carriage is stuck. The typewriter just keeps typing on the same spot.* □ *Be careful not to get that long necklace of yours caught in the carriage.*

carriage bolt   a long, heavy bolt with coarse threads and a wide area beneath the head that keeps the bolt from turning when the nut is tightened. □ *The tree house was held together with good, solid carriage bolts.* □ *The carpenter drilled a pilot hole for the carriage bolt.*

carriage return   **1.** a key on a computer or electric typewriter keyboard that moves the CURSOR or the CARRIAGE to the beginning of the next line. (Compare with ENTER.) □ *With the wraparound feature of this word processor, you don't need to hit the carriage return at the end of every line.* □ *Press the carriage return after you have typed in the command.* **2.** a lever that moves a manual typewriter CARRIAGE to the beginning of the next line. □ *I heard the click of the typewriter keys, then the thud of the carriage return.* □ *She pushed the carriage return several times.*

cartridge   **1.** a small, enclosed container of something. □ *The fountain pen ran out of ink. I need a new ink cartridge.* □ *She snapped a film cartridge into the camera.* **2.** a shell containing shot or a bullet, gunpowder, and the material needed to fire it. □ *I bought a box of cartridges for my shotgun.* □ *The automatic ejected the empty cartridge.* **3.** a small unit containing the STYLUS for a record player. (See also NEEDLE, STYLUS.) □ *Your record player isn't sounding so good. You might need a new cartridge.* □ *Do you sell cartridges for this brand of turntable?*

carving fork   a large, heavy fork used to hold meat in place while it is being carved. (See also CARVING KNIFE.) □ *The turkey's ready. Get the carving fork and knife.* □ *Our mouths watered while she skewered the roast with the carving fork and proceeded to carve it into thin, tender slices.*

carving knife   a long, sharp knife used for carving meat. (See also CARVING FORK.) □ *He sharpened the carving knife* *on a sharpening steel.* □ *The carving knife went through the meat as if it were butter.*

casement window   a window that opens by swinging out like a door. □ *The old house had quaint, diamond-paned, casement windows.* □ *She unlatched the casement window and pushed it open.*

cash machine See AUTOMATIC TELLER MACHINE.

cash register   a machine that adds up purchases, gives a receipt, and stores the money paid in a drawer. □ *I watched the display on the cash register to make sure I was being charged the correct price for each item.* □ *The clerk opened the cash register drawer and gave me my change.*

cash register tape   paper in a narrow strip, used in a CASH REGISTER to print out a receipt. □ *The clerk ran out of cash register tape and had to put in a new roll.* □ *There are coupons printed on the back of this cash register tape.*

casserole   **1.** a mixture of several foods, often including noodles or rice, baked and served in a covered dish. (See also HOT DISH.) □ *I asked my mother how to make tuna fish casserole, the kind with green beans and cream of mushroom soup.* □ *JOE: What do you put in that casserole? MARY: Just seasoned ground beef, cheddar cheese, rice, tomatoes, and corn bread over the top.* **2.** the covered dish in which a CASSEROLE is baked. □ *I use my two-quart casserole for all kinds of things.* □ *Layer the ingredients in a well-greased casserole.*

cassette   a small, flat case, especially one containing audio or videotape. □ *He put a cassette in the tape player.* □ *What did you record on this cassette? It doesn't have a label.*

cassette deck   a machine that plays and records audio CASSETTE tapes, especially one that is part of a stereo system including a separate amplifier and speakers. □ *He has a professional-quality cassette deck that can dub recordings from one cassette to another.* □ *She hooked up the cassette deck to the amplifier.*

cassette player a machine that plays audio CASSETTES. □ *Let's take the cassette player to the beach.* □ *The car radio also has a cassette player.*

caster a wheel that allows a piece of furniture to move around easily. □ *The chair is on casters, so you can move it around.* □ *He attached casters to the bottom of the footstool.*

castor oil oil from the seed of the castor oil plant, used as a medicine to empty the bowels. □ *My grandmother used to give us castor oil when we had stomach aches.* □ *The doctor said that castor oil was too harsh to give to little children.*

cathode ray tube AND **CRT** a tube in which a beam of electrons causes areas of a screen to glow. (CRT is often used to refer to a computer monitor containing a CATHODE RAY TUBE.) □ *As he turned the knob on the oscilloscope, he watched the cathode ray tube.* □ *This computer display isn't a CRT. It's an LCD.*

cat litter AND **kitty litter** small clay pellets usually placed in a tray for cats to eliminate in. (KITTY LITTER is informal.) □ *Please change the cat litter! It smells!* □ *I bought a bag of kitty litter at the pet store.*

catsup AND **ketchup** a sauce made from tomato paste, vinegar, and sugar. □ *May I have some catsup for these French fries?* □ *He put ketchup on his burger.*

catwalk a narrow walkway. □ *A catwalk just under the ceiling of the theater gives us access to the stage lights.* □ *The prison guard stood on the catwalk, where he had a good view of the prisoners in their cells.*

caulk **1.** a flexible substance used to seal a crack. □ *What kind of caulk should I use to seal the edge of the bathtub?* □ *She removed the brittle, old caulk from around the window frame.* **2.** to seal a crack with a flexible substance. □ *He caulked around the edge of the tile.* □ *She caulked the soles of her shoes to make them waterproof.*

CB radio See CITIZENS BAND RADIO.

C-clamp a metal clamp shaped like the letter C and adjusted by turning a screw. □ *The C-clamp held the two boards together while the glue dried.* □ *Use a C-clamp to hold that piece of wood steady on the workbench.*

CD See COMPACT DISC.

CD-ROM See COMPACT DISC READ-ONLY MEMORY.

ceiling fan an electric fan attached to a ceiling. □ *Turn on the ceiling fan. Let's get a breeze going in here.* □ *We installed a ceiling fan in the living room.*

CE key See CLEAR ENTRY KEY.

cell an electric battery. □ *The tape player takes six C cells.* □ *I need a couple D cells for my flashlight.*

cell(ular) phone a portable telephone that can be used anywhere. □ *Thanks to my cellular phone, I can make calls while I'm riding the commuter train.* □ *I gave my daughter a cell phone to keep in her car, in case of emergencies.*

centerpiece a decoration placed in the center of a dining table. □ *The guests brought a floral centerpiece as a gift to their host.* □ *She made a Thanksgiving centerpiece that included gourds and tiny ears of corn.*

central air AND **C/A** an air-conditioning system that cools an entire building. (See also CENTRAL HEATING.) □ *We installed central air in our house.* □ *2 bedroom apartment, C/A, no pets.*

central heating a heating system that heats an entire building. (See also CENTRAL AIR.) □ *This building has central heating.* □ *The central heating in the apartment building broke down. Everyone was freezing.*

Central standard time AND **CST** the time in the time zone that covers the middle part of the United States. (See also EASTERN STANDARD TIME, MOUNTAIN STANDARD TIME, PACIFIC STANDARD TIME.) □ *Chicago is on Central standard time.* □ *The program will air at 8:00 PM CST.*

Centronics™ cable   See PARALLEL CABLE.

cereal   **1.** a grain. □ *It is important to get plenty of cereals in your diet.* □ *Hominy grits are a favorite cereal in the South.* **2.** a breakfast food made of grain, sometimes with nuts, fruit, sugar, or other flavors added. □ *Shredded wheat is my favorite cereal.* □ *We had hot cereal for breakfast.*

cesspool   a tank that collects sewage and lets it seep into the ground. (See also SEPTIC SYSTEM, SEPTIC TANK.) □ *Cesspools are very unsanitary.* □ *Instead of a cesspool, we installed a septic tank.*

chafing dish   a metal dish in which food is kept warm while it is served. □ *The guest served themselves from the chafing dishes on the buffet.* □ *Keep the sauce warm in a chafing dish.*

chain guard   a metal shield that covers a BICYCLE CHAIN. □ *The chain guard kept my pants cuffs from getting caught in the chain.* □ *The ten-speed bike didn't have a chain guard.*

chain link fence   a fence made of woven metal rods. (See also CYCLONE™ FENCE.) □ *The yard was surrounded with a chain link fence.* □ *The little boy climbed up the chain link fence.*

chain saw   a power saw that cuts by moving a chain around a guide bar at high speed. □ *The workers used a chain saw to cut down the dead tree.* □ *I have an electric-powered chain saw.*

chaise longue   a narrow sofa, designed for one person to lie down on. (Also spelled "chaise lounge.") □ *She reclined on the chaise longue.* □ *The old chaise longue was my favorite place to sit and read.*

chalk   a crumbly, white substance usually used to make markings. □ *The teacher took a piece of chalk and wrote the equation on the blackboard.* □ *The dressmaker used chalk to mark the pattern details on the fabric.*

champagne flute   a tall, narrow, stemmed glass for serving champagne. □ *I bought a set of champagne flutes to match*

my other crystal. □ *He poured the bubbly liquid into cham-*
pagne flutes.

chandelier   a hanging lamp, especially one with lights on
several arms. □ *A crystal chandelier hung in the dining*
room. □ *The old theater has a beautiful stained-glass*
chandelier.

changer   **1.** a device that changes gears on a bicycle. (See
also DERAILLEUR.) □ *The changer doesn't work. I can't get*
the bike out of third gear. □ *The changer slipped while I*
was pedalling, and I suddenly found myself in first gear. **2.** a
device that puts a new CD or LP record on the turntable. □
The CD machine has a six-disc changer. □ *The changer*
dropped the next record onto the turntable.

channel   a television signal from a particular source. □
What channel is that program on? □ *This independent chan-*
nel does not belong to a network.

channel selector   a device that changes the CHANNEL that
a television set is receiving. □ *Turn the channel selector all*
the way counterclockwise. □ *Use the channel selector on the*
cable box, not the one on the television itself.

Chap Stick™   a brand of lip balm, a substance applied to
the lips to keep them from drying. □ *"Do you have some*
Chap Stick I could use?" Jill asked. □ *Mom said, "Put on*
some Chap Stick before you go out in the sun."

character   a symbol, such as a letter or number. □ *Com-*
puter file names can be eight characters long. □ *Numbers*
and letters are alphanumeric characters.

chassis   a frame, especially the frame of a car. □ *This*
model has a good, solid chassis and a powerful engine. □
The chassis is bent and cannot be repaired.

check cashing card   an identification card that permits
you to pay by check in a particular store. □ *May I see your*
check cashing card, please? □ *Would you like to apply for a*
check cashing card?

check-in   the act of showing that you are present. (Airline flights and hotels often require CHECK-IN.) □ *Passenger Smith, please proceed to the airline ticket counter for check-in.* □ *The airline will issue you a boarding pass at check-in.*

check-out line   a line of people waiting to pay for things in a store. □ *It seemed like I stood in that check-out line for an hour!* □ *The woman ahead of me in the check-out line suddenly ran back to the soup aisle to get something she forgot.*

cheese board   a board on which cheese can be sliced and served. □ *There were six different kinds of cheese on the cheese board.* □ *She arranged some crackers on the cheese board.*

cheesecloth   cotton cloth with a fairly coarse weave. □ *Strain the mixture through a cheesecloth.* □ *The kitchen towel was made of cheesecloth.*

cheese plane   a tool for cutting very thin slices of cheese. (Compare with CHEESE SLICER.) □ *Slice the cheese with a cheese plane.* □ *NANCY: How did you make these thin little curls of cheese? BILL: I used a cheese plane.*

cheese slicer   a tool for slicing cheese. (Compare with CHEESE PLANE.) □ *The grater has a blade that works as a cheese slicer.* □ *The cheese slicer has a stiff wire that passes through the cheese.*

cherry pitter AND **cherry stoner**   a tool that removes the pits from cherries. □ *This cherry pitter is handy when I want to make cherry pie.* □ *She went to work with her cherry stoner, and had a quart of cherries pitted in no time.*

cherry stoner   See CHERRY PITTER.

cherry tomato   a small, bite-sized tomato. □ *Let's put cherry tomatoes in the salad.* □ *I grew cherry tomatoes in my garden.*

chest of drawers   a piece of furniture with drawers, usually used to store clothes. (See also BUREAU.) □ *The* *bedroom set includes a bed frame and a matching chest of drawers.* □ *I keep my shirts in the closet and my underwear in the chest of drawers.*

Chicago-style   [of a pizza] having a thick crust. (Popular in Chicago.) □ *We are the only restaurant in Tulsa that makes genuine Chicago-style pizza.* □ *Would you like thin crust, or Chicago-style?*

chili   a stew made of beans, tomatoes, ground beef, and hot spices. □ *Chili and corn bread is a popular meal.* □ *The camp cook made a big pot of chili.*

chimney   a brick or stone structure on a roof, forming the top of a shaft that allows hot air and smoke to escape from a fireplace. □ *They must have a fire going. There's smoke coming out of their chimney.* □ *Something must be clogging the chimney. The smoke's not getting out.*

china   **1.** porcelain clay. □ *The figurine is made of china.* □ *Be careful with that china cup.* **2.** dishes made of porcelain clay. □ *She displayed her antique china in a china cabinet.* □ *I set the table with my best china.*

china cabinet   See CHINA CUPBOARD.

china cupboard AND **china cabinet**   a cabinet for displaying fine dishes. (See also BREAKFRONT, HUTCH.) □ *The china cupboard was crammed with dishes, crystal, and knick-knacks.* □ *Put the teacups back in the china cabinet, please.*

chinos   pants made of cotton TWILL fabric. □ *I put on chinos and a polo shirt.* □ *Can I wear chinos, or is that too casual?*

chipboard   See PARTICLE BOARD.

chisel   a tool with a flat, beveled point, used to cut or chip something. □ *The stonecutter hit the chisel with a hammer.* □ *I made a little groove in the wood with the chisel.*

choke   a device that limits the amount of air in the mixture of fuel and air entering an engine. □ *He adjusted the* *choke so that the car would run better when the engine was cold.* □ *The choke was stuck in one position. That's why the engine was racing.*

chopper   a tool, usually with a curved blade, for chopping food. □ *This chopper makes it easy to cut up vegetables for salsa.* □ *He got out the chopper and chopped up the garlic.*

chopping board AND **cutting board**   a board on which food is cut up. □ *I need to cut up some onions. I better get the chopping board.* □ *Don't dice those peppers on the countertop! Use a cutting board.*

chowder   a thick soup, usually containing seafood. □ *New England clam chowder is one of my favorite dishes.* □ *The inn was famous for its fish chowder.*

chrome   the metal trim on a car. □ *I washed and waxed the car and polished the chrome.* □ *It wasn't a serious car accident. I got a little dent in the chrome, that's all.*

chuck   the part of a drill or a ratchet screwdriver that holds the drill bit in place. □ *I loosened the chuck and removed the* ³⁄₈-*inch bit.* □ *Make sure the bit is seated firmly in the chuck.*

chuck key   a tool that tightens or loosens the chuck of a power drill, so that the drill bit will stay in place. □ *You will need to use the chuck key when you change the bit.* □ *This universal chuck key will fit any drill.*

chuck (roast)   a cut of beef from the animal's back, just behind the neck. □ *He browned the chuck roast in fat and then put it in the oven.* □ *You can use brisket or chuck in this stew.*

church key   a tool that punches a triangular hole in the end of a can. □ *She used the church key on the can of juice.* □ *I punched two holes in the can with the church key.*

circuit   a complete path for an electric current. (The wiring in a building is divided into CIRCUITS.) □ *The two outlets in this room are on two different circuits.* □ *The refrigerator has its own circuit.*

circuit board   a flat piece of plastic with electric components attached to it. □ *I opened up the VCR and looked at the circuit boards inside.* □ *The technician replaced an element on the circuit board.*

circuit breaker   a device that breaks the flow of electric current in a CIRCUIT if there is too much current. (Too much current in a CIRCUIT could cause the wiring to overheat and start a fire. Compare with FUSE.) □ *I see why the lights went out. The circuit breaker tripped.* □ *Why did the circuit breaker go? What's overloading that circuit?*

circular saw   a power saw with a circular blade. □ *He guided the circular saw along the cutting line he had marked on the plywood.* □ *Always wear goggles when using the circular saw. You don't want to get wood particles in your eyes.*

circulating pump   a pump that moves hot water through a heating system. □ *When the thermostat indicates that the room is too cold, the circulating pump forces hot water into the radiators.* □ *The circulating pump is located in the cool-water return line.*

citizens band radio AND **CB radio**   a two-way radio band that the public can use. □ *There's a citizens band radio in the car, so you can send for help if you get in trouble.* □ *The truckers used CB radio to tell each other where the police were laying speed traps.*

claw hammer   a hammer with two prongs on the opposite side of the head from the surface used for striking. (The prongs, or claw, of a CLAW HAMMER are often used to grasp nails and pull them out. See also BALL-PEEN HAMMER, HAMMER.) □ *The carpenter always kept a claw hammer within easy reach, in case she had to pull out a nail.* □ *Claw hammers are often used for working with wood, and ball-peen hammers for working with metal.*

cleanser   a substance that cleans something. □ *She sprinkled cleanser into the bathtub and scrubbed away with a sponge.* □ *This facial cleanser helps eliminate blemishes.*

clear entry key AND **CE key**   a key on a calculator, labeled "CE", that removes the most recently entered number from the display and from memory, without removing the rest of the calculation. (Compare with CLEAR (KEY).) □ *You put in the wrong number. Hit the clear entry key.* □ *He noticed that he had entered the number with the digits reversed, so he pressed the CE key.*

clear (key)   a key on a calculator, often labeled "C," that clears the numbers from the display and clears the calculation from the memory. (Compare with CLEAR ENTRY KEY.) □ *Having finished her calculation, she hit the clear key.* □ *I'm all messed up. I'll just press clear and start again.*

cleat   **1.** a shoe with small spikes in the sole that dig into the ground and give a good grip. (Usually plural.) □ *Have you seen my football cleats?* □ *The soccer players wore cleats.* **2.** a piece of metal with two prongs around which rope is wrapped to anchor it. □ *The sailor made the rope fast to the cleat.* □ *I hauled the flag up the flagpole, then wrapped the end of the rope around the cleat.*

cleaver   a heavy knife with a wide blade, used for chopping food. □ *He chopped the meat with a cleaver.* □ *She crushed the garlic by hitting it with the flat side of the cleaver.*

click on something   to place the CURSOR on an icon on the computer screen and press the mouse button once. (See also DOUBLE CLICK ON SOMETHING.) □ *Click on the word "File" on the menu bar.* □ *Click on "OK" in the dialog box.*

clip   **1.** to make short cuts with SCISSORS. □ *She sewed the seam and then clipped the curves, making little cuts from the edge of the fabric toward the seam.* □ *The barber clipped the customer's hair.* **2.** a cartridge holding a number of bullets. □ *He put another clip into the pistol.* □ *The ammunition for this gun comes in six-round clips.*

clock radio   an ALARM CLOCK and a radio built into one unit. (CLOCK RADIOS typically play the radio instead of sounding an alarm.) □ *I woke to an early-morning talk show* *on my clock radio.* □ *I opened my eyes and saw the glowing digital display of the clock radio.*

clog **1.** something that blocks the flow in a pipe. □ *There's some kind of clog in the drain. The water is backed up into the sink.* □ *I used a plunger to remove the clog.* **2.** to block a flow of gas or liquid. □ *What's clogging the bathtub drain?* □ *Cat hair had accumulated on the air filter and clogged the air conditioner.* **3.** a step-in shoe with a thick sole. □ *I like to wear these clogs around the house.* □ *His clogs thudded across the floor.*

closet auger AND **toilet auger** a tool for drilling clogs out of a toilet. □ *The plunger isn't working. Get the toilet auger.* □ *Using a closet auger, he worked the blockage out.*

closet bend a pipe, bent at 90 degrees, that drains waste out of a toilet. □ *The closet bend should rest on a solid support.* □ *The plumber hooked up the new toilet to the closet bend.*

clothes chute a passage that allows clothes to drop down into the place where they will be washed. □ *The upstairs bathroom has a clothes chute.* □ *A pile of dirty clothes accumulated under the clothes chute in the laundry room.*

(clothes) hamper AND **laundry hamper** a container in which dirty clothes can be collected. □ *Don't leave your dirty clothes on the floor. Put them in the clothes hamper.* □ *The hamper in the bathroom was jammed full. It was time to do the laundry.* □ *I carried the laundry hamper to the washing machine.*

clothesline a line on which wet clothes can be hung to allow them to dry. (See also DRYING RACK.) □ *There's a clothesline in the backyard.* □ *I set up a clothesline in the basement for the winter months.*

clothespin a clip for fastening clothes to a CLOTHESLINE. □ *I don't have enough clothespins to hang up all the clothes.* □ *He pulled the dry clothes free from the clothespins.*

clove **1.** a pungent, dried flower, used as a spice. □ *She spiced the apple cider with cloves.* □ *We need ground cloves for the spice cake.* **2.** a small bulb, part of a head of garlic. □ *Chop two cloves of garlic.* □ *How many cloves should we put in the spaghetti sauce?*

cloverleaf a highway intersection in the form of four loops. (See also INTERCHANGE.) □ *The car sped along one of the ramps of the cloverleaf.* □ *There's a cloverleaf ten miles north of town.*

clutch a device that allows an engine's power to be gradually applied to or removed from a transmission shaft. □ *The car won't stay in gear. I wonder if something's wrong with the clutch.* □ *Take your foot off the clutch once the gear is engaged.*

coach (class) AND **tourist (class)** an inexpensive class of airplane travel with crowded seating. □ *I always travel coach class, because it's cheap.* □ TRAVEL AGENT: *Would you like to travel first class or coach?* CUSTOMER: *Coach.* □ *On international flights, you may choose between first class, business class, and tourist class.*

coaster a small mat placed underneath a drinking glass to keep it from marking the surface beneath. □ *There was a set of coasters on the coffee table.* □ *Please use a coaster. Don't just set your glass down.*

coaster brake(s) a bicycle brake that works by moving the pedals backwards. (Compare with HAND BRAKE.) □ *It's a clunky old three-speed bike with coaster brakes.* □ *The coaster brake wasn't working. I checked the mechanism.*

coat a layer of paint. □ *Let the first coat dry before you apply another one.* □ *They applied several coats of paint to the car.*

coax(ial cable) a cable with a core of conductive material surrounded by a tube of conductive material and covered with insulation. (COAX is pronounced CO-acks.) □ *A length of coaxial cable ran between the VCR and the cable TV outlet* on the wall. □ *The computers in the network are connected with coax.*

cobbler a pastry made of fruit baked under a crust. (Compare with CRISP.) □ *Dessert was peach cobbler.* □ *I picked a quart of cherries today. I plan to make a cherry cobbler.*

cock **1.** a device that can start or stop a gas or liquid from flowing through. □ *He opened the cock on the radiator to let more steam in.* □ *The drain cock on the boiler is dripping. Better tighten it up.* **2.** to pull back the hammer or firing pin of a gun so that it is ready to be fired. □ *His gun was cocked and ready.* □ *She loaded the automatic and cocked it.*

cocoa **1.** a brown powder made from cacao beans. (Chocolate is also made from cacao beans.) □ *Add four tablespoons of cocoa to the batter.* □ *She sprinkled a little cocoa on top of each cup of cappuccino.* **2.** a drink made of COCOA or chocolate, sugar, and hot milk. □ *A hot cup of cocoa is wonderful on a cold day.* □ *If you want some cocoa, I'll start heating up the milk.*

CO detector See CARBON MONOXIDE DETECTOR.

CO₂ extinguisher See CARBON DIOXIDE EXTINGUISHER.

coffee cake a dense, sweet cake often served for breakfast or eaten with coffee. □ *Would you like a piece of this apricot coffee cake?* □ *They drank their coffee and nibbled their coffee cake.*

coffee can a can in which coffee is packaged and sold. □ *He used an empty coffee can to boil water in.* □ *There isn't much left in the coffee can.*

coffee cone a cone-shaped filter for a COFFEE MAKER. (See also COFFEE FILTER.) □ *I bought a box of coffee cones.* □ *She placed a coffee cone in the coffee maker.*

coffee filter a filter that holds ground coffee beans and lets hot water pass through. (See also COFFEE CONE.) □ *Don't put the coffee directly into the machine. Put a coffee* *filter in the basket first.* □ *This coffee filter can be washed and used again.*

coffee grinder   a device that grinds coffee beans. □ *I buy coffee in the bean. I have a coffee grinder at home.* □ *I woke to the sound of the coffee grinder in the kitchen.*

(coffee) grounds   used ground coffee beans. □ *She threw away the used filter and coffee grounds.* □ *The coffee was bitter and full of grounds.*

coffee maker   a device that makes coffee. (See also DRIP COFFEE MAKER.) □ *I poured the water into the coffee maker.* □ *This coffee maker has a ten-cup capacity.*

coffee measure AND **coffee scoop**   a spoon or small cup that measures the amount of ground coffee needed to make one cup of coffee. □ *Use the coffee measure to gauge the amount of coffee you need.* □ *One coffee scoop is equivalent to about one and a half tablespoons.*

coffeepot   a pot in which coffee is brewed. □ *She put the coffeepot on the stove.* □ *He poured another cup out of the coffeepot.*

coffee scoop   See COFFEE MEASURE.

coffee urn   a container for making and serving a large quantity of coffee. □ *The coffee urn on the left is regular coffee, and the one on the right is decaffeinated.* □ *She served her guests from a silver coffee urn.*

coil   **1.** something that is wound in a spiral. (See also ROLL.) □ *CUSTOMER: I would like to buy a hundred postage stamps. CLERK: You can buy them in sheets of fifty, or you can buy a coil of one hundred.* □ *The jacket is ornamented with coils of gold braid.* **2.** a length of tubing wound in a spiral or back and forth. □ *The condenser coil on the back of the air-conditioning unit discharges heat into the outside air.* □ *He felt the coils on the back of the refrigerator to see if they were warm.*

cola a soft drink flavored with the extract of cola nuts. □ *What brand of cola do you prefer?* □ *I'd rather have cola than lemon-lime.*

colander a bowl-shaped container with a number of holes that allow liquid to drain out. □ *Wash the lettuce and put it in a colander to drain.* □ *I drained the spaghetti in a colander.*

cold cuts a slice of cold meat. (COLD CUTS are often used in sandwiches. See also LUNCH MEAT.) □ *He made a sandwich of cold cuts and cheese.* □ *The guests made their own sandwiches from a platter of cold cuts.*

cold frame a clear glass or plastic frame that protects plants from the cold and allows sunlight to warm them. □ *I put cold frames over the vegetable plot. I was afraid there would be an early frost.* □ *She grew cabbage and onions in a cold frame.*

cold storage a place where things are stored and kept cold. □ *The store clerk went back into the cold storage to get more ice cream.* □ *She kept her fur coat in cold storage during the summer.*

cold water pipe a pipe that carries cold water into a building. (Contrasts with HOT WATER PIPE.) □ *The cold water tap should be hooked up to a cold water pipe.* □ *There was condensation on the cold water pipe.*

cole slaw a salad made of shredded cabbage and salad dressing. □ *Bring some cole slaw to the picnic.* □ *Cole slaw is a nice summertime dish.*

color showing all the colors in a picture. (Contrasts with BLACK AND WHITE.) □ *Is that color film or black and white?* □ *I bought a color TV.*

combination lock a lock that is opened by a sequence of numbers rather than a key. □ *The storage bin was locked with a combination lock.* □ *I got a combination lock for my bicycle.*

combination wrench   a wrench with a box-end wrench on one end and an open-end wrench of the same size on the other. □ *Combination wrenches are handy. You can try either end and see which works best.* □ *I have a set of combination wrenches for working on my car.*

comforter   a thick, quilted blanket. (See also THROW.) □ *My grandmother made this beautiful comforter.* □ *She tucked the comforter around her legs.*

co-mingled   mixed together. (Usually describes items to be recycled.) □ *This bin is for co-mingled items: paper, metal cans, and plastic.* □ *We have three recycling bins: one for cans, one for glass, and one for co-mingled newsprint and other paper.*

commemorative stamp   a stamp with a picture that honors someone or something. □ *Many people wanted the commemorative stamp with Elvis Presley's picture on it.* □ *A new line of commemorative stamps honors favorite children's books.*

compact disc AND **CD**   a disc with music or information digitally recorded on it. □ *I bought my favorite band's new CD.* □ *He listened to the compact disc on his portable CD player.*

compact disc read-only memory AND **CD-ROM**   a disc with computer-readable information recorded on it. □ *I got a new CD-ROM encyclopedia.* □ *This computer game is stored on compact disc read-only memory.*

comparison shop   to compare the price and quality of similar items, or the price of the same item at different stores. □ *We did a lot of comparison shopping before we decided which microwave to buy.* □ *Don't just buy the first dress that fits you. You should comparison shop.*

compass rose   a symbol on a map that shows which direction on the map corresponds to north, south, east, and west. □ *I couldn't find the compass rose on the map, so the directions were confusing.* □ *She drew a decorative compass rose on the finished map.*

compatible   able to work together. (When used to describe computers, COMPATIBLE means able to use the same software and accessories.) ☐ *This is an IBM-compatible laptop.* ☐ *The printer is Macintosh compatible.*

compost   waste material from plants and animals, allowed to rot and used to fertilize growing plants. (See also COMPOST HEAP.) ☐ *I covered the garden plot with a layer of compost.* ☐ *The gardener worked the compost into the sandy soil.*

compost heap AND **compost pile**   a pile of plant and animal waste that is being set aside to rot. (See also COMPOST.) ☐ *Don't throw those banana peels away. Put them on the compost heap.* ☐ *All kinds of trash can go into the compost pile, for instance, sawdust, dead leaves, coffee grounds, manure, etc.*

compost pile   See COMPOST HEAP.

compote   **1.** cooked fruit in syrup. ☐ *The meat was garnished with a cranberry compote.* ☐ *For dessert, we had a pear compote with ice cream.* **2.** a bowl on a stem, usually with a lid. ☐ *He served the jelly in a cut-glass compote.* ☐ *She spooned the pickle relish into a compote and carried it to the table.*

compressor   a device, part of a heat pump or air conditioner, that compresses refrigerant fluid in order to let heat escape. ☐ *There are two motors in the air conditioner. One runs the fan, and the other runs the compressor.* ☐ *The compressor and the condenser are located in a unit outside the house, so that the people inside don't hear the noise they make.*

computer-aided design AND **CAD**   the use of a computer program to make technical drawings and designs. (See also COMPUTER-AIDED MANUFACTURE.) ☐ *The engineers developed computer-aided design software for designing printed circuits.* ☐ *We can load a design from the CAD system directly to the software that controls manufacturing.*

computer-aided manufacture AND **CAM**   the use of a computer program to create a model of how a structure will behave. (See also COMPUTER-AIDED DESIGN.) □ *The engineers presented their CAM analysis of how the bridge would behave in high winds.* □ *This computer-aided manufacture software can run on a home computer.*

computer paper   paper designed to run through a computer printer, usually in one continuous strip, perforated and folded between pages, with evenly-spaced holes along the edges to fit the sprockets on the printer. □ *I printed out the sales figures on computer paper.* □ *He clipped the computer paper into the track feed on the printer.*

concentrate   a fluid from which most of the water has been removed. □ *I bought a can of orange juice concentrate.* □ *To reconstitute, add a few drops of the concentrate to two cups of water.*

concourse   a set of gates at an airport. □ *Your flight will be departing from gate 12 on the gold concourse.* □ *To get to my connecting flight, I had to run to a concourse at the other end of the airport.*

condensed milk   milk from which most of the water has been removed. (CONDENSED MILK with sugar added is called SWEETENED CONDENSED MILK. See also EVAPORATED MILK, POWDERED MILK.) □ *She added condensed milk to her coffee instead of cream.* □ *The cookie recipe calls for one can of sweetened condensed milk.*

condenser (coil)   a device, part of a cooling system, that allows hot refrigerant gases to condense into a liquid and so release heat. □ *This fan blows the heat from the condenser coil into the outside air.* □ *This tube conducts the refrigerant vapor into the condenser.*

condiment   a food used to add flavor to a dish. □ *Ketchup, mustard, and pickle relish are popular condiments for hamburgers.* □ *She served an assortment of condiments in little glass pots.*

confectioner's sugar   See POWDERED SUGAR.

console   **1.** a panel containing buttons, dials, switches, or other controls. □ *Press the "power" button on the VCR control console.* □ *The air conditioner controls were clearly labeled on the dashboard console of the car.* **2.** a large cabinet. □ *It took two people to move the television console.* □ *The stereo was set in a wooden console.*

consumer electronics   electronic devices that people use in their homes, such as televisions, VCRs, stereos, and personal computers. □ *We're the number one store for consumer electronics.* □ *Their shop repairs all kinds of consumer electronics.*

contact lens   a lens worn directly on the eye. (See also DAILY WEAR (CONTACT) LENS.) □ *I used to wear glasses, but now I have contact lenses.* □ *She took out her contact lenses and put them in their case.*

Con-Tact™ paper   a brand of plastic-coated paper with adhesive on one side. □ *"I always line my shelves with Con-Tact paper to protect them from spills," Joe said.* □ *"I like the way you decorated the notebook cover with Con-Tact paper," the teacher told his student.*

container   an object that can hold something else. □ *Put the lid back on that paint container.* □ *She poured the flour out of the bag into a plastic container with an airtight lid.*

continuity tester   a device that tests the flow of current through a circuit. □ *He touched the probes of the continuity tester to the wire, and the indicator light went on.* □ *The continuity tester shows that there is no current passing through this electrical cord.*

contraceptive   something that prevents pregnancy. (See also FAMILY PLANNING.) □ *The doctor can give you information about contraceptives.* □ *Condoms are a popular contraceptive.*

contrast   a control that increases or decreases the contrast between dark and light areas on a television or computer screen. □ *I fiddled with the contrast knob until I could read the words on the screen.* □ *The contrast was set so low that I could barely see the picture.*

control   a knob, button, switch, or other device that, when moved, makes a change in the way a machine operates. □ *Where's the brightness control on your TV?* □ *Don't mess with the controls on the furnace unless you know what you're doing.*

control (key) AND **Ctrl**   a key on a computer keyboard, labeled "Control" or "Ctrl." □ *Hit control-Q. That is, hold down the control key and press Q.* □ *Ctrl-"C" will interrupt the procedure.*

convection oven   an oven that operates by moving the hot air inside it. (Compare with MICROWAVE (OVEN).) □ *I use my microwave to heat liquids, but I use a convection oven for all my baking.* □ *There are both electric and gas convection ovens.*

convector   a device through which hot water flows in order to heat a room. (See also RADIATOR.) □ *The hot water heating system in this building uses baseboard convectors.* □ *This thermostat controls the convectors in the upstairs bedrooms.*

convenience store   a small store that is open long hours. □ *The kids went to the convenience store after school and bought some candy.* □ *I stopped by the convenience store on my way home to get a quart of milk.*

converter (box)   a box containing electronic components that convert the signal from a television cable into a form that can be viewed on a television set. □ *To change the channel, use the channel selector on your converter box.* □ *I connected my VCR to the converter.*

convertible   a car on which the roof folds down, leaving the top open. □ *It's a beautiful day. Let's take the convertible out for a spin.* □ *His pride and joy was his 1959 Chevy convertible.*

cookie cutter a tool that cuts a decorative shape out of flattened dough. □ *Oh, look! A cookie cutter shaped like the state of Texas!* □ *She used cookie cutters to make cookies shaped like stars, hearts, and diamonds.*

cookie gun a device that, when its trigger is pressed, squeezes a small amount of dough from a tube through an opening with a decorative shape. (Compare with COOKIE PRESS.) □ *Making a big batch of cookies is easy with this cookie gun.* □ *I clicked the trigger of the cookie gun, and a flower-shaped cookie appeared on the baking sheet.*

cookie jar a large, often decorative jar in which cookies are stored. □ *The cookie jar was shaped like a cat.* □ *There's some cookies in the cookie jar.*

cookie press a device that pushes dough from a tube through an opening with a decorative shape. (Compare with COOKIE GUN.) □ *The cookie press comes with six different discs, each one with a different shape cutout.* □ *You will need a cookie press to make these cookies.*

cookie sheet See BAKING SHEET.

cookware items which are used for cooking, such as pots, pans, knives, etc. □ *This store specializes in quality cookware.* □ *You can order this gourmet cookware through our catalog.*

coolant a substance that is used to cool something because it easily absorbs or releases heat. □ *There was not enough coolant in the car's cooling system.* □ *What kind of coolant does that refrigerator use?*

cooler an insulated container that keeps food cool or hot. □ *We put some sodas in the cooler and headed for the beach.* □ *Whenever I go on a long car trip, I like to take along some food in a cooler, in case I can't find a restaurant I like.*

cooling coil See EVAPORATOR (COIL).

cooling rack AND **cake rack; wire rack** a rack that allows air to flow over and under warm food in order to cool it.

☐ *After removing the cake from the oven, place it on a cooling rack until it is completely cool.* ☐ *Remove the cookies from the baking sheet and put them on a wire rack to cool.* ☐ *He took the muffins out of the pan and put them on the cake rack.*

coping   a structure that protects the top of a brick or stone wall. ☐ *It was a brick wall with a sandstone coping.* ☐ *The coping keeps rainwater from seeping into the wall.*

coping saw   a saw with a curved handle and a long, pointed blade, used for cutting curves and holes. ☐ *He made the cutout shapes with a coping saw.* ☐ *She carefully worked the coping saw around the curve.*

copy machine   See PHOTOCOPIER.

cordial glass AND **liqueur glass**   a small, stemmed glass used for serving cordials or liqueurs (sweet alcoholic liquors). ☐ *She sipped her cordial glass of Amaretto.* ☐ *He had a set of pink crystal liqueur glasses.*

cordless drill   an electric drill that does not need a cord to operate. ☐ *When you're done with the cordless drill, put it back in its bracket and let it recharge.* ☐ *This cordless drill is very convenient. For one thing, there's no cord for me to trip over.*

cordless (tele)phone   a telephone with the handset not attached to the base by a cord. ☐ *I like this cordless telephone. It lets me move from room to room while I talk.* ☐ *She took the cordless phone into the backyard with her.*

core   **1.** the woody, inedible center of a fruit such as an apple or a pear. ☐ *Toss your apple core on the compost heap.* ☐ *He ate the apple all the way down to the core.* **2.** to remove the CORE from a piece of fruit. ☐ *Core and slice the apples.* ☐ *She cored the pineapple with a paring knife.*

corned beef   beef that is cured in salt water and spices. ☐ *She sliced the corned beef very thin.* ☐ *Corned beef and cabbage is a favorite dinner at our house.*

cornice   a decorative edging or molding. □ *There was an ornamental carving on the cornice.* □ *The cornice hung some two feet past the wall of the house.*

Corning Ware™   a brand of ceramic baking dishes. □ *"Can Corning Ware be used in the microwave?" I asked the salesperson.* □ *"I would like a set of Corning Ware casseroles with matching lids," said Mary.*

corn syrup   a sweet liquid made from corn. □ *Corn syrup is an ingredient in many candies.* □ *Heat the corn syrup until it bubbles.*

correction fluid   a paint used to cover up mistakes on a typed or printed page.(See also LIQUID PAPER™.) □ *I dabbed correction fluid onto the misspelled word.* □ *On the letter, the addressee's name had been blocked out with correction fluid.*

corrosion   the eating away of a metal. □ *The salt air was responsible for the rapid corrosion of the cars in the seaside town.* □ *This enamel paint resists corrosion.*

corrugated cardboard   cardboard made of two flat, thin layers with a pleated layer between them. □ *Corrugated cardboard is accepted for recycling here.* □ *The box was made of corrugated cardboard.*

cosmetics   substances that people use to improve or change the way they look or smell. (See also MAKE-UP.) □ *The medicine chest was full of cosmetics: lipstick, nail polish, eye shadow, rouge, mascara, perfume, etc.* □ *The drugstore also sells cosmetics.*

cottage cheese   soft, white, loose curds of cheese. □ *I had some fruit salad with cottage cheese.* □ *For an appetizer, we had tomatoes stuffed with cottage cheese.*

cottage fries AND **home fries**   potatoes cut into thick pieces and fried. (See also (FRENCH) FRIES.) □ *All the sandwiches on the menu come with a side of cottage fries.* □ *We make home fries in our deep fryer.*

cotter pin   a piece of metal bent in half, used to fasten metal together. ☐ *Pass the cotter pin through the hole in the metal shaft, then bend the ends outward to secure it.* ☐ *A cotter pin kept the axle from slipping through the hole in the middle of the wheel.*

cotton swab   a small stick with a cotton tip at one or both ends. ☐ *She cleaned out her ear with a cotton swab.* ☐ *I used a cotton swab dipped in alcohol to clean the tape recorder head.*

cough drop AND **throat lozenge**   a small candy containing medicine to soothe a cough. (COUGH DROP is informal.) ☐ *I couldn't stop coughing, so I took a cough drop.* ☐ *A throat lozenge might make your sore throat feel better.*

counter   a horizontal surface that is roughly waist high. ☐ *She stacked the bowls on the kitchen counter.* ☐ *I stepped up to the airline counter and asked what time the flight would depart.*

counterpane   a decorative blanket placed on top of other linens on a bed to protect them from dust and dirt. (See also (BED)SPREAD.) ☐ *She folded back the counterpane and plumped up the pillows.* ☐ *This counterpane was woven by my great-great-grandmother.*

countersink   to fasten a screw or a nail in place so that the head is below a surface. ☐ *Countersink the screws so that they do not project from the surface of the wood.* ☐ *He used a nail set to countersink the nail.*

counterweight   a weight that balances an object at the other end of a pulley or a lever. ☐ *As the elevator went down, the counterweight went up.* ☐ *A counterweight keeps the record player's tone arm from falling too heavily onto the record.*

coupe   a car with two doors, a front and back seat, and a trunk in the rear. ☐ *Come in and take a look at our new luxury coupe.* ☐ *Test-drive this sporty new coupe!*

coupler   a latch that connects rail cars. □ *The engine backed up to the car, and the coupler engaged.* □ *The workers released the coupler and moved the cars apart.*

coupling   a threaded metal or plastic tube used to join plumbing pipes. □ *I joined short lengths of pipe with couplings until I had the length I needed.* □ *A reducing coupling attaches a larger pipe to a smaller one.*

coupon   a ticket that allows you a discount on a purchase. □ *I have a coupon for ten percent off.* □ *You can find a lot of good coupons in the Sunday paper.*

courtesy booth   a counter in a store where customers can get help with problems. □ *To return merchandise, please go to the courtesy booth on the second floor.* □ *At the courtesy booth in the grocery store, you can buy postage stamps and cash checks.*

cover crop   a crop that is grown in order to enrich the soil. □ *The farmer planted winter wheat as a cover crop.* □ *Soybean is a good cover crop. It puts nitrogen back into the soil.*

cover plate   See SWITCH PLATE.

cradle   the part of a telephone that holds the receiver in place. □ *He placed the receiver back in the cradle.* □ *The handset isn't seated in the cradle. The phone is off the hook.*

cramp   a piece of metal used to brace a brick wall. □ *They shored up the wall with a cramp.* □ *The cramps were all that was holding the wall together.*

crank   **1.** a handle that can be turned in order to move something. □ *Turn the crank to move the film through the microfilm reader.* □ *He raised and lowered the chalkboard with a crank.* **2.** to turn a CRANK. □ *You have to crank the old-fashioned record player to make it go.* □ *Crank the food mill until all the nuts are ground.*

crankcase   the part of an engine block that houses the CRANKSHAFT. □ *Drain the oil out of the crankcase.* □ *The* *bearings that hold the crankshaft are mounted inside the crankcase.*

crankshaft   a rod rotated by the pistons in an engine. □ *A flywheel at the end of the crankshaft engages with the clutch.* □ *When all the pistons are firing in the correct order, the crankshaft turns smoothly.*

crash   [for a computer] to fail. (Slang. See also SYSTEM CRASH.) □ *The power outage made my computer crash.* □ *The office system crashed, so we couldn't do any work all afternoon.*

crawl space   an area between the ground and the floor of a building that gives access to water and sewer pipes. □ *The plumber went down into the crawl space, trying to find the source of the bad smell.* □ *She lifted a panel in the floor and reached through the opening into the crawl space.*

cream   **1.** the fatty liquid that rises to the top of whole milk. □ *She poured a little cream into her coffee.* □ *Remove the soup from the heat and add one cup of cream.* **2.** to beat something, especially butter, until it is light and fluffy. □ *Cream the butter and the brown sugar.* □ *Cream the butter before adding the vanilla.*

creamed   served in a sauce made with milk or CREAM. □ *Help yourself to that creamed corn.* □ *At camp, we often ate creamed tuna on toast.*

creamer   a small pitcher used to serve CREAM. □ *On my breakfast tray, I found a pot of coffee and a creamer brim-full of fresh cream.* □ *I'd like to get a creamer to match my china sugar bowl.*

Cream of Wheat™   a brand of cooked wheat breakfast cereal. (See also FARINA.) □ *"There's nothing like a hot bowl of Cream of Wheat on a cold winter morning," said Ellen, rubbing her hands.* □ *"I like Cream of Wheat with milk and brown sugar," said the little boy.*

cream sauce   a sauce of thickened milk or CREAM. □ *Our special tonight is pasta in a delicate cream sauce.* □ *I have all the ingredients for spinach in cream sauce.*

crepe   a thin PANCAKE. □ *The main dish was crepes filled with sautéed vegetables.* □ *The dessert crepes were topped with whipped cream.*

crepe pan   a flat-bottomed pan designed for cooking CREPES. □ *She drizzled the batter into the crepe pan.* □ *He lifted the delicate pancake from the crepe pan.*

Crescent™ wrench   a brand of wrench with jaws that open or close to fit many sizes of nuts or bolts. □ *He used a Crescent wrench to remove the spark plugs.* □ *Hand me the Crescent wrench. I'm not sure what size this bolt is.*

crew neck   a shirt or sweater neck with a round opening that fits close around a person's neck. (See also BOAT NECK, SCOOP NECK, V NECK.) □ *That crew neck sweater looks good with the button-down shirt underneath.* □ *Most T-shirts have crew necks.*

crib   a tall-sided bed for a small child. □ *A brightly-colored mobile hung above the baby's crib.* □ *The baby was standing up, peeking over the side of the crib.*

crimp   to pinch or press something together. □ *He crimped the two wires together.* □ *The dressmaker crimped the edge of the fabric with a special crimping iron.*

Crisco™   a brand of vegetable shortening. (See also SHORTENING.) □ *Jane asked, "Did you make these cookies with butter?" "No, I used Crisco," Joe replied.* □ *"Fry the chicken in Crisco," Dad suggested.*

crisp   **1.** a baked dessert made of fruit with a sweet, crunchy crust on top. (Compare with COBBLER.) □ *What a delicious apple crisp!* □ *The pear crisp is all ready to go into the oven.* **2.** a molded, fried, crispy snack food—very much like a potato chip—made from tiny bits of potato. ☐ *John opened a can of crisps and ate them all himself!* ☐ *Would you like chips or crisps? Crisps break more easily.*

crisper   a drawer or compartment in a refrigerator that keeps vegetables moist and crisp. ☐ *Put the celery in the crisper.* ☐ *This refrigerator model has a dairy compartment, a meat compartment, and a crisper.*

Crockpot™   an electric device that cooks food slowly, at low temperatures. ☐ *"In the morning, I throw some meat and a few vegetables into the Crockpot, and when I get home, I have a nice pot of stew," Jim said.* ☐ *"I like to use the Crockpot for making pea soup," said Jane.*

croquette   finely-chopped food formed into a small patty, breaded, and fried. ☐ *For lunch, I made ham croquettes and a green salad.* ☐ *The restaurant's salmon croquettes are a big favorite.*

cross section   a picture or display showing how something would look if it were cut down the middle. ☐ *In this cross section, you can see how the piston fits into the chamber.* ☐ *The cross section of the mattress shows the springs and the different layers of padding.*

crosswise   from side to side. (Compare with LENGTHWISE.) ☐ *Cut the carrot crosswise into little rounds.* ☐ *He folded the blanket crosswise.*

crouton   a cube of dry, seasoned bread, often used as a GARNISH. ☐ *May I have some croutons for my salad?* ☐ *She sprinkled croutons on top of the soup.*

crowbar AND **pinch bar**   a steel bar with one end bent into a hook, used for prying things apart. ☐ *You'll need a crowbar to get that door open. It's rusted shut.* ☐ *They used pinch bars to pry up the floorboards.*

CRT   See CATHODE RAY TUBE.

cruet a glass bottle with a stopper, usually used to hold vinegar or oil for salad dressing. □ *The waiter brought me a vinegar cruet for my salad.* □ *She served the worcestershire sauce in a cruet.*

cruise control a device that keeps a car going at a set speed. □ *I set the cruise control at 65 miles per hour.* □ *He liked to use the cruise control on long highway trips.*

crumb a small, irregular fragment, especially of bread. □ *She wiped the crumbs off the tabletop.* □ *He threw his toast crumbs out the window for the birds to eat.*

crumb tray a tray at the bottom of a toaster that catches CRUMBS. □ *He emptied the crumb tray into the garbage can.* □ *I removed the crumb tray and shook the crumbs out of the toaster.*

crust the outer layer of a bread. □ *This French bread has such a nice, thick crust.* □ *She cut the crusts off the sandwiches.*

CST See CENTRAL STANDARD TIME.

Ctrl See CONTROL (KEY).

cueing a control on a phonograph turntable that raises or lowers the TONE ARM. □ *This lever controls the cueing. Lift it, move the tone arm over to the song you want to play, and then move the lever down.* □ *Don't just drop the tone arm onto the record. Use the cueing control!*

cuff a band of fabric around the end of a sleeve or a pants leg. □ *He unbuttoned his cuffs and rolled up his sleeves.* □ *Dirt got caught in my pants cuffs.*

Cuisinart™ a brand of FOOD PROCESSOR. □ *"Just pop those carrots into the Cuisinart, and they'll be grated in a jiffy,"* Larry said as he grated the cheese. □ *"I use my Cuisinart to mix bread dough," said Debby.*

culottes   pants or shorts with very full legs. □ *Is that a skirt or culottes?* □ *Do you think these shoes go with my culottes?*

cupcake   a small cake, roughly the size of a cup. □ *The children love to have cupcakes for dessert.* □ *I frosted the chocolate cupcakes with vanilla frosting.*

cupcake liners   See BAKING CUPS.

curb service   service that brings something out to or picks something up from the curb. □ *The restaurant has curb service. They'll bring your carry-out right to your car.* □ *JANE: Do you have to take your recyclables to the recycling center downtown? BILL: No, we have curb service. A truck comes by once a week and picks everything up.*

curbside recycling   the service of picking up recyclable items from the curb by your house. □ *The sanitation company now offers curbside recycling.* □ *Curbside recycling collects on Wednesday mornings.*

curler AND **(hair) roller**   a cylinder around which hair is wrapped in order to curl it. (See also HOT ROLLERS.) □ *She came to the door in her bathrobe and curlers.* □ *I like these foam hair rollers. You can sleep on them.*

curling iron   a cylindrical, heated device used for curling hair. □ *Plug in the curling iron and I'll curl your hair for you.* □ *She used the curling iron to make curls at the end of her ponytail.*

current   a flow of electricity. □ *Use the continuity tester to see if there is any current coming through that wire.* □ *Current is measured in amperes.*

cursor   a symbol on a computer screen that shows where characters will appear as you type them in. □ *She pressed the "up"-arrow key, and the cursor moved up one line.* □ *You can position the cursor with the mouse or with the arrow keys.*

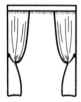

curtains AND **draperies; drapes**   pieces of cloth that hang from a rod above the inside of a window and can be pulled together to cover it. (DRAPERIES and DRAPES are formal. To draw CURTAINS, DRAPERIES, or DRAPES is to open or shut them.) ☐ *Shut the curtains. There's too much light in here.* ☐ *The draperies matched the blue of the pattern in the rug.* ☐ *She drew the drapes in the evening.*

cushion   a cloth-covered pad. ☐ *The chair cushion was so thin I could feel the springs underneath it when I sat down.* ☐ *She put a cushion behind her back.*

custard   a soft food made of cooked eggs and milk. (CUS-TARD can be either boiled or baked.) ☐ *Pour the custard into individual custard cups and bake for fifty minutes at 300 degrees.* ☐ *Dessert was chocolate custard.*

custard cup   a small dish in which CUSTARD can be baked and served. ☐ *She poured the pudding into custard cups.* ☐ *Set the filled custard cups in a tray of hot water and place them in the oven to bake.*

cut   to remove words or pictures from a computer screen. (See also PASTE.) ☐ *She selected the text she wanted to cut.* ☐ *Does this word processor allow you to cut and paste?*

cut in   to combine shortening with flour or other dry ingredients by cutting the shortening into tiny pieces. ☐ *After you have mixed the dry ingredients, cut in the butter.* ☐ *Cut in the shortening using two knives or a pastry cutter.*

cutlery   **1.** knives used for preparing or eating food. ☐ *This store specializes in cutlery. We should be able to get a good butcher knife here.* ☐ *She carefully sharpened the kitchen cutlery.* **2.** knives, forks, and spoons. (See also FLATWARE, SILVERWARE.) ☐ *Each place at the table was set with gleaming silver cutlery.* ☐ *She rinsed the cutlery before putting it in the dishwasher.*

cutting board   See CHOPPING BOARD.

cycle selector   a control on a WASHING MACHINE, DISH-WASHER, or DRYER that selects the temperature and length of the washing or drying cycle. ☐ *Set the cycle selector to "cold* *wash." □ The cycle selector has settings for small or normal loads.*

Cyclone™ fence   a brand of fence made of metal links. (See also CHAIN LINK FENCE.) □ *"Hey, kids! Don't you climb that Cyclone fence," she shouted. □ "No way my dogs could have got out," he protested. "The Cyclone fence keeps them in the yard."*

cylinder   **1.** the part of a revolver that holds a set of cartridges and moves them into place for firing. □ *She swung out the cylinder to remove the spent cartridges. □ There are six chambers in the cylinder. The gun can fire six bullets before reloading.* **2.** See (LOCK) CYLINDER.

cylinder block   the part of an engine that houses the cylinders, the chambers in which the pistons go up and down. □ *The exhaust manifold is bolted to the cylinder block. □ Locate the rocker arm cover, on top of the cylinder block.*

D

dado **1.** a groove cut into a piece of wood. □ *This saw blade makes a clean, straight dado.* □ *She cut dadoes for the brackets to fit into.* **2.** the lower part of an inside wall. □ *The dado is paneled with cherry wood.* □ *She had wallpaper on the upper part of the wall, while the dado was painted white.*

daily wear (contact) lens a contact lens that is worn during waking hours. (See also CONTACT LENS.) □ *I used to have daily wear contact lenses, but now I have disposables.* □ *I can't sleep in these contacts. They're daily wear lenses.*

dairy compartment See BUTTER COMPARTMENT.

daisy wheel a plastic wheel with letters of type around the edge, part of an electric typewriter or computer printer. □ *The daisy-wheel printer makes a lot of noise. The letters on the daisy wheel clatter against the paper.* □ *The typewriter has a number of different daisy wheels, each with a different typeface.*

dam a structure that holds water back. □ *They built a dam across the river.* □ *If the dam breaks, the whole town will be flooded.*

damper a flap that opens or closes an opening between a fireplace and a chimney. □ *Open the damper before you light a fire in the fireplace. Otherwise the smoke will fill the room.* □ *It was a windy day. I closed the damper to keep the wind from blowing in through the fireplace.*

damper pedal See FORTE PEDAL.

dark meat the thighs and legs of a cooked fowl. (Contrasts with WHITE MEAT.) □ *Would you prefer white meat or dark meat?* □ *I like dark meat. Give me a leg off that turkey.*

dart a fold sewn together in order to make fabric fit a curved shape. □ *The tailor put bust darts into the blouse so* *that it would fit the customer's figure.* □ *She marked the position of the darts on the front of the dress.*

dash   a very small quantity of liquid or powder. □ *Add a dash of hot sauce.* □ *She put a dash of nutmeg into the hot apple cider.*

dash(board)   the panel facing the front seats of a car, where the gas gauge, speedometer, radio, and other controls are located. (DASH is informal.) □ *The cigarette lighter is on the dashboard, to the left of the radio.* □ *He rested his coffee cup on the dash.*

database   **1.** a set of data in computer-readable form. □ *The company has a giant database containing the names, addresses, and phone numbers of all its customers.* □ *All the books in the library are indexed in this database.* **2.** a computer program that creates and works with DATABASES. □ *Can you recommend a good database?* □ *This software package contains a word processor, database, and a spreadsheet.*

Daylight savings time AND **DST**   one hour later than standard time. (Most areas in the United States use DAYLIGHT SAVINGS TIME in the spring and summer.) □ *When do we go on Daylight savings time? It's this Sunday, isn't it?* □ *It's nine-thirty by the time the sun sets, now that we're on Daylight savings time.* □ *The time is 2:00 PM, DST.*

DC   See DIRECT CURRENT.

dead bolt   a lock that thrusts a metal bolt from the edge of a door into a corresponding hole in the doorjamb. □ *Lock the dead bolt before you go to bed.* □ *The hotel door had both a doorknob lock and a dead bolt.*

decanter   a glass container with a spout or lip for pouring liquids out. (See also CARAFE.) □ *She poured the drinks out of a crystal decanter.* □ *The coffee decanter will hold twelve cups.*

deck   a platform attached to the side of a house. □ *Joe's out on the deck, putting some steaks on the grill.* □ *The sliding door in the kitchen opens out onto the deck.*

deck chair   a folding chair long enough for a person to lie down on. □ *She set up a deck chair on the lawn.* □ *He lay on the deck chair and sunbathed.*

decongestant   a drug that reduces swelling, especially in the nose. □ *This cold medicine contains a decongestant.* □ *He used a decongestant spray.*

decor   the way a place is decorated. □ *I love the country decor in that restaurant.* □ *They bought the painting because it went well with their living room decor.*

decorating bag   a cone-shaped bag with a metal tip, through which frosting is squeezed to make decorations. (See also PASTRY BAG.) □ *She scooped the blue icing into a decorating bag.* □ *He used a decorating bag with a flat tip to make these sugar roses.*

dedicated   built and used for only one purpose. □ *You don't need a computer if all you want to do is word processing. You can get a dedicated word processor.* □ *A dedicated phone line connects the computers in the network.*

deep dish   baked in a deep pan; thick. □ *For dessert, I baked a deep dish apple pie.* □ *Tony's Ristorante makes an excellent deep dish pizza.*

deep fry   to fry something in enough oil or fat to cover it. (Compare with PAN FRY.) □ *We deep fried the onion rings in vegetable oil.* □ *The chef at that restaurant deep fries everything.*

deep fryer   a device that heats a large quantity of fat or oil for frying food. □ *We use our electric deep fryer for making French fries.* □ *She carefully removed the fish sticks from the deep fryer.*

defogger   See DEFROSTER.

defrost   to thaw something out. □ *I defrosted the frozen spinach in the microwave.* □ *Defrost the turkey before you put it in the oven.*

defroster AND **defogger**   a device that heats a car window so that ice and fog will not form on it. □ *Turn on the defroster while I try to scrape the ice off the windshield.* □ *The windows were steaming up, so I turned on the defogger.*

dehumidifier   a device that removes moisture from the air. □ *An air conditioner and a dehumidifier maintain an ideal climate for these rare manuscripts.* □ *Without the dehumidifier, it would be awfully muggy in here in the summertime.*

de-icer   a chemical that removes ice. □ *I squirted some de-icer into the frozen lock on my car door.* □ *There was a solid layer of ice on the windshield. He sprayed it with de-icer.*

deli(catessen)   a place that sells prepared foods. □ *I went to the delicatessen and got some sandwiches.* □ *She picked up some olives and potato salad at the deli on her way home.*

deli-style   of the kind sold in a DELI(CATESSEN). □ *These deli-style pickles have extra garlic and spices.* □ *Our deli-style meats are the best in town.*

demitasse   a small cup with a handle, often used for serving coffee. □ *She poured espresso into the demitasse.* □ *After the meal, I had a demitasse of Turkish coffee.*

denim   a thick cotton fabric with a twill weave. (Blue jeans are made of DENIM.) □ *My blue denim jacket is one of my favorite things to wear.* □ *Denim shirts are very popular.*

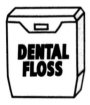

dental floss AND **(tooth) floss**   a thin fiber used to clean between teeth. □ *The dentist gave me a new toothbrush and a container of dental floss.* □ *She worked the tooth floss in between her teeth.*

deodorant   a preparation that eliminates or covers up the smell of perspiration. (See also ANTIPERSPIRANT.) □ *I took a shower and put on some deodorant.* □ *This deodorant has a spicy smell.*

department store   a store that sells many different kinds of things. □ *At the department store, I got a shirt, a bed-*

spread, and a new garden hose. □ *The department store is having a sale on bakeware.*

depilatory   a preparation that removes hair. □ *She used a depilatory on her upper lip.* □ *This depilatory cream will not irritate your skin.*

deposit   an amount of money paid as a guarantee. □ *There's a ten-cent deposit on glass bottles in this state. When you return the bottle to the store, you get your ten cents back.* □ *We put down a deposit on the dining room set we wanted.*

deposits   substances left behind when water evaporates. (See also BUILDUP.) □ *The water is full of iron, and it leaves rust deposits in the sink.* □ *She scrubbed at the lime deposits on the bottom of the tub.*

derailleur   a device that changes gears on a bicycle by moving the bicycle chain from one set of sprockets to another. (See also CHANGER.) □ *She moved the gear lever, and the derailleur smoothly moved the chain into the next gear.* □ *The bent chain would not move through the derailleur.*

descending order   [of numbers] from largest to smallest; of letters, from Z to A. (Compare with ASCENDING ORDER.) □ *I sorted the zip codes in descending order.* □ *Just for a change, the teacher called out the students' names in descending order.*

desktop (computer)   a full-sized personal computer, the right size to sit on a desk. (Compare with LAPTOP (COMPUTER), NOTEBOOK (COMPUTER), PALMTOP.) □ *The desktop computer comes with mouse, monitor, and several popular software packages already installed.* □ CUSTOMER: *I'd like to look at some computers.* SALESPERSON: *Were you interested in a desktop or a laptop?*

desktop publishing   designing and publishing printed materials using a personal computer. □ *I have six years' experience at desktop publishing.* □ *This graphics program can export images into a word-processing file, so it's great for desktop publishing.*

dessert plate   a small plate on which dessert is served; part of a formal table setting. □ *On each dessert plate, a cream puff rested in a shining pool of chocolate sauce.* □ *The hostess took our dinner plates and brought in a stack of dessert plates.*

dessert spoon   a small spoon used for eating desserts. □ *The silver service included tablespoons, soup spoons, tea-spoons, and dessert spoons.* □ *The waiter brought me a dessert spoon and a goblet full of chocolate mousse.*

detergent   a substance used for cleaning. □ *I put laundry detergent into the washing machine.* □ *The dishwasher requires a special dishwashing detergent.*

deviled   mixed with spicy seasonings. □ *What delicious deviled eggs!* □ *These sandwiches are deviled ham on toast.*

dew point   the temperature at which dew forms. (A measure of humidity.) □ *It's 85 degrees right now, with a dew point of 72.* □ *The humidity today is very high. The dew point is almost the same as the temperature.*

diagonal parking   a parking arrangement in which cars are parked side by side, at an angle. (Compare with PARAL-LEL PARKING.) □ *I like diagonal parking because it's easy to get the car into the parking space.* □ *The parking lot at the mall is marked for diagonal parking.*

dial   **1.** a control that you twist clockwise or counterclock-wise in order to change the way a machine is operating. (See also KNOB, SWITCH.) □ *The big dial on the front of the TV is the channel selector.* □ *Turn your radio dial to 101.7 FM.* **2.** to place a call on a telephone. □ *Every time I dial that number, I get a busy signal.* □ *You must have dialed incorrectly.*

dialog box   a box appearing on a computer screen that requires you to make a choice. □ *Click on "OK" in the dialog box.* □ *A dialog box will appear, asking you if you want to save changes to the file.*

dial tone a steady tone heard through a telephone receiver when the receiver is off the hook but there is no call in progress. □ *He hung up. I heard a dial tone.* □ *Something's wrong with the phone. I don't even get a dial tone when I pick up the receiver.*

diaper a piece of material worn between a baby's legs and fastened around the waist, used to contain the baby's urine and feces. □ *Do you use cloth diapers or disposables?* □ *I think the baby needs a new diaper.*

diaper pail a pail in which dirty DIAPERS are collected. □ *Twice a week, the diaper service comes to collect the diaper pail.* □ *The diaper pail needs to be cleaned thoroughly.*

diaper service a business that collects and cleans dirty DIAPERS and delivers clean ones. □ *The young parents thought that getting a diaper service would be a good idea.* □ *The diaper service came and emptied the diaper pail.*

diaphragm **1.** a device that controls the amount of light that can pass through a camera lens. □ *As the diaphragm closes, the aperture gets smaller, and the picture will have greater depth of field.* □ *She set the camera for an aperture of f/2. The diaphragm was wide open.* **2.** a thin metal plate that vibrates when sound waves hit it. (Part of a microphone.) □ *The diaphragm in the telephone receiver had to be replaced.* □ *This magnet converts the vibration of the diaphragm to an electrical signal.*

dice to cut something into very small cubes. □ *Dice the eggplant.* □ *I need you to dice two onions for me.*

(dietary) fiber fiber from fruits, vegetables, and grains that helps the intestines move food along the digestive tract. □ *One serving of this cereal provides five grams of dietary fiber.* □ *Joe was suffering from constipation. His doctor recommended getting more fiber in his diet.*

differential a device on a car axle that allows the wheel on the outside of a turn to spin faster than the wheel on the inside, so that the car is easier to control. □ *I'm having diffi-culty handling the car around turns. I think something may be wrong with the differential.* □ *You may need a different lubricant in the differential.*

digital   1. having to do with formed numbers rather than markings on a clock face. □ *Tom wears a digital watch.* □ *I can tell time better from an analog watch than I can from a digital one.* **2.** having to do with the kind of coded informa-tion used by a computer and similar devices. □ *I cannot un-derstand any of this digital date.* □ *You are not supposed to be able to red digital data.*

digital display   a display that shows numbers, rather than a pointer on a scale. □ *The gas gauge has a digital display that tells you exactly how many gallons are left in the tank.* □ *I could see the glowing red numbers on my alarm clock's digital display.*

digital watch   a watch that shows the time in numbers, rather than hands on a dial. □ *His digital watch beeped, in-forming him that it was five o'clock.* □ *This digital watch can display the time and date, and it can also function as a stopwatch.*

dike   a structure that holds floodwater back. (See also LEVEE.) □ *The dike sprang a leak, and the whole street flood-ed.* □ *The river swelled with the heavy rains, but the dikes held.*

dill pickle   a cucumber pickled in vinegar, salt, dill, and other spices. □ *I like a few slices of dill pickle on my ham-burger.* □ *She bit into the crunchy dill pickle.*

dime store   a store that sells a variety of inexpensive things. (See also FIVE AND TEN (CENT STORE).) □ *I bought a few post cards at the dime store.* □ *The dime store is having a sale on craft supplies.*

diner   a restaurant that serves inexpensive, quickly pre-pared food. □ *They have good French fries at that diner.* □ *I usually have breakfast in a little diner on the way to work.*

dining room   a room used for serving meals. □ *Come on into the dining room. Dinner is served.* □ *In the dining room there was a table with matching chairs, a china cupboard, and a buffet.*

dinner plate   a large plate used for the main course of a dinner; part of a formal table setting. □ *After the soup plates were removed, the dinner plates were brought in.* □ *We crowded our dinner plates with good things from the buffet.*

diode   an electrical device that allows current to flow through in only one direction. □ *The diode in the car's alternator failed.* □ *The AC/DC adapter contains a diode.*

dip   a sauce into which other foods, such as chips, crackers, or cut-up vegetables, are dipped. □ *Sour cream is the main ingredient in many kinds of dip.* □ *Jane makes a wonderful dip with mayonnaise and artichoke hearts.*

dipstick   a thin metal rod that is dipped into a car's engine to measure the oil level. □ *The mechanic pulled out the dipstick, wiped it clean, pushed it back in, and read the oil level.* □ *I opened the hood and checked the dipstick.*

direct current AND **DC**   an electrical current that flows in only one direction. (Compare with ALTERNATING CURRENT.) □ *This machine operates on direct current.* □ *You will need a DC adapter for this laptop computer.*

directory   a group of computer files. (See also FOLDER.) □ *My personal correspondence is in a directory labeled LETTERS.* □ *I can't find that file in this directory.*

disassemble   to take something apart. □ *To disassemble the chair, first remove the bolts that hold the back part of the frame to the seat.* □ *In order to clean the carburetor, you will have to disassemble it.*

disc brakes   brakes where the brake pads are pressed against a metal disc. (Compare with DRUM BRAKES.) □ *The car has disc brakes on the front axle and drum brakes on the rear.* □ *The mechanic put new brake pads on the disc brakes.*

disc camera a camera that uses film in the shape of a disc. (A DISC CAMERA can advance film quickly.) □ *I need some film for my disc camera.* □ *The disc camera is easy to carry because it's fairly flat.*

discount store a store that sells things at low prices. □ *I do most of my shopping at the discount store.* □ *When the new discount store opened up, the local department store was afraid it would drive them out of business.*

dish drainer AND **dish rack** a rack on which clean, wet dishes are placed to dry. (See also DRYING RACK.) □ *I put away the dishes that were in the dish drainer.* □ *The dish rack has special brackets for cups and silverware.*

dish rack See DISH DRAINER.

dish soap soap used to wash dishes. □ *He squirted dish soap into the sink full of hot water.* □ *This dish soap really cuts grease.*

dish towel a small towel used to dry dishes. □ *He wiped his hands on the dish towel.* □ *She got a clean dish towel and dried the dishes.*

dishwasher a machine that washes dishes. □ *After the dinner guests left, I loaded up the dishwasher.* □ *Those plastic bowls should go in the top rack of the dishwasher.*

dishwasher safe able to be safely washed in a DISHWASH-ER. □ *What about these wineglasses? Are they dishwasher safe?* □ *These storage bowls are microwaveable and dishwasher safe.*

disinfectant a substance used to kill bacteria, especially on non-living things. □ *The hospital room was cleaned with disinfectant.* □ *This bathroom cleanser acts as a disinfectant.*

(disk) drive **1.** a device that reads from and writes on computer disks. (DISK DRIVES are usually labeled with letters.) □ *The computer has a 5¼-inch disk drive.* □ *Put the data disk in the B drive.* **2.** See HARD DISK.

diskette AND **floppy (disk)** a portable, removable computer disk. (Compare with HARD DISK. FLOPPY is informal.) □ *This machine takes 3½-inch diskettes.* □ *I'll copy the report onto a floppy disk for you.* □ *It took six floppies to back up that file.*

disk operating system AND **DOS** a type of computer operating system. □ *"I can write programs using disk operating system commands," said Jane, "but I don't know any programming languages."* □ *"Is that PC a DOS machine?" the customer asked the computer salesperson.*

dismantle to take something apart completely. □ *We'll have to dismantle those bookshelves before we can move them.* □ *They had to practically dismantle my computer to figure out what the problem was.*

dispenser a device that lets out a certain amount or quantity of something. □ *There's no toothpaste mess with this new toothpaste dispenser.* □ *I took a few napkins from the napkin dispenser.*

display panel a panel or window that shows something. □ *When the VCR is recording, you will see the letters REC on the display panel.* □ *The display panel on the answering machine says that I have three calls.*

disposable designed to be thrown away after use. □ *I use disposable diapers when I take the baby on a trip.* □ *She forgot to bring her camera with her, so she bought a disposable one at the drugstore.*

Disposall™ a brand of machine that grinds up food waste. (See also GARBAGE DISPOSER.) □ *"What shall I do with the orange peels?" I asked. "Put them down the Disposall," said Bill.* □ *"We had a Disposall installed in the kitchen sink," Mary informed us.*

distilled water pure water, obtained by boiling it to remove impurities and then allowing it to recondense. (See also TAP WATER.) □ *Dissolve the tablet in distilled water.* □ *I use distilled water in developing my photographs.*

distributor   a device that delivers electrical current to the spark plugs in an engine. □ *The engine is misfiring because there is a crack in the rotor arm of the distributor.* □ *Locate the wire leading from the distributor to the spark plug.*

ditch   a long, narrow hole dug in the ground, usually designed to drain water from higher levels or carry water to lower levels. □ *Rainwater ran off the surface of the road and collected in the ditch.* □ *He dug a ditch from the creek to his garden patch.*

diverter (valve)   a device that directs the flow of water from one outlet to another. □ *The diverter valve beneath the spout on the kitchen sink changes the water flow from the spout to the spray head.* □ *He pulled the lever on the bathtub spout, and the diverter made the water come out of the shower.*

document   a computer file containing text. □ *To create a document, choose CREATE on the File menu.* □ *She edited the document, saved her changes, and closed the file.*

Dolby™   a brand of system for reducing noise in an audio signal. □ *"Let's go to the new movie theater," Jim suggested. "It has a Dolby sound system."* □ *"Can your tape deck play Dolby cassettes?" Linda asked.*

dollop   a medium-sized portion of a mushy substance. □ *He put a dollop of whipped cream on each piece of pumpkin pie.* □ *She added a dollop of red tempera paint to the color she was mixing.*

dolly   a handcart used for moving large objects. □ *They put the refrigerator on a dolly and wheeled it out of the kitchen.* □ *I loaded the dolly with heavy boxes.*

dolman sleeve   a sleeve that is full where it meets the bodice and tapered to be tight around the wrist. □ *The dolman sleeves on that sweater are flattering to the figure.* □ *This blouse has dramatic dolman sleeves.*

doorbell   a bell used to signal that someone is waiting at the door. □ *The door-to-door salesperson went to the next* *house and rang the doorbell.* □ *Instead of just ringing, "ding-dong," the doorbell played a few bars of Beethoven.*

doorjamb   the frame around a door. □ *He leaned against the doorjamb and stuck his head into the room.* □ *The dead bolt fits into a hole in the doorjamb.*

door knocker   a piece of metal attached to a door and used to make a loud knock. □ *They had a brass door knocker engraved with the family name.* □ *I rapped on the door knocker, but no one came to the door.*

doorstep   a step just outside a door. □ *When I got home, there was a package waiting for me on the doorstep.* □ *I sat down on the doorstep to wait for my friend.*

doorstop   **1.** a weight or a wedge used to hold a door open. □ *We used a cement block as a doorstop.* □ *She slid the rubber doorstop under the door and wedged it firmly open.* **2.** a small spring with a padded end, attached to a wall to keep a door from banging against the wall. □ *He pushed the door open, and it bounced against the doorstop.* □ *After the second time the doorknob punched a hole in the wall, I decided to install a doorstop.*

dormer (window)   a window in a structure that projects out from a roof. □ *The house had a charming pair of dormer windows.* □ *A dormer window is a good, cosy place for a window seat.*

DOS   See DISK OPERATING SYSTEM.

dot matrix (printer)   a computer printer that forms characters and symbols out of small dots. □ *My dot matrix printer needs a new ribbon.* □ *A dot matrix is cheap, but the print quality is not as good as a laser printer.*

double bed AND **full bed**   a bed big enough for two people to sleep in. □ *The hotel room had two double beds.* □ *I need sheets to fit a full bed.*

double boiler   two cooking pots that fit together, one on top of the other. (Water is usually boiled in the bottom pot, in order to cook foods in the top one over steady, gentle heat.) □ *Combine the sugar, flour, and egg yolks in the top of a double boiler.* □ *Melt the chocolate in a double boiler.*

double click on something   to place the cursor on an item on a computer screen and press the mouse button twice, quickly. (See also CLICK ON SOMETHING.) □ *Double click on the name of the file you want to open.* □ *Double click on the corner of the window to close it.*

double-hung window   a window with a top section that can slide down, and a bottom section that can slide up. □ *The old house had double-hung windows in wooden sashes.* □ *The sashes of the double-hung window are raised and lowered with a cord that runs over a pulley.*

dough   an uncooked, mushy or elastic mixture of flour and other ingredients. □ *He mixed up a big batch of cookie dough.* □ *Knead the bread dough for fifteen minutes.*

dowel   a cylindrical length of wood. (The size of a DOWEL is given by its diameter in inches.) □ *The chair was held together with small pegs made of dowel.* □ *The mug stand is made out of half-inch dowel.*

download   to copy information from a computer or information service onto your computer or computer diskette. (Contrasts with UPLOAD.) □ *I downloaded the information I wanted from the library's CD-ROM onto this disk.* □ *It was a large file. It took several minutes to download it.*

downspout   a pipe that drains rainwater from the gutters on a roof to the ground. □ *I looked out the window and saw water pouring out of the downspout.* □ *Leaves and twigs were clogging the downspout, so water was accumulating on the roof.*

drain   **1.** a hole through which water travels to a sewer. □ *Something's clogging the drain in the bathroom sink.* □ *There was a drain in the basement floor.* **2.** to allow water or other liquid to run out. □ *He drained the oil out of the* *crankcase.* □ *The hole in the bottom of the flowerpot will drain the excess water.*

drainage   the capacity to let excess water run out. □ *She dug a ditch in the backyard to improve the drainage.* □ *The building had constant problems with drainage, because it was located at the bottom of a hill.*

drainer   a slotted tool for lifting foods out of cooking liquid, letting the liquid DRAIN away. □ *Use the drainer to remove the French fries from the oil.* □ *He carefully scooped the boiled mushrooms out of the water with the drainer.*

drain opener   a chemical that dissolves clogs. (See also DRANO™.) □ *This new liquid drain opener works fast.* □ *The plunger didn't work, so I tried a drain opener.*

drainpipe   an open pipe that collects rainwater from the edge of a roof and DRAINS it away. □ *The water ran down the drainpipe and out the downspout.* □ *The water in the drainpipe froze.*

Drano™   a brand of drain opener. (See also DRAIN OPENER.) □ *"The sink's backed up," Anna called from the bathroom. "Get some Drano."* □ *"All I did was pour Drano into the drain," said the plumber. "You could have done that yourself."*

draperies   See CURTAINS.

drapes   See CURTAINS.

drawbridge   a bridge with a hinge at one end, so that the other end can be raised and lowered. (Compare with LIFT BRIDGE.) □ *They raised the drawbridge over the canal so that the boat could go by.* □ *The drawbridge was lowered again, and the cars drove across.*

drawer   an open box that fits into a space in a piece of furniture. □ *The drawer in the little table contained a bag of rubber bands, a note pad, and a pencil.* □ *The drawers in her bureau were stuffed with clothes.*

drawer liner   material, usually paper, placed in the bottom of a DRAWER to protect it from dirt and stains. □ *He measured the drawer liner so it would fit the drawer.* □ *The drawer liner was getting yellow and brittle, so I decided it was time to change it.*

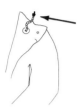

drawstring   a string that runs around an opening and can be pulled in order to tighten or shut it. □ *There is a drawstring around the waist of those pants so you can adjust them to fit you.* □ *I pulled the drawstring on my sleeping bag until the top part fit snugly around my head.*

dredge   to coat something in flour or meal. □ *Dredge the chicken breasts in cornmeal.* □ *Dredge the vegetables in flour before frying.*

dredger   a device that sprinkles flour or meal onto something. □ *I put some flour, salt, and pepper in the dredger.* □ *He shook the dredger over the slices of fish.*

drill bit   the sharp tip of a drill, the part that cuts the hole. (DRILL BITS are measured by diameter.) □ *I need a ³⁄₈-inch drill bit to drill a pilot hole for this screw.* □ *She loosened the chuck and removed the drill bit.*

drill press   a machine that lowers a DRILL BIT into something placed on the attached table. □ *He used a drill press to drill two holes precisely an inch apart.* □ *This drill press can drill holes in metal.*

drip coffee maker   a device that makes coffee by dripping hot water onto ground coffee beans. (See also COFFEE MAKER.) □ *This coffee is specially ground for use in drip coffee makers.* □ *I bought a ten-cup drip coffee maker.*

drippings   melted fat that drips from cooking meat. □ *Baste the roast with the drippings.* □ *I roasted the potatoes in the drippings from the leg of lamb.*

drive-in   a restaurant or a theater that people attend in their cars. □ *What's showing at the drive-in?* □ *We took the kids out for root-beer floats at the drive-in.*

driver a computer program that runs a particular device, such as a printer or a speaker. □ *Did this printer come with a driver?* □ *She installed the driver for her new sound card.*

driver's seat the seat directly behind the steering wheel of a car, where the driver sits. □ *I can't reach the glove box from the driver's seat.* □ *The driver's seat adjusts independently from the passenger seat.*

driveshaft the car axle that is driven by the engine. □ *The differential transfers power to the driveshaft.* □ *If the driveshaft can be rotated while the brakes are on, it needs repair.*

drizzle **1.** to drip a thin stream of liquid onto or into something. □ *Drizzle the top of the casserole with melted butter.* □ *Drizzle a little sesame oil into the soup.* **2.** rain falling in thin streams. □ *A cold drizzle was falling.* □ *The drizzle fell all afternoon.*

drop cookie a cookie formed by dropping a spoonful of dough onto the baking sheet. (See also BAR (COOKIE), PRESSED COOKIE.) □ *Chocolate chip cookies and peanut butter cookies are both drop cookies.* □ *Because it does not require shaping or cutting, the dough for drop cookies does not need to be very firm.*

drop leaf table a table with one or more hinges that allow part of the tabletop to fold down. (The folding parts are sometimes called "leaves." See also GATE LEG TABLE.) □ *When I have guests, I put up both sides of the drop leaf table, and when I'm by myself, I put them down.* □ *The drop leaf table can fit into small spaces when the leaves are folded down.*

drugstore a store that sells drugs and, usually, many other items. (See also PHARMACY.) □ *I went to the drugstore and got some cough syrup.* □ *You can get candy, cosmetics, and magazines at the drugstore.*

drum the cylindrical, rotating part of a DRYER. □ *The drum is rotating, but there's no heat in the dryer.* □ *Don't put so many clothes into the drum. You're overloading it.*

drum brakes   brakes that work by pressing against the inside of a hollow drum located on the axle. (Compare with DISC BRAKES.) □ *This car has disc brakes on the front and drum brakes on the rear.* □ *The emergency brake lever works the rear drum brakes.*

drumstick   the leg of a fowl. □ *I bought a half dozen turkey drumsticks at the butcher shop.* □ *The kids each wanted a drumstick.*

dry cell   a battery containing powdered (not liquid) chemicals. □ *Dry cells are convenient because they don't leak.* □ *Dry cells can be deposited at the fire station for recycling.*

dry-clean   to clean cloth with chemicals rather than with water. □ *You'd better dry-clean those curtains.* □ *The label on the silk jacket said, "Dry-clean only."*

dry cleaning   items that have been DRY-CLEANED or need to be dry-cleaned. □ *I collected the dry cleaning and dropped it off at the cleaner's.* □ *The dry cleaning will be ready on Thursday.*

dryer   a machine that dries clothes. □ *I put the wet clothes into the dryer.* □ *The dryer needs a vent into the outside air.*

dryer sheet   a piece of thin material that is placed in a clothes DRYER, where it releases a substance that softens clothes. (See also FABRIC SOFTENER.) □ *Did you remember to put a dryer sheet in with that load?* □ *Each dryer sheet is good for two loads.*

drying rack   a rack on which something, usually clothes or dishes, is placed to dry. (See also CLOTHESLINE, DISH DRAINER.) □ *He hung the wet laundry on the drying rack.* □ *She set the clean dishes in the drying rack.*

dry ingredients   flour and other powdered ingredients in a recipe. (DRY INGREDIENTS might include salt, baking powder, or baking soda.) □ *Mix the dry ingredients, then add the egg and vanilla.* □ *Sift all the dry ingredients together.*

dry measure   a measure for fruits and vegetables. (Note: DRY MEASURE quarts and pints are about 1/16 larger than LIQUID MEASURE quarts and pints. Contrasts with LIQUID MEASURE.) □ *A pint of strawberries is a dry measure pint.* □ *A peck is equivalent to eight quarts, dry measure.*

dry mustard   ground mustard seeds. (Compare with (PRE-PARED) MUSTARD.) □ *Use one half teaspoon of dry mustard.* □ *Put in just a dash of dry mustard.*

drywall   a building material made of a sheet of plaster covered with heavy paper on both sides. □ *The walls of this room are made of drywall.* □ *You will need a plastic sheath to anchor the screw into the drywall.*

DST   See DAYLIGHT SAVINGS TIME.

dub   to copy material onto an audiotape or videotape. □ *I dubbed the song onto a tape for you.* □ *He hooked up two VCRs so he could dub videotapes.*

duct   a pipe or passage that conducts a gas or liquid from one place to another. □ *We need to clean out the furnace ducts.* □ *This duct allows the hot, moist air to escape from the dryer.*

duct tape   a strong cloth tape backed with gray or silver plastic. □ *He wrapped duct tape around the pipe to seal the leak.* □ *She fixed the cables in place with duct tape.*

dumb terminal   an electronic device that allows you to communicate with a computer but that does not itself run programs. □ *I have a dumb terminal at home that I use to dial up the mainframe at work.* □ *CHARLIE: Is that a PC? JANE: No, it's a dumb terminal.*

dumpling   a lump of dough, sometimes filled with fruit, vegetables, or meat, and either boiled, baked, steamed, or fried. □ *She made chicken soup with dumplings.* □ *We filled the dumplings with seasoned pork and then dropped them into the hot oil.*

Dumpster™   a brand of container for collecting the trash from a building. □ *"Please take the trash out to the Dumpster," said Bill.* □ *"Oh, look," Jane said. "Somebody put this perfectly good lamp in the Dumpster."*

dust   **1.** small particles of dirt. □ *The table was covered with dust.* □ *I shook the bedspread, and a cloud of dust flew into the air.* **2.** to remove DUST from something. □ *I'd better dust the living room before the company comes.* □ *The fancy carvings on that bookcase make it hard to dust.* **3.** to sprinkle something with a powder. □ *Dust the tops of the cupcakes with powdered sugar.* □ *Dust the bread dough with flour.*

dust bag   See VACUUM BAG.

Dustbuster™   a brand of hand-held vacuum cleaner. □ *"Don't worry," Mary said when I spilled the flour. "The Dustbuster will pick that up in a jiffy."* □ *"That Dustbuster is awfully handy for cleaning the upholstery," said Carol. "You ought to get one."*

dust cloth AND **dust rag**   a cloth used to wipe DUST away. □ *I got out the dust cloth and went to work on the bookshelves.* □ *He went out to the porch and shook out the dust rag. Dust went flying everywhere.*

dust cover   a cover placed on something to protect it from DUST. □ *She snapped the dust cover onto her computer keyboard.* □ *The lid of the phonograph turntable acts as a dust cover.*

dust mop   a mop used to remove DUST. □ *I used a dust mop to get the cobwebs out of the corners of the ceiling.* □ *She cleaned the Venetian blinds with a dust mop.*

dustpan   a flat, usually triangular tray, used to collect the dirt swept together by a broom or brush. □ *You hold the dustpan, and I'll sweep.* □ *He swept the bathroom floor with a whisk broom and a dustpan.*

dust rag   See DUST CLOTH.

dust ruffle   a decoration of pleated fabric around the bottom of a piece of furniture. □ *The bedspread comes with a matching dust ruffle.* □ *She had calico dust ruffles on all her armchairs.*

dutch oven   a large pot with a tight-fitting cover. □ *He cooked the roast in a dutch oven.* □ *She heated up some oil in the bottom of the dutch oven.*

duvet   a thick, padded blanket. (Pronounced du-VAY.) □ *It was a cold night, but the duvet kept me warm.* □ *She wrapped herself up in the duvet.*

dwarf variety   a fruit tree or vegetable that grows only to a very small size. □ *They planted an orchard of dwarf variety apple trees.* □ *This dwarf variety tomato plant is suitable for growing indoors.*

E

earphones devices that transmit sound directly into the ear. (See also HEADPHONES.) □ *He turned on the radio and fit the earphones into his ears.* □ *If you want to watch the in-flight movie, you will need these earphones.*

earpiece the part of a telephone containing the speaker that transmits sound to your ear. (Compare with MOUTH-PIECE, RECEIVER.) □ *His voice was so loud that I could hear him even when I held the earpiece six inches away from my ear.* □ *A strange crackling noise came out of the earpiece.*

ease **1.** extra fabric in a piece of clothing to allow the wear-er to move more easily. □ *The pattern has plenty of ease at the shoulder.* □ *The ease at the waistline makes these pants very comfortable.* **2.** to put small folds into a piece of fabric in order to make it the same length as a smaller piece of fabric. □ *Match the notches on the sleeve cap and the arms-eye. Ease.* □ *Ease the front panel of the blouse and join it to the back panel.*

Eastern standard time AND **EST** the time in the time zone that includes the East Coast and eastern parts of the United States. (See also CENTRAL STANDARD TIME, MOUN-TAIN STANDARD TIME, PACIFIC STANDARD TIME.) □ *When we crossed the border into Georgia, we set our clocks ahead to Eastern standard time.* □ *The movie will be broadcast at 9 PM EST.*

easy chair a padded chair with arms and a high back. □ *I relaxed in my easy chair, reading the paper.* □ *That old easy chair needs to be reupholstered.*

eaves the parts of a roof that stick out over the side of a building. □ *It began to rain. We took shelter under the eaves of a nearby house.* □ *There was a wasp's nest under the eaves by the front porch.*

EBB See ELECTRONIC BULLETIN BOARD.

economy (class)   the cheapest class of airplane travel. □ *TRAVEL AGENT: Would you like first class, business, or economy class? CUSTOMER: Economy.* □ *First class is five hundred dollars, and economy class is only two hundred and seventy.*

economy size   a very large size. □ *I get the economy size laundry soap, because it's cheaper per ounce than the smaller size.* □ *My grandkids are coming over this weekend. I'll get the economy size package of hot dog buns.*

edger AND **weed whacker**   a device that can cut grass in narrow spaces, such as the edge of a lawn where it meets the pavement. (WEED WHACKER is slang. See also WEED EATER™.) □ *When I was done with the lawn mower, I got to work with the edger.* □ *Use the weed whacker to trim the grass around the base of the tree.*

edit   to change text in a computer file. □ *Type in the file name of the file you wish to edit.* □ *This is a read-only file. You can't edit it.*

egg beater   a hand-cranked device with one or two rotating whisks, used to beat raw eggs and other liquids. □ *She whipped the eggs with an egg beater.* □ *I whisked the cocoa into the hot milk with an egg beater.*

egg-beater drill   a straight, hand-cranked drill that looks like an EGG BEATER. (See also BRACE AND BIT.) □ *It's hard work to drill a hole through an inch of wood with an egg-beater drill.* □ *He used the egg-beater drill for small holes, and the power drill for large ones.*

egg cup   a cup in which a boiled egg is served in the shell. □ *He brought in a breakfast tray with muffins, fruit, and a hard-boiled egg in a china egg cup.* □ *I bought a pretty, hand-painted egg cup for my daily breakfast egg.*

egg poacher   a shallow metal cup in which an egg can be poached. (Some EGG POACHERS have more than one cup for more than one egg.) □ *She set the egg poacher in the boiling water and cracked an egg into each of the wells.* □ *Brush an egg poacher with melted butter.*

egg salad a mixture of chopped, hard-boiled eggs, may-onnaise, and seasonings. □ *I would like an egg salad sand-wich, please.* □ *He puts pickle relish in his egg salad.*

egg separator a device that catches the yolk of a raw egg and lets the white fall through. □ *This egg separator is aw-fully convenient when I'm making lemon meringue pie.* □ *She used an egg separator to keep the yolks from breaking and leaking into the egg white.*

egg slicer a device that cuts a boiled egg into thin slices, using a set of parallel wires. □ *She put the hard-boiled egg into the egg slicer.* □ *The egg slicer cut the egg into perfect slices.*

egg timer a device that measures the time needed to cook a hard-boiled egg. (Small hourglasses are sometimes used as EGG TIMERS.) □ *When the water is boiling, turn the egg timer over.* □ *The egg timer beeped. I took the eggs out of the hot water.*

egg topper a device that cuts off the top of a boiled egg in its shell. □ *He clipped off the top of the egg with an egg top-per.* □ *After using the egg topper, she spooned up the tender, soft-boiled egg.*

egg white the clear part of a raw egg that turns white when cooked. (See also (EGG) YOLK.) □ *This recipe calls for four egg whites.* □ *The main ingredient of meringue is whipped egg white.*

(egg) yolk the opaque, bright yellow part of a raw egg. (See also EGG WHITE.) □ *The custard is made with egg yolks.* □ *The yolk is my favorite part of a hard-boiled egg.*

18-wheeler a truck with eighteen wheels on five axles. (Informal.) □ *Jim drives an 18-wheeler for a living.* □ *I hate having to pass those 18-wheelers on a two-lane road.*

800 number a telephone number with an area code of 800. (There is no charge for calling an 800 NUMBER. Com-pare with 900 NUMBER.) □ *If you have any questions about* *our product, please call our 800 number.* □ *Is there an 800 number for that airline?*

eject   to push something out. □ *How do I get the computer to eject my disk?* □ *The machine ejected the video cassette.*

eject button   a button that causes a machine to EJECT something. □ *Where is the eject button on this VCR?* □ *She pushed the eject button, and the CD popped out of the machine.*

(electrical) outlet   an opening in which an electrical plug can be connected to the current. □ *There is an electrical outlet on each wall of this room.* □ *I'm looking for an outlet to plug in my laptop.*

electrical tape   black plastic tape, usually used to wrap electrical wires. □ *He mended the appliance cord with electrical tape.* □ *She wrapped electrical tape around the exposed wires.*

electric blanket   a blanket that is heated by electricity. □ *I couldn't face these bitter cold winter nights without my electric blanket.* □ *The electric blanket keeps the bed warm even when the furnace is turned down low.*

electric fan   a rotating fan powered by electricity. □ *He put an electric fan in the window in order to get a breeze going through the room.* □ *An electric fan in the attic blew the hot air out to the outside.*

electric fry pan AND **electric skillet**   a flat-bottomed pan heated by electricity. □ *The temperature control on the electric fry pan allows you to adjust the temperature precisely.* □ *She made fried chicken in the electric skillet.*

electric knife   a vibrating knife powered by electricity. □ *The electric knife is great for slicing meat.* □ *The electric knife sliced the bread in no time.*

electric meter   a device that measures how much electricity has been used. □ *Once a month, a meter reader comes*

to write down the numbers from the electric meter. □ *Each apartment has its own electric meter.*

electric mixer an electric-powered device that mixes food with rotating metal whisks. □ *I use the electric mixer to mix cake mixes.* □ *He whipped the egg whites in the electric mixer.*

electric razor See ELECTRIC SHAVER.

(electric) receptacle the set of holes in an electrical outlet into which an electric plug fits. □ *The wires are connected to the electric receptacle.* □ *You can't fit a three-prong plug into a two-slot receptacle.*

electric shaver AND **electric razor** an electric device that cuts hair by means of small, rotating blades. □ *This electric shaver gives a good, close shave.* □ *There's no outlet in the bathroom, so I can't use my electric razor.*

electric skillet See ELECTRIC FRY PAN.

electric toothbrush a vibrating toothbrush powered by electricity. □ *The batteries in my electric toothbrush gave out.* □ *The electric toothbrush really gets my teeth clean and shiny.*

electric typewriter a typewriter in which electric power is used to strike the type element against the paper. (Compare with MANUAL TYPEWRITER.) □ *The keys on the electric typewriter are easy to push.* □ *This electric typewriter has a feature that allows you to erase mistakes easily.*

electrode an electrical TERMINAL separated from another terminal by a gap. □ *I adjusted the gap between the side electrodes of the spark plug.* □ *He cleaned off the chemical deposits on the battery electrode.*

electronic bulletin board AND **EBB** a service that allows people to leave computer messages for one another. □ *I dialed up the gourmet cooking EBB to see if there were any new and interesting recipes.* □ *I've made many new friends through this electronic bulletin board.*

electronic mail AND **e-mail**   **1.** a system for sending messages from one computer to another. □ *Do you have e-mail?* □ *I sent him an electronic mail message.* **2.** messages sent by computer. □ *I checked my e-mail and found a note from my buddy in Venezuela.* □ *If you want to send me electronic mail, I can give you my e-mail address.*

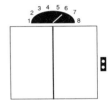

elevator   a device that moves people or large objects up and down between the floors of a building. □ *I was waiting for the elevator that would take me to the fifteenth floor.* □ *In the morning, all the office workers crowded into the elevator.*

elevator music   soft, mild background music. (Derogatory. See also MUZAK™, PIPED MUSIC.) □ *I hate the elevator music they play in the doctor's waiting room.* □ *Elevator music was piped into the store.*

elevator shaft   the passage up and down which an ELEVATOR moves. □ *It was a terrible accident. Someone fell down the elevator shaft.* □ *When the elevator got stuck between floors, the repair worker had to go into the elevator shaft to repair it.*

Elmer's™ glue   a brand of glue. (See also WHITE GLUE.) □ *"Use your Elmer's glue to fasten the pictures onto the poster board," the teacher told the class.* □ *"Does Elmer's glue work on fabric?" Joan asked.*

e-mail   See ELECTRONIC MAIL.

emergency brake AND **hand brake; parking brake**   a brake that locks a car's wheels while it is standing still. □ *The brakes went out on me. I had to use the emergency brake to stop the car.* □ *I put the car in neutral and pulled up on the hand brake.* □ *You should set the parking brake when you park on a hill.*

emery board   a narrow strip of abrasive material, usually used to smooth the tips of fingernails or toenails. (See also (FINGER)NAIL FILE.) □ *She smoothed her toenails with an emery board.* □ *After I trimmed my fingernails, I evened them up with an emery board.*

emission material let out into the atmosphere. ☐ *The car's exhaust was tested for harmful emissions.* ☐ *The emissions from some plastics can be toxic.*

enamel **1.** a hard, glossy paint. ☐ *I used white enamel on the woodwork.* ☐ *The saucepan has a protective enamel coating.* **2.** the hard surface of a tooth. ☐ *I have very hard, thick enamel, so the dentist has to use a special drill on me.* ☐ *The tooth decay had eaten through the enamel.*

encrypt to put a computer file in code. ☐ *For security reasons, I encrypted the file.* ☐ *I can't read this document. It must be encrypted.*

end grain the rough surface where wood has been cut across the grain. ☐ *Nails driven into the end grain do not hold very well.* ☐ *The carpenter sanded the end grain until it was perfectly smooth.*

engine **1.** a device that converts fuel into mechanical energy. ☐ *The diagram showed the cylinders and pistons in an automobile engine.* ☐ *My car won't start. I don't know if it's a problem with the engine or with the ignition system.* **2.** the part of a train that houses the ENGINE and pulls or pushes the rail cars attached to it. (See also LOCOMOTIVE.) ☐ *It took three engines to haul the long coal train.* ☐ *The commuter trains have diesel engines.*

engine block a block of metal housing the cylinders and crankshaft of an ENGINE. ☐ *The winters are cold here. You'll want an electric heater to keep the oil from freezing in your engine block.* ☐ *The mechanic used a winch to hoist the engine block out of the truck.*

English muffin a flat round of spongy, chewy baked dough. (See also MUFFIN.) ☐ *Would you like an English muffin or toast with your eggs?* ☐ *She spread butter on her English muffin.*

enter a key on a computer keyboard, usually labeled with a bent arrow or the word "Enter" and used to mark the end of a line or a command. (Compare with CARRIAGE RETURN.)

□ *Type EXIT and press "enter."* □ *Hit "enter" twice to begin your e-mail session.*

entertainment system a television, VCR, stereo, or other entertainment devices all housed in one place. □ *An entire wall of the living room was taken up with a state-of-the-art entertainment system.* □ *Their entertainment system included a video game player and dozens of video game cartridges.*

entrance ramp AND **on ramp** a ramp that leads onto a highway. (ON RAMP is informal. Contrasts with EXIT RAMP.) □ *Increase your speed on the entrance ramp, so that you will be able to merge with the highway traffic.* □ *My car broke down on the on ramp.*

entrée AND **main dish** a food served as the main part of a meal. (ENTRÉE is formal. See also SIDE DISH.) □ *The menu listed appetizers, soups, entrées, and desserts.* □ *Baked chicken was the main dish, with mixed vegetables on the side.*

entry(way) a small room or area just inside the front door of a building. (See also FOYER, LOBBY.) □ *I took off my wet boots in the entryway before going into the house.* □ *The letter carrier waited in the entry while I got the money for the C.O.D. package.*

environment **1.** the surroundings. □ *The factory was polluting the environment.* □ *The book suggested several ways for an ordinary family to help the environment.* **2.** the way a computer program has been set up. □ *I'm running this word processor in a DOS environment.* □ *You can customize your environment by setting up the prompt you want to see, the terminal emulation you want to run, whether or not you want the time and date displayed, and so forth.*

EP See EXTENDED PLAY.

equalizer an electronic device that adjusts the balance of high and low tones; part of a stereo system. □ *I think the equalizer really makes a difference in the sound of the stereo.*

□ *He adjusted the equalizer until the bass tones made the floor shake.*

error message   a message on a computer screen indicating that something is wrong. □ *I'm doing what the manual told me to do. Why am I getting an error message?* □ *The error message says that the disk is full.*

escape (key)   a key on a computer keyboard, labeled "Escape" or "Esc." □ *To interrupt the search, press the escape key.* □ *You can always use "escape" to go back to the previous menu.*

escutcheon (plate)   a piece of metal that protects the area around a doorknob or a faucet. □ *There is a small rubber gasket in between the spout and the escutcheon plate.* □ *There was a heavy brass escutcheon behind the doorknob.*

espalier   to train a plant to grow flat against a wall or fence. □ *The cherry trees had been espaliered against the south wall.* □ *To espalier a young tree, you will need to keep it carefully pruned.*

espresso   strong coffee made by passing steam through ground coffee beans. □ *I had a cup of espresso after the meal.* □ *I'd like a double espresso, please.*

espresso maker   a device that makes ESPRESSO. □ *He put the espresso maker on the stove.* □ *She buys a special blend of coffee for her espresso maker.*

EST   See EASTERN STANDARD TIME.

ethnic food   food from some particular ethnic group. (Some popular kinds are Chinese, Mexican, and Italian.) □ *You can get taco shells in the ethnic food aisle at the grocery store.* □ CHARLIE: *What restaurant shall we go to?* JANE: *How about a place with ethnic food?*

evaporated milk   milk from which some of the moisture has been removed. (See also CONDENSED MILK, POWDERED

MILK.) □ *He poured evaporated milk into his coffee.* □ *She stirred the evaporated milk into the batter.*

evaporator (coil) AND **cooling coil**   a coil of metal tubing that removes heat from the air that passes over it; part of a refrigeration system. □ *The evaporator coil is located just above the blower.* □ *The cold air from the evaporator passes up through this duct.* □ *The cooling coil is located on the front of the window unit air conditioner.*

Excel™   a brand of spreadsheet. □ *"I use Excel to keep track of the budget," said the secretary.* □ *"Enter the information into Excel, and print it out as a chart," my boss suggested.*

excelsior AND **packing material**   soft or fluffy material used to protect something packed in a container. □ *I opened the box that I got in the mail. It was so full of excelsior that it looked as though there was nothing else in it!* □ *She pulled out the styrofoam packing material, then gently took the radio out of the box.*

exhaust fan   a fan that moves unwanted gases out of a system or a room. □ *The exhaust fan in the attic pushes the hot air out of the house.* □ *We installed an exhaust fan in the garage so that the toxic car exhaust won't accumulate in there.*

exhaust manifold   a set of tubes that moves exhaust gas from an engine into the exhaust system. □ *There seems to be a leak in the exhaust manifold.* □ *The mechanic carefully fit the new gasket to the exhaust manifold before bolting it back in place.*

exhaust (pipe) AND **tailpipe**   the pipe at the back of a car that lets the waste gases flow out. □ *The exhaust pipe was rusted through.* □ *The exhaust is connected to the muffler.* □ *The technician put a probe in the tailpipe to measure the chemicals in the exhaust.*

exit ramp AND **off ramp**   a ramp that leads traffic off a highway. (Contrasts with ENTRANCE RAMP.) □ *When you* *reach the end of the exit ramp, turn left.* □ *There was a mile-long line of cars waiting to get onto the off ramp.*

ExLax™ a brand of LAXATIVE. □ *"If you're feeling consti-pated, take some ExLax," said Mom.* □ *"I'm sorry your stom-ach hurts. Would you like some ExLax?" Jim asked.*

expansion slot a space in a computer for extra electronic components. □ *I put a second serial port card into the ex-pansion slot.* □ *This computer has several expansion slots, so you can add a sound card if you want.*

exploded view a picture that shows all the separate parts of something and indicates how they fit together. □ *I studied the exploded view of the carburetor in the car manual.* □ *Locate the bearings on the exploded view of the bicycle hub.*

exposure **1.** one act of allowing light to fall on photo-graphic film. □ *How many exposures have you taken today?* □ *Light leaked into the camera and ruined several expo-sures.* **2.** a photograph. (Film is often measured in EXPO-SURES.) □ *This is a 36-exposure roll of film.* □ *How many exposures per roll?*

extended play AND **EP** a recording containing more than one song but not as many as a full CD or LP. □ *The band just released a new EP.* □ *That song is only available on an extended play.*

extension characters following a dot in the name of a computer file. □ *In the file name LETTER.DOC, LETTER is the file name, and .DOC is the extension.* □ *All of the files with the extension .BAK are backup files.*

extension cord an electrical cord that plugs into an outlet at one end, and has one or more receptacles in the other end where other devices can plug in. □ *I want to put the lamp on the other side of the room from that outlet. I'll have to use an extension cord.* □ *He ran an extension cord out from the garage to power the electric drill he was using in the backyard.*

extract   a substance or quality, such as a flavor taken out of something else. □ *The cookies are flavored with vanilla extract.* □ *Cocoa butter is an extract of the cacao bean.*

eye   **1.** the narrow opening at one end of a needle. □ *I can't get the thread through the eye of this needle.* □ *The yarn needle has a fairly large eye.* **2.** the area on a potato where a stalk is beginning to grow. (To *eye* a potato is to remove these EYES.) □ *This potato is no good. It's all eyes.* □ *She cut out the potato eye.*

eye bolt   a bolt with a metal loop at one end. □ *He screwed an eye bolt into the wall, and then fastened a rope to the eye.* □ *The hammock was hung on eye bolts at either end of the porch.*

eye cup   a cup-shaped piece of plastic or rubber that fits around the eye. □ *These binoculars have rubber eye cups.* □ *The eye cup on the video camera shaded the photographer's eye from the sun.*

eyedrops   liquid medicine that is dropped into the eye. □ *The doctor prescribed some eyedrops to reduce the inflammation in my eyes.* □ *The ophthalmologist dilated my eyes with special eyedrops.*

eyelet   a fabric decorated with tiny holes with embroidered edges. □ *The skirt was edged with eyelet lace.* □ *She wore a white eyelet sundress.*

F

fabric softener a substance added to clothes in the WASH-ING MACHINE or DRYER to make them feel soft. (See also DRYER SHEET.) □ *She measured the fabric softener into the washing machine basket.* □ *These towels are so soft! What fabric softener do you use?*

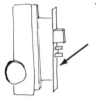

faceplate the part of a door lock that fits on the edge of the door. □ *The latch comes out of a hole in the faceplate.* □ *He screwed the faceplate onto the edge of the door.*

facing a band of fabric used to line the edge of a garment. □ *She sewed a facing into the neck of the blouse.* □ *The facings on the hems are made of contrasting fabric.*

facsimile AND **fax** an image sent electronically through telephone lines. □ *There's an urgent fax for you.* □ *Please confirm our telephone agreement by letter or facsimile.*

family planning AND **birth control** exercising control over when to become pregnant; using some method to prevent unwanted pregnancy. (See also CONTRACEPTIVE.) □ *The clinic educates young people about family planning.* □ *What form of birth control do you use?*

fan a device that moves air. □ *Turn on the fan. It's too warm in here.* □ *The fan in the air conditioner is making an awful noise.*

fan belt a loop of tough material that connects the cooling FAN in a car engine to the alternator. □ *The fan belt broke, so the alternator wasn't recharging the battery.* □ *You should replace the fan belt from time to time.*

fanlight a semicircular window above a door. □ *The sun streamed in through the fanlight.* □ *I would like to install a fanlight above the front door.*

fanny pack a bag worn around the waist. (Some people wear these bags over their buttocks. FANNY is U.S. slang for the buttocks.) ☐ *The cyclist put her wallet into her fanny pack.* ☐ *Instead of a purse, I use a fanny pack.*

fare box   a box for collecting money from passengers on a bus or train. ☐ *I slid my dollar into the fare box.* ☐ *Please have exact change ready. Fare box does not make change.*

farina   somewhat coarsely ground wheat, often cooked and eaten as a breakfast food. (See also CREAM OF WHEAT™.) ☐ *He stirred the farina.* ☐ *This fruit pudding is made with farina.*

fascia   a part of the trim of a house that covers the end of the roof rafters. ☐ *The gutters are nailed to the fascia.* ☐ *We had to replace the rotting fascia on our house.*

fastener   something that holds things together. ☐ *What kind of fastener should I use—a nail, a brad, or a screw?* ☐ *You will find snaps, buttons, and other fasteners in the notions section of the store.*

fast-food   food that is quickly prepared. ☐ *We stopped at a fast-food restaurant on our way to the movie.* ☐ *Is there a good fast-food place in the neighborhood?*

fast-forward   **1.** to quickly move audiotape or videotape forward through a machine. (Contrasts with REWIND.) ☐ *This part of the movie is boring. Let's fast-forward past it.* ☐ *He fast-forwarded the tape to the song he wanted to hear.* **2.** a button which makes audiotape or videotape move quickly forward through a machine. ☐ *Hit the fast-forward. I want to see the end of the tape.* ☐ *I can't find the fast-forward on this tape player.*

fatigue   the weakening of metal. ☐ *The shelf bracket was showing signs of fatigue, so we replaced it.* ☐ *The workers spotted the fatigue in the bridge girders.*

faucet   a tube out of which water flows, usually into a sink or tub. ☐ *I turned on the hot water, but the water coming out of the faucet was cold.* ☐ *She pivoted the faucet over to the left side of the sink.*

faulty not working correctly. □ *I'm afraid there is a faulty board in your computer.* □ *The faulty gasket failed to seal the space between the pipes, and water leaked over everything.*

faux finish paint that makes a surface look like something it is not. □ *The faux finish makes the plastic countertop look like marble.* □ *The decorator loved to use faux finishes when he designed a room.*

fax See FACSIMILE.

fax machine a device that transmits an image across phone lines. □ *I can fax you a copy of the contract if you have a fax machine.* □ *The fax machine beeped and started printing the message it was receiving.*

fax modem a device that can send and receive computer information and FAX transmissions. □ *I used my fax modem to fax a letter to the office and to follow it up with an e-mail message.* □ *The computer comes with an internal fax modem.*

feather duster a bundle of feathers on a handle, used to remove dust from surfaces. □ *The housekeeper whisked a feather duster across the shelves.* □ *He used a feather duster to clean the porcelain figurine.*

feature something special about an item. □ *This refrigerator has a frost-free feature.* □ *You can use the spell-check feature of this word processor to proofread your documents.*

feedback the return of sound from a speaker into a microphone, causing a loud, shrill, unpleasant noise. □ *Get those speakers out in front of the microphone so you don't have to worry about feedback.* □ *The sound system in the auditorium was having a terrible problem with feedback.*

feminine hygiene concerning products for cleaning the vagina. (A euphemism.) □ *Douches and other feminine hygiene products can be found in aisle 10.* □ *This feminine hygiene spray comes in scented and unscented.*

feminine napkin See SANITARY NAPKIN.

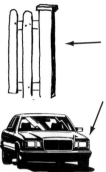

fence post a post that forms part of a fence. □ *Barbed wire was fastened to the fence posts with staples.* □ *The fence posts were set in concrete.*

fender a metal shield that protects the wheel of a car or bicycle. □ *There's a dent in the fender.* □ *A big piece of trash got caught up underneath the fender and was scraping against the tire.*

ferrule **1.** the band of metal that holds an eraser on the end of a wooden pencil. □ *Nervous, she gnawed on the ferrule of her pencil.* □ *The ferrule was too loose, and the eraser fell out.* **2.** the tip of an umbrella or walking stick. □ *The umbrella's metal ferrule scratched the floor.* □ *The cane had a rubber ferrule to help it grip smooth surfaces.*

fertilizer a substance put into soil to nourish plants. □ *She used a special kind of fertilizer for her rosebushes.* □ *He sprayed liquid fertilizer on the garden.*

FF See FORM FEED.

fiber See (DIETARY) FIBER.

fiber optic transmitting a signal through clear glass or plastic fibers. □ *The computers are linked in a fiber optic network.* □ *The surgeon used a fiber optic camera to examine the patient's incision.*

filament a coil of thin wire that produces light; part of an incandescent light bulb. □ *The filament must have broken. I can hear it rattling around in the light bulb.* □ *The three-way bulb has two filaments.*

file a set of data stored by a computer. □ *To open a file, choose "Get" on the File menu.* □ *To see the files on your disk, double-click on the disk icon.*

fillet a piece of meat with the bones removed. □ *The grocery store is having a special on catfish fillets.* □ *Trim the fat from the fillet of beef.*

filling   a food paste placed between or inside layers of other food. □ *She used raspberry jam as a filling between the layers of chocolate cake.* □ CHARLIE: *What's the filling in these cabbage rolls?* MARY: *Ground walnuts, onions, and cheese.*

film advance   a control on a camera that moves the film along. □ *I forgot to turn the film advance after I took that shot, so I wound up with a double exposure.* □ *This lever is the film advance.*

finger bowl   a small bowl filled with water for washing the fingertips; part of a formal table setting. □ *Each guest had a finger bowl of steaming water.* □ *Each finger bowl had a tiny flower floating in it.*

finger food   food that can be easily picked up by the fingers and eaten. □ *She served popcorn, pretzels, cookies, and other finger foods.* □ *We brought some finger foods to eat while we watched the movie.*

(finger)nail file   a flat piece of metal with a ridged surface, used for smoothing or shaping the fingernails. (See also EMERY BOARD.) □ *After she trimmed her nails, she shaped them with a fingernail file.* □ *The nail file quickly took off the rough edge on my thumbnail.*

finger tight   as tight as it can be made by hand. □ *Make all the nuts finger tight before you go to work on them with the wrench.* □ *The butterfly nut just needs to be finger tight. Tighten it more than that, and you're liable to break something.*

finger towel   a small towel for drying the hands. □ *She put out fresh finger towels for her guests to use.* □ *I bought some special holiday finger towels with "Happy New Year" embroidered on them.*

finial   a pointed ornament on top of something, especially a lamp. □ *I replaced the lampshade and screwed the finial back on top.* □ *The finials on the bedposts were shaped like acorns.*

fire alarm a signal used to warn that there is a fire in the building. □ *When they heard the fire alarm, all the residents of the apartment building went outside.* □ *He smelled smoke, so he turned on the fire alarm.*

firearm a weapon that uses burning gunpowder to shoot something. □ *Handguns, rifles, and shotguns are all firearms.* □ *He was carrying an unlicensed firearm.*

firebrick a kind of brick that resists fire and does not melt. □ *The chimney was lined with firebrick.* □ *They built a kiln out of firebrick.*

fire extinguisher a device that puts out a fire by spraying it with water or chemicals. (See also CARBON DIOXIDE EXTINGUISHER.) □ *I bought a fire extinguisher for the kitchen.* □ *He sprayed the fire extinguisher at the base of the fire.*

(fire) hydrant AND **fire plug** an outlet for a main water line, primarily used for firefighters to connect their hoses to the water supply. (FIRE PLUG is folksy.) □ *It is illegal to park in front of a fire hydrant.* □ *The firefighters hooked up the hose to the nearest hydrant.* □ *The fire plugs in that town are painted bright yellow.*

fireplace an opening, usually lined with brick or stone, in which a fire can safely burn. □ *We sat around the fireplace, watching the flames.* □ *He swept the ashes out of the fireplace.*

fire plug See (FIRE) HYDRANT.

firing pin a metal rod in a gun that strikes a cartridge, causing the gunpowder to ignite. □ *When you pull the trigger, it releases the spring that drives the firing pin.* □ *He opened the breech and examined the firing pin.*

first class the most expensive travel class, with many amenities. □ *The first-class passengers get wider, more comfortable seats.* □ *We decided to travel first class on our train trip. We had a nice, roomy compartment all to ourselves.*

fish burger a patty of fish served on a hamburger bun. □ *I don't eat red meat, so at fast-food restaurants, I usually have a fish burger.* □ *She put some tartar sauce on her fish burger.*

fisheye lens a camera lens that distorts an image, making objects in the center appear larger. □ *The photographer made the actor appear ugly by shooting him with a fisheye lens.* □ *The landscapes taken through the fisheye lens have a strange, nightmarish quality.*

fishhook a bent piece of wire with a sharp end, used to catch fish. □ *I put a worm on my fishhook and cast my line into the lake.* □ *The angler landed the fish in her boat and worked the fishhook out of its mouth.*

fish poacher a long, narrow metal pan used for cooking a fish over boiling water. □ *Our mouths watered as Jill lifted the steaming fish from the fish poacher.* □ *Place the fish poacher across two oven burners.*

fish scaler a tool that scrapes the scales off a fish. □ *This handy pocketknife even has a fish scaler attached.* □ *She gutted the fish and scraped it with the fish scaler.*

fish stick a rectangular piece of breaded fish. □ *I arranged the frozen fish sticks on a baking sheet and put them in the oven.* □ *Serve the fish sticks with cocktail sauce.*

fitted sheet a bed sheet with elastic at the corners, so that it fits tightly around a mattress. (Compare with FLAT SHEET.) □ *The sheet set includes one flat sheet, one fitted sheet, and two pillow cases.* □ *The elastic in this fitted sheet is wearing out. It keeps sliding off the mattress.*

fitting a device that connects lengths of pipe. □ *This fitting joins two pipes at a right angle.* □ *If you're using copper pipes, you'll need copper fittings.*

five and ten (cent store) a store that sells a variety of inexpensive things. (The earliest FIVE AND TEN CENT STORES sold things that cost between five and ten cents. See also

DIME STORE.) □ *The kids love the dozens of kinds of candy they can get at the five and ten cent store.* □ *I'm going to go to the five and ten and get some school supplies.*

fixative   a chemical sprayed onto a picture to keep it from smudging. □ *The artist sprayed fixative onto her charcoal sketch.* □ *Fixative protected the old drawing.*

fixings   foods that are usually served with a main dish. (Folksy.) □ *For just $3.99 you get a slice of turkey and all the fixings.* □ *She served the catfish with all kinds of fixings.*

flange   **1.** a projecting edge. □ *The flange on the edge of this plastic sleeve keeps it from falling into the hole.* □ *The flange on the lid of the blender helps to make a tight seal.* **2.** a metal ring that anchors a pipe to an opening in a wall or floor. □ *I removed the flange from the wall behind the sink.* □ *The pipe screws into this flange.*

flannel   fabric with a fuzzy texture. □ *I wear flannel pajamas when the weather's cold.* □ *He wore a checked flannel shirt.*

flan ring   a metal ring in which flan, a kind of CUSTARD, is baked. □ *Line an 8-inch flan ring with a pastry crust.* □ *Set the flan ring on a cookie sheet and fill it with the egg mixture.*

flap   the part of an envelope that folds over and seals. □ *I licked the flap and sealed the envelope.* □ *He slid a letter opener under the flap.*

flapjack   See PANCAKE.

flare   a bright light used to give a warning or signal for help. □ *The trucker put a line of flares around his broken-down truck.* □ *A police officer saw our flare and came to see what was wrong.*

flash   extra material left by a mold on a molded object. □ *I trimmed the flash from the plastic pieces in the model airplane kit.* □ *A little piece of flash was keeping the pen from screwing together as it should.*

flash(bulb)   a light used to light up the subject of a photograph. □ *What kind of flashbulbs does that camera take?* □ *It's dark in here. I'll have to use my flash.*

flashers AND **four ways**   flashing lights at all four corners of a car, used to signal trouble. (Informal.) □ *That car up there has the flashers on. I wonder what the matter is.* □ *The engine died. I turned on the four ways as I guided the car onto the shoulder.*

flask   a container with a narrow neck, used to hold liquid or powder. (Often used to describe a flat bottle of liquor.) □ *He always carried a flask of whiskey with him.* □ *The hunter carried a flask of gunpowder.*

flat   a tray full of plants, fruit, or vegetables. □ *I bought a flat of petunias to plant alongside the front walk.* □ *Tomatoes are $2.00 for a carton, $7.99 for a whole flat.*

flat-felled seam   a seam with one raw edge tucked under the other and sewed down. □ *A flat-felled seam is strong and attractive.* □ *Use a flat-felled seam for seams that will be visible on the finished garment.*

flats   women's shoes with very low heels. (Compare with (HIGH) HEELS.) □ *This skirt looks good with flats.* □ *I wish I could wear flats to work. They're so much more comfortable than heels.*

flat sheet   a bed sheet, a rectangular piece of cloth big enough to cover a bed. (Compare with FITTED SHEET.) □ *I need a queen-sized flat sheet.* □ *This flat sheet comes with a matching fitted sheet.*

flat (tire)   a tire that does not have enough air in it. (FLAT is informal.) □ *I tried to pump up the flat tire.* □ *My bicycle had a flat.*

flatware   knives, forks, and spoons made of a metal other than silver. (See also CUTLERY, SILVERWARE.) □ *She got a four-place setting of stainless steel flatware.* □ *I have a set of silverware in addition to the flatware I use every day.*

flea collar   an animal collar containing a substance that repels fleas. □ *The dog's flea collar isn't working. I just saw a flea hop off him.* □ *If your cat's going to go outside, he'll need a flea collar.*

flier   a step in a straight FLIGHT OF STAIRS. □ *All the fliers should be the same width.* □ *Eight fliers led up to the first landing.*

flight(s) of stairs   a series of steps in an indoor staircase. □ *Go through the door to your left and up the flight of stairs.* □ *I had to go up six flights of stairs to get to the apartment.*

float   a hollow ball that floats on the water in a toilet tank and works the mechanism that refills the tank after a flush. □ *The float was punctured, so the toilet didn't work.* □ *The float is attached to a metal arm called the float arm. The float arm is attached to the water inlet valve.*

floor joist   a wood or metal beam that supports a floor. □ *The floor joists are squeaking in this corner of the room.* □ *The workers replaced the rotten floor joist.*

floppy (disk)   See DISKETTE.

floss   See DENTAL FLOSS.

flour   **1.** very finely-ground grain, usually wheat. □ *Use two cups of flour.* □ *Add two tablespoons of flour to the boiling milk.* **2.** to coat something with FLOUR. □ *Grease and flour two cake pans.* □ *Lightly flour a bread board.*

flour sifter   a device that pushes FLOUR through a fine mesh, giving it a very even texture. □ *She turned the crank on the flour sifter, and the flour came out in a fluffy pile.* □ *I put all the dry ingredients into the flour sifter.*

flowerpot   a container that holds dirt for a plant to grow in. (FLOWERPOTS are measured by diameter.) □ *I bought an eight-inch flowerpot for my begonia.* □ *This plastic flowerpot has a saucer attached, to catch the excess water.*

flue   a passage that lets hot air escape. □ *I opened the fire-place damper so that the smoke from the fire rose up into the flue.* □ *There is a flue above the stove.*

fluorescent bulb   a light bulb in which electricity causes a gas to glow. (A FLUORESCENT BULB is more efficient than an INCANDESCENT BULB.) □ *The light fixture in the kitchen takes a fluorescent bulb.* □ *This fluorescent bulb will fit in an ordinary lamp socket.*

flush   at exactly the same level. □ *Is the head of the screw flush with the wood?* □ *The front of the drawer was flush with the surface around it.*

fly   an opening from the waist to the crotch in the front of a pair of pants. □ *He zipped up the fly of his blue jeans.* □ *You forgot to close your fly.*

flywheel   a weighted wheel that keeps something moving smoothly. □ *A flywheel keeps the crankshaft rotating evenly.* □ *A belt connects the "oars" of the rowing machine to a flywheel.*

FM   See FREQUENCY MODULATION.

foam rubber   rubber with a spongy texture. □ *This cheap mattress is just a sheet of foam rubber.* □ *They packed the computer printer in a box and cushioned it with foam rubber.*

focus   **1.** sharpness and clarity. (Frequently used in the expression IN FOCUS, sharp and clear.) □ *I got the picture in focus and snapped the shutter.* □ *Turn this ring on the lens until the image is in focus.* **2.** to get an image in FOCUS. □ *I focused the camera on the distant mountain.* □ *The TV camera was focused on the president's face.*

focusing knob   a control that adjusts the sharpness of a picture; part of a projector. □ *He turned the focusing knob until the picture was clear and sharp.* □ *Adjust the focusing knob until the image is in focus.*

fold   **1.** to bend something back on itself. □ *He folded the paper in half.* □ *Fold the fabric lengthwise and place the* *edge of the pattern piece along the fold.* **2.** to stir something gently into something else. □ *Fold the beaten egg whites into the cake batter.* □ *Fold the whipped cream into the sugar mixture.*

folder　**1.** a folded piece of thick paper, used to protect papers or group them together. □ *I opened the client's folder and found a copy of the last invoice we had sent her.* □ *He set up a folder for each letter of the alphabet.* **2.** a group of files on a computer. (See also DIRECTORY.) □ *Open the BUDGET folder.* □ *Why not group all the spreadsheets together in one folder?*

folding chair　a chair that can be folded flat. □ *I got out the card table and four folding chairs.* □ *We keep some folding chairs in the closet, in case we need extra seating.*

fondue　a heated sauce, often melted cheese, into which other food is dipped. □ *She served a cheese fondue, and the guests enjoyed dunking chunks of bread into the savory cheese.* □ *The main dish fondue was boiling, seasoned oil, with a variety of raw meats and seafoods to put into it.*

fondue fork　a long-handled fork for holding food in a hot liquid. □ *Each fondue fork had a different-colored handle, so everybody could keep track of which one belonged to him or her.* □ *She speared the strawberry with her fondue fork and dipped it into the hot chocolate sauce.*

fondue pot　a pot for keeping a FONDUE liquid hot. □ *I got an electric fondue pot, because I like to serve fondue.* □ *The fondue pot was full of melted cheese.*

font　a set of letters, numbers, and characters in the same style. □ *This printer can print out in a number of fonts.* □ *The word processor allows you to format text in twenty different fonts.*

font cartridge　a cartridge that fits into a computer printer and allows it to print different FONTS. □ *This font cartridge has ninety-nine different fonts, each in six different sizes.* □ *She put in the font cartridge that included the Old English font.*

food coloring a dye that can be safely added to food. □ *The cook added blue food coloring to the frosting.* □ *The candy gets its color from food coloring.*

food dehydrator a device that dries food. □ *We arranged slices of fruit on the racks of the food dehydrator.* □ *We use our food dehydrator to preserve fruit and vegetables from our garden.*

food mill a hand-cranked machine that grinds or mashes food. □ *Put the tomatoes through a food mill.* □ *I used the food mill to grind the nuts.*

food processor a machine that can chop, slice, grind, and mix food. □ *The food processor comes with dough hooks for kneading bread dough.* □ *I put the carrots in the food processor, pressed a button, and had carrot slices in practically no time.*

food warmer a device that keeps food warm. □ *This hamburger tastes like it sat in a food warmer for hours.* □ *I put Bill's dinner on the food warmer to keep it warm till he got home.*

foolproof impossible to wreck. □ *Try these easy, foolproof recipes.* □ CHARLIE: *I don't want to use your coffee maker. I'm afraid I'll break it.* JANE: *Oh, come on, Charlie. It's foolproof.*

footboard the structure across the foot end of a bed frame. (Contrasts with HEADBOARD.) □ *I hung an extra quilt over the footboard.* □ *Bolt the footboard to the side rail.*

footbridge a bridge for people to walk across. (See also PEDESTRIAN WALKWAY.) □ *There was a footbridge across the busy street.* □ *A picturesque wooden footbridge led across the river.*

footer a piece of text in the bottom margin of a page. (Compare with HEADER.) □ *Do you want to put the page number in the header or the footer?* □ *The word processor allows you to add a footer up to two lines long.*

footstool   a piece of furniture for resting the feet on. □ *She drew the footstool up to the old easy chair.* □ *We bought a chair and a matching footstool.*

forced air heat   a heating system in which a fan blows hot air through the ducts into the rooms. □ *MARY: Does your apartment have forced air heat? JANE: No, it has hot water heat.* □ *We decided to replace the boiler and radiators with forced air heat.*

foreign object   something from outside; something that is not supposed to be where it is. □ *The baby had pushed some kind of foreign object into his nose.* □ *Remove any foreign objects you find in the sink trap.*

fork   **1.** an eating and cooking tool with several points, called TINES, at one end. □ *She speared the last shrimp on her fork.* □ *Hold the meat steady with your fork while you cut it.* **2.** the metal structure that holds the front wheel of a bicycle. □ *The fork was bent, so the wheel couldn't turn.* □ *The front wheel snaps in and out of the little hooks at the bottom of the fork.*

form feed AND **FF**   a button on a computer printer that pushes the paper through to the end of the page. (Compare with LINE FEED.) □ *Push FF and see if you can get the printer to spit out that page.* □ *When it finishes printing, hit the form feed.*

Formica™   a brand of hard plastic. □ *"These Formica countertops are so easy to clean!" said Lisa.* □ *"This table has a Formica top," the salesperson pointed out.*

form letter   a standard letter sent to a number of people. □ *I wrote to my representative in Congress, but I only got a form letter in reply.* □ *I used the word processor to write a form letter, then printed out a copy for everyone in the database.*

forte pedal AND **damper pedal; sustain pedal**   a pedal that lifts the damper on the strings of a piano, so that the notes are sustained. □ *This mark tells you to press the forte* *pedal.* □ *The damper pedal is the one on the right.* □ *The pianist held down the sustain pedal and banged out a storm of sound.*

45 an audio disc that plays at 45 revolutions per minute. (Informal. A 45 usually contains only one song per side.) □ *She has a collection of 45s of great hits of the 1960s.* □ *Will this turntable play a 45?*

foundation the part of a building that is anchored in the ground. □ *The foundation of this house is a concrete slab.* □ *First, the construction workers dug a hole for the foundation of the new building. Then they reinforced it with cement blocks.*

foundation (garment) AND **girdle** an undergarment that squeezes the body to make it look thinner. (GIRDLE is informal.) □ *I need a foundation to get into my old dresses.* □ *The lingerie department sells a variety of foundation garments.* □ *I can't wait to get home and take off this girdle! I can hardly breathe!*

fountain pen a pen that writes with a stream of ink coming through a small slot in the tip. □ *He used a fountain pen to sign important documents.* □ *My fountain pen leaked all over my pocket.*

four-cylinder engine an engine with four cylindrical chambers and four pistons. (FOUR-CYLINDER ENGINES burn less gasoline and produce less power than engines with more cylinders.) □ *The compact car had a four-cylinder engine.* □ *Is that a four-cylinder engine or a six-cylinder engine?*

four ways See FLASHERS.

four-wheel drive **1.** the ability to transfer the power of a vehicle's engine to either one or both of its axles. □ *This pickup truck has four-wheel drive.* □ *You'll need the four-wheel drive to get up that slippery hill.* **2.** a vehicle with FOUR-WHEEL DRIVE. □ *When I moved to this town in the mountains, I bought a four-wheel drive.* □ *We took our four-wheel drive on the camping trip.*

foyer   a room just inside a front door. (See also ENTRY(WAY), LOBBY.) □ *The foyer of the office building was lit with a crystal chandelier.* □ *I stood in the foyer, looking out the front door at the rain.*

frame advance   a control that allows you to view a videotape one frame at a time. □ *The baseball fan used the frame advance to watch the double play in detail.* □ *I hit the still button, then used the frame advance to see the action frame by frame.*

frank(furter) AND **hot dog; wiener**   a kind of sausage. (WIENER and HOT DOG are informal.) □ *We stopped at a frankfurter vendor for lunch.* □ *The kids roasted wieners over the campfire.* □ *The diner serves all-beef hot dogs.*

freezer   a device that freezes things inside it. □ *I store a lot of meat in the freezer in the garage.* □ *I filled the ice cube tray with water and put it in the freezer.*

freezer paper   thick paper for wrapping food stored in a FREEZER. (Compare with FREEZER WRAP.) □ *The butcher wrapped the meat in freezer paper.* □ *I wrapped the chicken in plastic wrap and freezer paper and labeled it with the date.*

freezer wrap   a sheet of foil or plastic for wrapping food stored in a FREEZER. (Compare with FREEZER PAPER.) □ *I covered the lasagna with freezer wrap and put the food in the freezer.* □ *I like this clear freezer wrap because you can see what's inside it.*

freight elevator   a large ELEVATOR for carrying goods. □ *Bring those packages up on the freight elevator.* □ *The apartment building has a freight elevator for residents to use when they move their furniture in and out.*

freight (train)   a train that carries goods, rather than passengers. □ *I had to wait at the railroad crossing while a long freight train went by.* □ *The freight was hauling fifteen boxcars full of machine parts.*

French curve   a flat piece of material with a curved edge, used for drawing curves. □ *The tailor used a French curve to*

draw a pattern for the coat sleeve. □ *Use a French curve to connect the two dots.*

French door   a door having many glass panes. (FRENCH DOORS often appear in pairs.) □ *She opened the French doors and walked out onto the patio.* □ *French doors led to the balcony.*

(French) fries   fried strips of potato. (FRIES is informal. See also COTTAGE FRIES.) □ *All the sandwiches on the menu come with French fries and a dill pickle.* □ *Would you like some fries with your hamburger?*

Freon™   a brand of refrigerant fluid. □ *The mechanic added some Freon to the car's air-conditioning system.* □ *The air conditioner is leaking Freon.*

frequency modulation AND **FM**   a kind of radio signal. (Compare with AMPLITUDE MODULATION.) □ *My favorite FM station is 101.9.* □ *Frequency modulation stations come in a lot clearer than amplitude modulation stations do.*

fricassee   a meat stew. □ *I made the leftover chicken into a fricassee.* □ *Our special today is pork fricassee.*

fringe   a decorative band of hanging cords, strings, or strips of material. □ *The curtains were royal blue with a gold fringe.* □ *A foot-long leather fringe hung from the shoulders of the jacket.*

fritter   a portion of fried dough or batter. (Folksy.) □ *I cooked up some corn fritters.* □ *You can put shrimp, fish, or crab into these seafood fritters.*

frontage road   a smaller road that runs alongside a highway or major road. (See also ACCESS ROAD.) □ *You have to get onto the frontage road to get to those roadside businesses.* □ *He exited the highway and went back along the frontage road.*

front porch   a roofed platform attached to the front of a house. □ *We sat on the front porch, watching the world go by.* □ *The kids keep their bicycles out on the front porch.*

frost free   [of a food freezer that] removes frost automatically. □ *This 11.5 cubic foot freezer is frost free.* □ *As she chipped the layer of ice from the inside of her freezer, Jill vowed for the twentieth time to buy a frost free model.*

frosting   a paste of sugar, shortening, and other ingredients, used to cover and decorate cakes and pastries. (Compare with GLAZE, ICING.) □ *She made a chocolate cake with lemon frosting.* □ *You'll need a cup of butter and two cups of powdered sugar for the frosting.*

frozen dinner AND **TV dinner**   a meal frozen on a tray in which it can be reheated and served. (TV DINNERS are called that because they can be eaten while watching television.) □ *It's going to be a busy week. I'll buy a bunch of frozen dinners instead of trying to cook.* □ *I left some TV dinners for the babysitter to heat up for the kids.*

fruit leather   mashed fruit dried to form a thin sheet. □ *I used the food dehydrator to make fruit leather.* □ *Fruit leather is Billy's favorite snack.*

fry   to cook something in hot fat. □ *Fry the onions in two tablespoons of butter.* □ *Over the campfire, the anglers fried the fish they caught.*

fry basket   a wire basket with a handle, used to place food in deep, hot fat. □ *I cut up the potatoes and put them in the fry basket.* □ *A fry basket is handy for deep-frying food.*

frying pan   a flat-bottomed pan with a handle, used for frying food. (Compare with GRIDDLE, SKILLET.) □ *I heated up some oil in the frying pan.* □ *Carefully pour the batter into a frying pan.*

F-stop   a setting that determines how much light can pass through a camera lens. □ *The higher the F-stop, the greater the depth of field in the picture.* □ *Adjust the aperture to an F-stop of f/2.*

fuel indicator AND **gas gauge**   a display that shows how much fuel is left. (GAS GAUGE is informal.) □ *Check the fuel* *indicator from time to time.* □ *The gas gauge says I've got a quarter tank.*

fuel injector   a device that sprays gasoline into an engine cylinder. □ *This car doesn't have a carburetor. It has a fuel injector.* □ *Something is clogging the fuel injector. That's why the truck won't accelerate.*

full bed   See DOUBLE BED.

full boil AND **rolling boil**   the state of being hot enough that large bubbles are continuously forming. □ *Bring the water to a full boil.* □ *When the soup has reached a rolling boil, drizzle in the beaten egg.*

full-service   doing everything possible for customers. (At a FULL-SERVICE gas station, the employees fill the cars with gas, wash the windshields, and check the oil levels. Contrasts with SELF-SERVICE.) □ *This gas pump is full-service. The self-service pump is over there.* □ *The grocery store will take your order over the phone and have it delivered. They'll also special order things for you. It's the last full-service grocery store in town.*

function key   one of a set of computer keys labeled with the letter "F" followed by a number. □ *The F1 function key will give you the help menu.* □ *You can set up the function keys to perform tasks you frequently do.*

fungicide   a preparation that kills fungus. □ *This fungicide ought to take care of your athlete's foot fungus.* □ *She dabbed fungicide onto her peeling fingernail.*

funnel   a hollow cone, used to pour a liquid or powder into a narrow opening. □ *He used a funnel to put the syrup into a smaller bottle.* □ *She put a paper funnel into the oil filling hole and poured the motor oil into the engine.*

furnace   a device that burns fuel to produce heat for a building. □ *This furnace burns natural gas.* □ *He lit the pilot light on the furnace.*

furnace filter a device that traps dust and dirt in the air flowing into a FURNACE. □ *It's time to replace the furnace filter.* □ *A clogged furnace filter will reduce the efficiency of the furnace.*

furniture polish a substance that is rubbed onto wooden furniture to make it shiny. □ *She sprayed furniture polish on the tabletop and rubbed at it with a soft cloth.* □ *The furniture polish had a pleasant, lemony scent.*

fuse a device that interrupts an electrical circuit by melting if too much current passes through it. (Compare with CIRCUIT BREAKER. When a fuse melts, it is said to BLOW.) □ *The fuse blew, so I replaced it.* □ *I looked at the fuse for the refrigerator. It was OK.*

fuse box an opening that gives access to the FUSES in a building's electrical circuits. □ *I shone the flashlight on the fuse box to see if a fuse had blown.* □ *The fuse box is in the basement.*

fusible element the part of a FUSE that melts if too much current passes through it. □ *I examined the fuse. The fusible element had melted.* □ *The fusible element will melt at currents higher than 20 amps.*

fusible interfacing a stiff material that will stick to fabric when heated. (See also INTERFACING. Compare with FUSIBLE WEB.) □ *She ironed in a layer of fusible interfacing to make the jacket hold its shape.* □ *Cut fusible interfacing to fit the pattern piece.*

fusible web a strip of material that will stick two layers of fabric together when heated. (Compare with FUSIBLE INTERFACING.) □ *Instead of sewing the hem, he used fusible web.* □ *The pockets were attached with fusible web.*

G

gadget a device. (Informal.) □ *I've got a helpful little gadget for removing a car's oil filter.* □ *This gadget grates cheese in a jiffy.*

gallery a roofed platform around more than one side of a house. (See also BALCONY, PORCH, VERANDA.) □ *A screened gallery ran around three sides of the old hotel.* □ *The gallery was crowded with flowering plants.*

garage a building in which vehicles are stored. □ *They built a two-car garage in back of the house.* □ *At the end of her shift, the bus driver took her bus back to the garage.*

garage door opener a device that opens and closes the door of a GARAGE automatically. □ *In the cold winter months, I'm really glad I have a garage door opener.* □ *He pushed the button on his garage door opener, and the garage door slid up.*

garbage can AND **garbage pail; trash can** a container for collecting garbage. □ *He threw the coffee grounds into the garbage can.* □ *I carried the full garbage pail out to the Dumpster.* □ *He picked up the litter from the street and put it in a trash can.*

garbage chute a passage that drops trash from the upper floors of a building into a place where it is collected or burned. (Apartment buildings often have GARBAGE CHUTES.) □ *I took the kitchen garbage out to the garbage chute.* □ *The little girl was crying because she had dropped her toy down the garbage chute.*

garbage collector someone whose job is to collect garbage from a neighborhood, place it into a truck, and take it to a dump or a landfill. □ MARY: *What day does the garbage collector come?* CHARLIE: *Wednesday.* □ *Early in the morning, I heard the garbage collector's truck in the alley.*

garbage compactor AND **trash compactor**   a device that crushes garbage into a small space. (Compare with GARBAGE DISPOSER.) □ *He put the garbage into the garbage compactor.* □ *With the trash compactor, we only put out one trash bin for the garbage collector every week. We used to put out three.*

garbage disposer   a device that grinds up food waste and washes it down a drain. (Compare with DISPOSALL™, GARBAGE COMPACTOR.) □ *Don't put those orange peels in the trash. Put them in the garbage disposer.* □ *This switch is for the light above the sink, and this one is for the garbage disposer.*

garbage pail   See GARBAGE CAN.

garbage truck   a truck in which a GARBAGE COLLECTOR gathers up garbage. □ *The garbage collector emptied the Dumpster into the garbage truck.* □ *The garbage truck went up one side of the street and down the other.*

garden clippers   a large pair of shears used to trim bushes and tree branches. (See also HEDGE CLIPPERS.) □ *She trimmed the hedge with the garden clippers.* □ *These garden clippers need sharpening.*

garden hose   a flexible tube used to bring water from a faucet to a place some distance away. □ *I hooked up the garden hose and watered the plants in the backyard.* □ *He rinsed off his car with water from the garden hose.*

garlic press   a device that mashes a clove of garlic into a paste. □ *Put two cloves of garlic through the garlic press and add them to the tomato sauce.* □ *She scraped the garlic from the bottom of the garlic press.*

garment bag   a piece of luggage that holds a garment laid flat and that can be hung up by a hook at one end. □ *He packed an extra suit in his garment bag.* □ *A garment bag helps keep clothes from wrinkling when you travel.*

garnish   **1.** an edible decoration for food. □ *Each plate had a sprig of parsley as a garnish.* □ *The chef cut cherry*

tomatoes into flower shapes and used them for a garnish.
2. to decorate food with a GARNISH. □ *The grapefruit half was garnished with a cherry.* □ *Garnish the roast with a few steamed vegetables arranged in an attractive shape.*

gas   **1.** See GAS(OLINE). **2.** a natural GAS that comes from the earth's crust and is used as a fuel for heating and cooking. (Informal.) □ *MARY: Is that a gas or electric stove? JANE: Gas.* □ *If you smell gas, leave the building immediately and call the gas company.*

gas gauge   See FUEL INDICATOR.

gas grill   an outdoor grill that produces cooking heat by burning GAS. □ *I don't have to mess with charcoal. I have a gas grill.* □ *She fired up the gas grill and got the hamburgers ready.*

gasket   a thin, flexible object used to seal the gap where two things are joined together. (See also SEAL.) □ *There is a ring-shaped rubber gasket between the faucet spout and the escutcheon.* □ *When you disassemble the carburetor, you will probably destroy the carburetor gaskets. You should have a new set ready.*

gas meter   a device that shows the amount of natural GAS used in a building or part of a building. □ *Something must be wrong with the gas meter. I can't believe we used that much gas last month.* □ *From time to time, I check the reading on my gas bill against the gas meter, to make sure the gas company isn't making a mistake.*

gas(oline)   a liquid fuel used in engines. □ *What grade of gasoline does your car use?* □ *Uh-oh. The car's out of gas.*

gas (pedal)   a pedal in a car or truck that pumps fuel into the engine when pressed. (GAS is informal.) □ *He stepped on the gas pedal, and the car accelerated.* □ *I hit the brake when I meant to hit the gas.*

gas pump   a device that pumps GAS(OLINE) from a storage tank at a GAS STATION into cars and trucks. □ *You parked* *your car too far away from the gas pump. I can't possibly get the hose out to your gas tank. □ She watched the gas pump carefully, measuring exactly eight gallons into her gas tank.*

gas station   a business that sells GAS(OLINE). (See also SER-VICE STATION) □ *I'm getting low on gas. I'd better stop at a gas station. □ The gas station is open 24 hours a day.*

(gas) tank   a chamber that holds GAS(OLINE), especially in a car or truck. □ *There's a leak in your gas tank. That could be dangerous. □ We filled the tank before we left on our trip.*

gate   **1.** a door in a fence or wall. □ *She unlatched the gate and went into the front yard. □ He pressed a button to open the gate into the parking lot.* **2.** the location in an airport where passengers get on and off a plane. □ *Flight 714 is now arriving at gate 21A. □ Andrew Williams, please meet your party at gate C49.*

gate leg table   a table with legs that swing in so that the sides can fold down. (See also DROP LEAF TABLE.) □ *When the sides are down, the gate leg table is very compact. □ She put a new finish on the antique gate leg table.*

gather   **1.** a small fold in a piece of fabric. □ *Make sure the gathers in the top of the skirt are even before you sew it to the waistband. □ She put tiny gathers in the ruffle at the bottom of the bedspread.* **2.** to put a series of small folds in a piece of fabric. □ *Gather the sleeve cap and fit it into the bodice. □ The full trousers were gathered into tight bands at the ankles.*

gearbox   a device containing a system of gears. □ *The manual transmission includes a clutch and a gearbox. □ The gearbox multiplies the rotating energy coming from the engine.*

gear shift AND **gear stick**   the control that changes gears on a car or bicycle. (GEAR STICK refers specifically to the control that changes gears on a car with manual transmission.) □ *She moved the gear shift to "reverse." □ Put in the clutch before you try to move the gear stick.*

gear stick   See GEAR SHIFT.

gelcap   an oval-shaped pill with a gelatin coating. (An advertising term. See also CAPLET, CAPSULE, TABLET.) ☐ *Try these extra-strength gelcaps on your next severe headache.* ☐ *One of these gelcaps contains twice as much medicine as one tablet of the other brand.*

generic   without a brand name. (GENERIC products are often cheap because the manufacturer does not spend any money to advertise them.) ☐ *This generic peanut butter tastes just as good as the brand-name stuff.* ☐ *The cat doesn't seem to like the taste of the generic cat food.*

giblets   the heart, liver, and GIZZARD of a fowl. ☐ *I made stuffing out of the chicken giblets.* ☐ *He used the turkey giblets for soup stock.*

gift box   an attractive box, suitable for containing a gift. ☐ *The sales clerk said, "I can put this in a gift box for you."* ☐ *I had the store put the sheets in a pretty silver gift box.*

gift wrap   **1.** decorative paper for wrapping a gift. (See also WRAPPING PAPER.) ☐ *I bought a roll of "Happy Birthday" gift wrap.* ☐ *After the holidays, many stores have sales on gift wrap.* **2.** to wrap something in decorative paper. ☐ *I bought a present for my sister and had it gift wrapped at the store.* ☐ *It took me all night to gift wrap the children's Christmas presents.*

gimlet   a handle attached to a steel tip, used for drilling small holes. ☐ *I used the gimlet to bore a starter hole for the screw.* ☐ *The gimlet drilled a neat hole in the drywall.*

gingham   fabric with a checked pattern. ☐ *There were red gingham curtains in the kitchen window.* ☐ *The little girl wore a dress of blue gingham.*

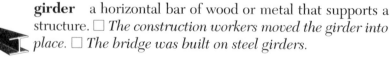

girder   a horizontal bar of wood or metal that supports a structure. ☐ *The construction workers moved the girder into place.* ☐ *The bridge was built on steel girders.*

girdle   See FOUNDATION (GARMENT).

gizzard   part of the digestive tract of a fowl. □ *The cook chopped up the chicken gizzard and used it in the stuffing.* □ *He likes to put turkey gizzards in his stew.*

(glass) insulator   a piece of glass used to protect wires on a power line. □ *She collects old-fashioned glass insulators.* □ *An insulator capped the place where the wire was attached to the power pole.*

glaze   **1.** a clear, shiny coating. (Compare with FROSTING, ICING.) □ *Make a glaze for the fruit out of sugar and gelatin.* □ *The glaze on the doughnut was very thick.* **2.** to put a clear, shiny coating on something. □ *He glazed the ham with honey.* □ *Glaze the top of the loaf with egg white.*

glazing   the glass or clear plastic in a window. □ *Cut the glazing about an eighth of an inch smaller than the opening of the window sash.* □ *I installed double-strength glazing in the patio door.*

glazing bead   a strip of putty or metal that holds a glass pane in a window frame. □ *After placing the pane of glass into the window frame, make a glazing bead with a rope of putty.* □ *The old glazing bead was rusting away.*

glitch   a flaw, especially in a computer program. (Slang.) □ *There's a glitch in this word processor. When you try to put a word in boldface and italics, it prints it out with an underline.* □ *A glitch in the program made the whole system crash.*

global   concerning every occurrence of something. □ *I wanted to replace the word "happy" with the word "glad" throughout the document, so I did a global replace.* □ *She needed to find every file that had to do with the Miller account, so she did a global search for "Miller."*

glove box AND **glove compartment**   a compartment in the DASH(BOARD) of a car. □ *I have a flashlight in the glove box.* □ *He kept a number of road maps in the glove compartment.*

glove compartment   See GLOVE BOX.

glue stick   a solid stick of glue. ☐ *He used the glue stick to put a line of glue along the top of the piece of fabric. ☐ She dabbed the glue stick on the back of the photograph.*

go off   [for an alarm] to sound. ☐ *Why did the fire alarm go off? There's no fire in the building! ☐ His alarm clock went off at six AM.*

gooseneck lamp   a light on a flexible rod. (The flexible part of this lamp looks like the neck of a goose.) ☐ *She adjusted the gooseneck lamp to shine onto the book she was reading. ☐ He bent the gooseneck lamp lower.*

gore   a triangular panel of cloth; part of a garment. ☐ *The six gores of this skirt make it flare out at the bottom. ☐ A gore under the arm gives this blouse its dramatic lines.*

governor   a device that controls how fast a motor or engine will run. ☐ *The governor kept the pump engine from overheating. ☐ I adjusted the governor on the lawn mower engine.*

graham cracker   a slightly sweet cracker made with whole wheat flour. ☐ *The children had graham crackers and a glass of milk for a snack. ☐ The crust of this pie is made of crushed graham crackers.*

graham flour   whole wheat flour, including the wheat germ. ☐ *Use 2 cups of graham flour. ☐ The bread recipe calls for graham flour.*

grain   the pattern of long fibers in wood. (With the grain means in the same direction as the GRAIN.) ☐ *The walnut paneling had a beautiful swirling pattern in the grain. ☐ The carpenter sanded the wood with the grain.*

grandfather clock   a pendulum clock in a tall cabinet. ☐ *The grandfather clock chimed on the hour. ☐ I heard the deep ticking of the pendulum on the grandfather clock.*

granny fork   a fork with a short, wooden handle and two sturdy TINES. □ *She poked the boiling potatoes with a granny fork to see if they were tender.* □ *He turned the broiling meat with a granny fork.*

granola   a mixture of whole grains, fruit, and nuts, often eaten as a breakfast cereal. □ *I bought some raspberry granola at the health food store.* □ *The hikers kept up their energy with handfuls of granola.*

granulated sugar   sugar in the form of small crystals. (Compare with POWDERED SUGAR.) □ *Add two cups of granulated sugar.* □ *Can I substitute granulated sugar for powdered sugar in this recipe?*

graphics   pictures or diagrams. □ *How can I add graphics to my newsletter?* □ *This computer program allows you to store graphics on disk.*

grate   to shred something by rubbing it across a rough surface. □ *Grate the carrots.* □ *She grated two pounds of potatoes.*

grater   a tool with a rough surface, used for grating foods. □ *Use this side of the grater if you want something coarsely grated.* □ *He rubbed the block of cheese across the grater.*

gravy   a sauce made of flour, animal fat, and liquid. □ *Would you like gravy on your mashed potatoes?* □ *He ladled gravy onto the roast beef.*

gravy boat   a boat-shaped bowl for serving GRAVY. □ *I bought a gravy boat in my china pattern.* □ *The sauce was served in a gravy boat.*

grease   **1.** solid or semi-solid oil or fat. □ *The mechanic put a little grease in the hinges of the car door.* □ *The roasting pan was covered with grease.* **2.** to put GREASE on something. (See also BUTTER.) □ *Grease the gasket before installing it.* □ *Grease and flour two eight-inch cake pans.*

Greek salad   a dish including lettuce, Greek feta cheese, olives, and tomatoes. □ *I ordered a Greek salad.* □ *She made a large Greek salad for dinner.*

griddle   a heavy, flat pan with a long handle. (Compare FRYING PAN, SKILLET.) □ *Heat the griddle till a drop of water will bounce on it.* □ *He poured pancake batter onto the griddle.*

griddle cake   See PANCAKE.

grill   **1.** a wire rack for cooking food directly over heat. (See also (BARBECUE) GRILL, HIBACHI.) □ *I put the chicken on the grill.* □ *The electric grill is easy to clean.* **2.** to cook something on a GRILL. □ *I grilled some tomatoes.* □ *Our special today is the grilled seafood platter.*

grinder   See SUB(MARINE) SANDWICH.

grit   the number of abrasive grains per square inch of SANDPAPER. □ *To finish your woodworking project, you'll need a fine sandpaper, about 250 grit.* □ *The carpenter sanded the end grain with a coarse, 40 grit sandpaper.*

grits   coarsely ground corn. □ *I had grits for breakfast.* □ *He ladled gravy onto his grits.*

grocery store   a store that sells foodstuffs. (See also SUPERMARKET.) □ *Stop at the grocery store on your way home and pick up some tomatoes and a quart of milk.* □ *Does this grocery store have a good meat department?*

gross   one hundred and forty-four; twelve dozen. □ *I bought a gross of brass nails.* □ *We needed several gross of hot dog buns for the company picnic.*

ground   an electrical connection leading to the ground, used to make an electrical system safer. □ *The third prong on a three-prong plug connects to ground.* □ *The neutral wire in the circuit is connected to ground.*

grout cement that fills the gaps between tiles. □ *He used a toothbrush to clean the grout in the bathroom.* □ *Let the fresh grout set for fifteen minutes, then wipe off the excess with a damp cloth.*

guarantee a legally binding promise that something will not fail. □ *The manufacturer's guarantee on this toaster says that they will replace it free of charge.* □ *The mechanic gave me a written guarantee on the repair work.*

guard rail a rail along the edge of a road, to keep vehicles from going past the edge. □ *The car crashed into the guard rail.* □ *A guard rail was constructed on the dangerous curve.*

guest towel a small towel for guests to dry their hands on. □ *The guest towels had the family name embroidered on them.* □ *The fancy guest towels had lace edgings. I was almost afraid to use them.*

gusset a piece of fabric sewn into a garment to give the wearer extra room to move. □ *Sew in the underarm gusset before sewing the side seam.* □ *She added a gusset to the pants crotch.*

gutter the metal or plastic channel that collects the water that flows off the roof. □ *I have to clean the leaves out of my gutter.* □ *Tom paints his gutters every five years.*

H

hacksaw   a saw with a metal frame holding a narrow, removable blade. □ *She used a hacksaw to cut through the plastic sheeting.* □ *He had a variety of blades for his hacksaw.*

hailer   a hand-held loudspeaker. (See also BULLHORN.) □ *The police officer spoke into a hailer.* □ *He addressed the crowd through a hailer.*

hair clip   a plastic or metal fastener that holds hair in place. □ *She fastened the ponytail with a hair clip.* □ *I bought a fancy rhinestone hair clip.*

hair clipper   an electric tool that cuts hair. □ *The hairdresser trimmed the hair on the back of my neck with a hair clipper.* □ *I bought a hair clipper so I could do haircuts at home.*

hair coloring   a preparation that changes the color of hair. □ *This brand of hair coloring is very gentle to the hair.* □ *The stylist applied a subtle hair coloring to bring out my highlights.*

(hair) conditioner   a preparation that makes hair easier to comb. □ *After shampooing, apply hair conditioner.* □ *This conditioner leaves your hair silky smooth and shiny.*

hair dryer   a device that dries hair by blowing hot air onto it. □ *This hand-held hair dryer is great for traveling.* □ *After the hair stylist put the curlers in my hair, I went to sit under the hair dryer.*

hair net   a net worn around the hair to keep it out of the way. □ *All food service employees must wear a hair net.* □ *There are hair nets to match every hair color.*

hair pin   a piece of wire bent into a U-shape and used to hold hair in place. (See also BOBBY PIN.) □ *Wind the braid*

142

into a coil and secure it with hair pins. □ *A hair pin fell out, and my whole hair style came undone.*

(hair) roller   See CURLER.

hair spray   a preparation that is sprayed onto hair to keep it in place. □ *She arranged her hair to her liking and sprayed it with hair spray.* □ *This hair spray works even in a strong wind.*

hair trigger   a gun trigger that will fire with a very slight amount of pressure. □ *He had a hair trigger on his shotgun. He could fire a shot the second he saw something move.* □ *You don't want a hair trigger on your pistol. It's dangerous!*

half-and-half   a mixture of half milk and half cream. □ *What would you like for your coffee? Cream, half-and-half, or milk?* □ *You can use half-and-half where the recipe calls for cream.*

hamburger   **1.** ground beef. □ *Hamburger is $1.50 a pound this week.* □ *I bought two pounds of hamburger for a meat loaf.* **2.** See (HAM)BURGER (SANDWICH).

hamburger patty   ground beef made into a flat, round shape. □ *I bought a box of frozen hamburger patties.* □ *He put the thick, juicy hamburger patties on the grill.*

(ham)burger (sandwich)   a cooked patty of ground beef served on a round bun. (BURGER is informal.) □ *Special this week—hamburger sandwich, $2.49.* □ *They make a pretty good hamburger sandwich at that diner.*

hammer   **1.** a tool with a long handle and a heavy head, used for pounding. (See also BALL-PEEN HAMMER, CLAW HAMMER.) □ *Do you have a hammer in your toolbox?* □ *She used a small hammer to drive the tacks into the molding.* **2.** to pound on something with a HAMMER. □ *I hammered the nail into the board.* □ *He hammered the metal flat.* **3.** the part of a gun that strikes the cartridge when the trigger is pulled. □ *Pull the hammer back to cock the gun.* □ *The next round moved into place in front of the hammer.*

hammock a large piece of cloth hung up by both ends and used as a place to lie down. □ *I hung the hammock between two tree trunks.* □ *He lay in the hammock, rocking and daydreaming.*

ham radio amateur radio, a hobby in which people contact each other by radio. □ *Do you have a ham radio license?* □ *The ham radio operator was able to receive signals from many thousands of miles away.*

hand brake 1. a bicycle brake operated by a lever on the handlebars. (Compare with COASTER BRAKE.) □ *The hand brake is sticking.* □ *The hand brake brought the bike to an immediate stop.* 2. See EMERGENCY BRAKE.

handgrip a piece of plastic or rubber that makes something easier to grip in the hand. □ *The handgrip on this hammer is peeling away.* □ *The bicycle handlebars had specially molded handgrips.*

handgun a gun that can be held and fired in one hand; a pistol. □ *She applied for a license to buy a handgun.* □ *He kept a handgun in the glove box of his car.*

hand-held able to be held in one hand. □ *I bought a hand-held video camera.* □ *The security guards used a hand-held device to screen the airline passengers for weapons.*

handlebar a horizontal bar used to steer the front wheel of a bicycle. □ *She leaned forward over the handlebars and pedaled hard.* □ *He wanted a ten-speed bike with racing handlebars.*

handrail See BANISTER.

handsaw a saw that is moved by hand. □ *She used a handsaw to cut the boards.* □ *It's hard to cut a straight line with a handsaw.*

handset See RECEIVER.

(hand) strap a loop of material hanging from the ceiling or a rail in a bus or train, held by standing passengers to keep themselves from falling. □ *At rush hour, every seat and every hand strap on the bus was taken.* □ *She grabbed the strap as the train went around a curve.*

hand towel   a towel used for drying the hands. □ *The hotel room was equipped with a bath towel, a hand towel, and a wash cloth for each guest.* □ *I bought a set of hand towels to match my bath towels.*

hangar   a building used for storing and repairing airplanes. □ *The plane rolled into the hangar.* □ *There was a row of hangars to one side of the runway.*

hanging file   a file folder that hangs from rails on either side of a drawer. □ *He installed a rack for hanging files in the file drawer.* □ *She made a label for the hanging file.*

hard boiled   [of an egg] boiled until the yolk is dry. (Compare with SOFT BOILED.) □ *WAITER: How would you like your egg? CUSTOMER: Hard boiled.* □ *The salad was garnished with slices of hard boiled egg.*

hard disk   a large-capacity computer disk that is more or less permanently installed. (Compare with DISKETTE.) □ *This laptop has a hard disk.* □ *This database is too big for a diskette. We'll have to store it on the hard disk.*

hard drive   a device that reads and writes information on a HARD DISK. □ *The hard drive is labeled "C:."* □ *This laptop has a 120 meg hard drive and two 3½-inch floppy drives.*

hardware   **1.** tools, metal and plastic fasteners, and other items used in building. □ *The grocery store sells some kinds of hardware.* □ *This kit includes all the hardware you will need to install a doorknob.* **2.** the physical parts of a computer. (Contrasts with SOFTWARE.) □ *Something's wrong with the computer, but I can't tell if it's a hardware or a software problem.* □ *She designs computer hardware.*

hard water   water that contains large amounts of minerals. (Contrasts with SOFT WATER.) □ *We got a water softener to improve the quality of the hard water that comes out of the* tap. □ *I can't seem to get anything clean with this hard water.*

hardwood floor   a floor made of parallel strips of wood. □ *The apartment had beautiful hardwood floors.* □ *He stripped the old varnish from the hardwood floor.*

hardy plant   a plant that can live through a cold winter. □ *In this northern climate, you will want a number of hardy plants in your garden.* □ *Strawberries are a hardy plant.*

harp   a metal frame that supports the lampshade on a lamp. □ *She fit the new lampshade in place on the harp and screwed in the end ornament.* □ *The harp screws in underneath the light bulb.*

hash   a mixture of chopped meat, vegetables, and seasonings. □ *I bought a can of beef hash.* □ *She made hash out of the leftover turkey.*

hash browns   fried, chopped, or shredded potatoes. □ *Two eggs, sausage, and hash browns cost $2.95.* □ *I like to put onions in my hash browns.*

hasp   a fastener with a hinged flap that fits over a loop. □ *The storage locker was fastened with a hasp.* □ *She put a padlock through the hasp.*

hatchet   a tool with a long handle and a sharp, heavy head, used for chopping. (See also AXE.) □ *She split the firewood with a hatchet.* □ *He used a hatchet to clear away the dead branches.*

head   a whole garlic root, composed of a number of CLOVES. □ *I put a couple heads of garlic in the oven to roast.* □ *She stored the garlic head in the refrigerator.*

headboard   a board fastened across the head end of a bed frame. (Contrasts with FOOTBOARD.) □ *The antique bed had a tall headboard.* □ *I like the headboard on that brass bed.*

head cleaner a device or a substance for cleaning the TAPE HEAD in an audio or video recorder or player. □ *This cassette is a head cleaner. Just play it once in your tape player, and it will scour the heads clean.* □ *She dabbed head cleaner onto the video head.*

header a text in the top margin of a page. (Compare with FOOTER.) □ *You can place the header at the left or right margin, or in the center.* □ *There should be a different header for each section of the book.*

headlamp AND **headlight** a light on the front end of a car or bicycle. □ *The bicycle had a battery-operated headlamp.* □ *It's getting dark. Turn on the headlights.*

headlight See HEADLAMP.

headphones a pair of speakers on a U-shaped frame, to be worn over a person's ears. (See also EARPHONES.) □ *She put on the stereo headphones.* □ *The radio operator listened to the signal coming in over the headphones.*

headset a device that holds speakers over a person's ears and a microphone to the person's mouth. □ *The telephone operators put on their headsets.* □ *The air traffic controller spoke into the headset.*

health food food that is good for one's health, often whole, unprocessed foods. □ *I bought some whole-wheat flour at the health food store.* □ *In the health food section at the grocery store, you can get many sugar-free, low-fat snacks.*

heaping more than full, with some amount heaped up on top. □ *Add a heaping teaspoon of sugar.* □ *He put a heaping handful of berries into the batter.*

heat exchanger a device that transfers heat to or from the air. □ *The compressor compresses the hot fluid in the heat exchanger, thus releasing the heat.* □ *A fan blows the warmed air from the heat exchanger into the cold room.*

heating element something that produces heat when electricity is passed through it. □ *The heating element on the electric burner was glowing red.* □ *I took the toaster apart and removed the broken heating element.*

heating pad a pad-shaped electric device that produces heat. □ *I put a heating pad on my aching muscles.* □ *He used a heating pad to relieve his stiff shoulder.*

heat pump a device that moves heat out of a building in hot weather and into the building in cold weather. □ *We replaced our furnace with a heat pump.* □ *The outdoor part of the heat pump contains the compressor and a heat exchanger coil.*

heavy cream AND **whipping cream** thick cream that contains a high percentage of fat. (WHIPPING CREAM is easily whipped to a fluffy texture.) □ *After removing the soup from the heat, add half a cup of heavy cream.* □ *Whip the whipping cream with an electric mixer.*

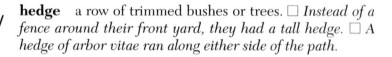

hedge a row of trimmed bushes or trees. □ *Instead of a fence around their front yard, they had a tall hedge.* □ *A hedge of arbor vitae ran along either side of the path.*

hedge clippers AND **hedge trimmers** a large pair of shears used to trim a HEDGE.(See also GARDEN CLIPPERS.) □ *Use hedge clippers to snip off any stray twigs.* □ *He pruned the fruit tree with his hedge trimmers.*

hedge trimmers See HEDGE CLIPPERS.

hem **1.** the bottom edge of a garment, folded under and sewed down to prevent fraying. □ *The hem of the skirt came just below her knees.* □ *The hem of those pants needs to be a little higher.* **2.** to fold under the bottom edge of a garment and sew it in place. □ *I'll get these pants hemmed right now.* □ *I'm almost finished sewing this blouse. I just have to hem it.*

herb **1.** a plant whose leaves or seeds are used to season food. (See also SPICE.) □ *Rosemary is a popular herb.* □ *I'm growing herbs in my garden.* **2.** a kind of leaf or seed used to season food. □ *The savory bread is made with herbs and cheeses.* □ *Oregano and basil are my favorite herbs.*

herbicide   a substance that kills weeds. □ *I spread herbicide on the front lawn.* □ *The farmer sprayed the corn crop with herbicide.*

hero (sandwich)   See SUB(MARINE SANDWICH).

hex key   See ALLEN™ WRENCH.

hex nut   a nut with six sides. □ *She threaded the hex nut onto the bolt and tightened it with a wrench.* □ *The wrench doesn't quite fit this hex nut.*

hex wrench   See ALLEN™ WRENCH.

hibachi   a charcoal grill. (Japanese. See also (BARBECUE) GRILL, GRILL.) □ *I lit the coals in the hibachi.* □ *He put the chicken wings on the hibachi and basted them with barbecue sauce.*

high beam   **1.** with car headlights on high power, aimed high. (Contrasts with LOW BEAM.) □ *There were no street lights on the dark, deserted stretch of road. She put her lights on high beam.* □ *Don't have the lights on high beam when it's foggy. The light just reflects off the water vapor in the air.* **2.** a headlight on high power, aimed high. (Informal. Usually plural.) □ *The car coming toward me had his high beams on. It was blinding.* □ *Turn off your high beams as you come into the town.*

high chair   a baby's chair with tall legs, so that the baby can sit at table height. □ *I put the baby in her high chair.* □ *The high chair has a strap to keep the baby from wiggling out.*

(high) heels   women's shoes with tall heels. (HEELS is informal. Compare with FLATS.) □ *I'm looking for a pair of high heels in patent leather.* □ *I can't wait to get home and get out of these heels! My feet are killing me!*

highlight   to draw attention to text on a computer screen by marking it, putting it in a different color, for instance. □

Click on the word to highlight it. □ *Underlined words will be highlighted.*

highlighter (pen)   a pen that makes a wide mark of bright, transparent ink. (HIGHLIGHTERS are used to mark other writing or printing in order to make it stand out.) □ *The student marked the key words in the textbook with a highlighter.* □ *I used a highlighter pen to emphasize the paragraphs I wanted removed from the document.*

hinge   a device made of two metal plates joined by a pin. (HINGES fasten two things together in such a way that one of them, such as a door or a lid, can swing. See also PIVOT, SWIVEL.) □ *The hinges on the front door are squeaking. They need oil.* □ *Joe held the door up to the door frame, and I screwed the hinges in place.*

hoe   a tool with a long handle and a flat blade at one end, used for chopping and digging. □ *He uprooted the weeds with a hoe.* □ *Loosen the soil with a hoe.*

hold button   a button on a telephone that puts a call "on hold," so that the person on the other end must wait for someone to take the call. □ *I asked the caller to hold, and I pushed the hold button.* □ *The hold button is blinking. Is there a call on hold?*

hole punch   a device that punches one or more holes, usually in paper. □ *I keep a small hole punch in my notebook, so I can punch holes in class handouts and file them in my notebook.* □ *The hole punch can take up to ten sheets of paper.*

Hollywood bed   a low bed with a HEADBOARD but no FOOTBOARD. □ *Most motel rooms have Hollywood beds.* □ *The bedroom was furnished with a Hollywood bed and a dresser.*

holster   a holder for a handgun. □ *He kept his Colt pistol in a fancy, tooled-leather holster.* □ *She had her gun concealed in a shoulder holster under her jacket.*

home fries   See COTTAGE FRIES.

hood   the metal lid that covers a car's engine. ☐ *I popped the hood open and took a look at the engine.* ☐ *This lever opens the hood.*

hood ornament   a decoration on the very front of a car's HOOD. ☐ *The car had a fancy hood ornament in the shape of the Cadillac logo.* ☐ *The Rolls Royce hood ornament is a winged woman.*

hook and eye   a clothing fastener with one half in the shape of a hook that fits into the other half, shaped like a loop. ☐ *The collar fastens in back with a hook and eye.* ☐ *The skirt zips up one side, and the waistband closes with a hook and eye.*

hook and loop fastener   a clothing fastener in which tiny plastic hooks on one half catch tiny loops on the other half. (See also VELCRO™.) ☐ *Press the halves of the hook and loop fastener together to close the opening.* ☐ *The cuffs on the coat are secured with hook and loop fastener.*

hookup   a place to connect to a service, such as electricity, cable TV, or running water. ☐ *The campsites have electric hookups.* ☐ *Is there a cable hookup in this apartment?*

hopper   a container that drops or moves its contents into something else. ☐ *I put the nuts into the hopper on the food mill.* ☐ *The garbage collector tossed the bags of garbage into the hopper of the garbage truck.*

hors d'oeuvre   small portions of food served before a meal or as a snack. (Pronounced ore-DERV. See also APPETIZER, CANAPÉ.) ☐ *The host passed a tray of hors d'oeuvres.* ☐ *I brought hors d'oeurves to the potluck dinner.*

horsepower AND **hp**   a unit of power; 746 watts. Used to measure the power that a motor or engine can deliver. ☐ *The sports car has a 200 horsepower engine.* ☐ *The vacuum cleaner motor can deliver 4 hp.*

hose clamp   a round metal clip that attaches a hose to a metal or plastic tube. ☐ *Remove the hose clamps that attach* the hoses to the fuel filter. □ She used a pair of pliers to open the hose clamp.

hosiery socks, tights, or stockings. □ *Our store specializes in hosiery.* □ *Men's hosiery is on the fifth floor.*

hotcake See PANCAKE.

hot dish a mixture of several foods, baked and served hot in a covered dish. (Regional. See also CASSEROLE.) □ *Can I get the recipe for your tuna hot dish?* □ *Everyone brought a hot dish to the church supper.*

hot dog See FRANK(FURTER).

hot pad See POT HOLDER.

hot plate a portable device for heating food. □ *I plugged in my hot plate and heated some water.* □ *I don't need a stove. I get along fine with just a hot plate.*

hot rollers heated curlers. (See also CURLER.) □ *I bought a set of hot rollers, hoping they would put some lasting curl in my hair.* □ *For best results, use the hot rollers on slightly damp hair.*

hot sauce a sauce made of spicy chili peppers. (See also TABASCO™ SAUCE.) □ *The hot sauce was so spicy that it made Jim's face turn red.* □ *I like to add a dash or two of hot sauce to my tomato soup.*

hot shoe the place on a camera where a flash unit can be attached. □ *The photographer slipped the flash onto the hot shoe.* □ *This flash unit won't fit the hot shoe on that camera.*

hot slot a slot in an electrical outlet connected to a hot wire in the electrical circuit. □ *This prong of the plug needs to connect to the hot slot.* □ *The black wire should be connected to the hot slot.*

hot tub a heated bath tub large enough for several people. □ *They have a hot tub in their backyard.* □ *After dinner, we can soak in the hot tub, if you like.*

hot water heat   a heating system that moves hot water through pipes into radiators that warm the air around them. □ *This building has hot water heat.* □ JANE: *What kind of heating system do you have in your house?* MARY: *Hot water heat.*

hot water heater   a device that heats water for use in a building. □ *I adjusted the temperature on the hot water heater so that the hot water taps would not run scalding hot.* □ *When I turn the hot water faucet, nothing but cold water comes out. Something must be wrong with the hot water heater.*

hot water pipe   a pipe that carries hot water through a building. (Contrasts with COLD WATER PIPE.) □ *I felt the two pipes to see which was the cold water pipe and which was the hot water pipe.* □ *The hot water pipe does not need to be connected to the toilet.*

hot wire   a wire carrying electrical current into a circuit. □ *Connect the hot wire to the hot slot in the outlet.* □ *The hot wire is connected to a terminal on the service panel.*

(household) pest   an animal not wanted in a house, such as a rat, mouse, or insect. □ *This spray kills fifteen different kinds of household pests.* □ *We hired an exterminator to get rid of the pests in the woodwork.*

houseplant   a plant, especially a decorative one, kept in the house. □ *A row of houseplants lined the windowsill.* □ *The coleus is a favorite houseplant because of its striking colors.*

housewares   things that are useful or pretty in the house. □ *You will find pots and pans in the housewares section, ground floor.* □ *Linens, kitchen goods, and china figurines are all 30% off in our great housewares sale.*

housing   a case or rigid cover for something. □ *He pried open the plastic housing of the electric shaver.* □ *There is a metal housing around the motor of the electric fan.*

hp   See HORSEPOWER.

hubcap AND **wheel cover** a cover for the center of a car wheel. □ *The car had shiny chrome hubcaps.* □ *He had decorative wheel covers fitted onto the car.*

hull 1. the body of a boat or ship. □ *The boat has a fiberglass hull.* □ *The bottom of the hull was covered with barnacles.* 2. the outer covering of a grain, nut, or seed. □ *She soaked the corn to make it easier to remove the hull.* □ *He picked off the papery hull of the walnut.* 3. the short section of stem at the end of a berry. □ *It was easy to pull the hulls off the ripe strawberries.* □ *I pinched the hull off the blueberry.* 4. to remove the HULL from something. □ *Hull two quarts of strawberries.* □ *This machine automatically hulls coffee beans.*

humidifier a device that puts moisture into the air. (See also VAPORIZER.) □ *A humidifier keeps the air from getting too dry in the winter.* □ *We bought a humidifier for the hot, dry summers.*

hutch a piece of furniture with shelves and drawers for displaying and storing dishes. (Folksy. See also BREAKFRONT, CHINA CUPBOARD.) □ *The hutch matched the country-style dining room furniture.* □ *I keep my collection of glass vases on the top shelf of the hutch.*

hygrometer a device that measures humidity. □ *According to the hygrometer, the humidity is sixty percent.* □ *I have a home weather station with a thermometer, a barometer, and a hygrometer.*

I

IBM™   International Business Machines, a brand of computer hardware and software. □ *MARY: Is that computer a Macintosh or an IBM? CHARLIE: IBM.* □ *I need an IBM-compatible printer.*

ibuprofen   a drug that relieves pain and reduces fever and inflammation. □ *I took two ibuprofen tablets for my headache.* □ *The doctor prescribed ibuprofen for Mary's muscle aches.*

icebox   See REFRIGERATOR.

ice bucket   a bucket for holding ice, often used to cool wine. (See also WINE COOLER.) □ *I went to the ice machine and filled my ice bucket.* □ *He put the champagne bottle in the ice bucket and surrounded it with ice.*

ice cream dipper   See ICE CREAM SCOOP.

(ice cream) float   a soft drink with ice cream floating in it. □ *We stopped at the sweet shop for an ice cream float.* □ *We bought a bottle of soda and a quart of ice cream so that we could make floats.*

ice cream freezer   See ICE CREAM MAKER.

ice cream maker AND **ice cream freezer**   a device in which ice cream is made. □ *Chill the ice cream maker in the freezer for at least four hours.* □ *We filled the ice cream freezer with ice and then poured cream into the chamber.*

ice cream scoop AND **ice cream dipper**   a tool for scooping up ice cream. □ *Using the ice cream scoop, he rolled up a perfect ball of ice cream and packed it into the ice cream cone.* □ *This ice cream's too hard to scoop with a spoon. Do you have an ice cream dipper?*

(ice cream) soda   a drink made with ice cream, carbonated water, and flavoring. □ *Bill had a hot fudge sundae, and I had an ice cream soda.* □ *Would you like whipped cream on your soda?*

ice (cube) tray   a tray in which water is frozen to form ice cubes. □ *I emptied the ice cube tray into an ice bucket.* □ *When you take the last ice cube out of the ice tray, please refill it and put it back in the freezer.*

ice maker   a machine that makes ice. □ *This refrigerator has an ice maker.* □ *Ice cubes rattled out of the ice maker into my glass.*

ice pick   a pointed tool for chipping ice. □ *I broke up the chunk of ice with an ice pick.* □ *She chipped some ice off the block with the ice pick.*

ice tongs   a tool for picking up ice cubes. □ *There's an ice bucket and ice tongs on the bar.* □ *She picked up an ice cube with the ice tongs.*

icing   a thick liquid or paste made of sugar and other ingredients and used to cover and decorate a cake or pastry. (Compare with FROSTING, GLAZE.) □ *Drizzle the icing on the cinnamon buns.* □ *The cake had chocolate icing.*

icing tip   a small metal cone with a specially-shaped hole at the small end. (Frosting or ICING is forced through this hole to make cake decorations. See also PASTRY TIP.) □ *Put an icing tip on the decorating bag.* □ *This icing tip makes a star-shaped decoration.*

icon   a picture on a computer screen, representing a disk, a program, a folder, a directory, or a file. □ *Highlight the disk icon, and choose "Eject" from the menu.* □ *To open the file, double click on the file icon.*

ID   See IDENTIFICATION.

identification AND **ID**   an official document that shows a person's name, age, description, or picture. (See also CALLER

IDENTIFICATION.) ☐ *In order to cash a check here, you will need to show some identification.* ☐ *I had to show my student ID in order to sign up for the class.*

idle **1.** [for a vehicle's engine] to run while the vehicle is standing still. ☐ *She put the car in neutral and let it idle.* ☐ *The bus was idling at the curb.* **2.** how smoothly an engine IDLES. ☐ *Something's wrong with the car. The idle sounds very rough.* ☐ *I heard the loud idle of a motorcycle engine.*

ignition (switch)   the switch in which a car key is inserted and turned, causing the ignition system to start. ☐ *I put the key in the ignition switch, but it wouldn't turn.* ☐ *I turned the key in the ignition, and the engine started up.*

ignition (system)   the system that delivers electric current to the spark plugs in a car engine. ☐ *The distributor is part of the ignition system.* ☐ MARY: *The car won't start.* JANE: *I bet there's something wrong with the ignition.*

inboard motor   a motor located within a boat's hull. (Contrasts with OUTBOARD MOTOR.) ☐ *The boat had an inboard motor.* ☐ *They installed an inboard motor in their fishing boat.*

incandescent bulb   a light bulb that produces light by passing electric current through a wire filament, which glows as it heats up. (See also FLUORESCENT BULB.) ☐ *This light fixture requires an incandescent bulb.* ☐ *The glowing incandescent bulb was hot to the touch.*

incinerator   a device that burns garbage. ☐ *The garbage trucks took the garbage to the incinerator.* ☐ *The garbage chute leads to an incinerator in the basement.*

indicator light   a light that signals something. ☐ *The indicator light on the coffee urn says that the coffee is still brewing.* ☐ *The red indicator light tells you that the battery is getting low.*

indoor/outdoor carpeting   WATERPROOF carpeting that can be used indoors and outdoors. ☐ *We installed indoor/*

outdoor carpeting on the back terrace. □ *The playroom floor was covered with rugged indoor/outdoor carpeting.*

infill   fencing material between fence posts. □ *The pickets in the picket fence are infill.* □ *The fence had stone posts and chain link infill.*

infuser   a device that holds tea leaves in hot water, allowing the water to pass through and brew the tea. (See also STEEPER. Compare with TEA BALL.) □ *I swirled the infuser back and forth in the teapot.* □ *She put a spoonful of tea leaves in the infuser.*

infusion coffeepot   a device that brews coffee by allowing the ground coffee beans to sit and steep in hot water. □ *I poured boiling water into the infusion coffeepot.* □ *I prefer the taste of coffee brewed in an infusion coffeepot to the kind you get from a drip coffee maker.*

ink cartridge   a device that releases the ink needed by a fountain pen, computer printer, or photocopier. □ *Does that printer take a ribbon or an ink cartridge?* □ *He removed the empty ink cartridge from his fountain pen.*

inkjet printer   a computer PRINTER that forms characters by spraying ink droplets onto the paper. □ *The print quality from this inkjet printer is quite good, and the printer itself is inexpensive.* □ *I would like to replace my dot matrix printer with an inkjet printer.*

inner tube   a rubber or plastic tube inside a bicycle or car tire. (Inflated INNER TUBES are often used for recreation, such as floating on water or sliding on snow.) □ *There was a leak in the inner tube, so the tire kept going flat.* □ *I floated down the river in my inner tube.*

in season   at the right time of year. □ *The restaurant serves fresh fruit, in season.* □ *Hot chocolate and spiced apple cider are available in season.*

insecticide   a preparation that kills insects. (See also INSECT REPELLENT, PESTICIDE.) □ *I sprayed insecticide into* *the crack where I had seen the ants.* □ *Boric acid is an insecticide.*

insect repellent AND **bug spray**   a preparation that keeps insects away. (BUG SPRAY is informal or slang. See also INSECTICIDE, PESTICIDE.) □ *The hikers put on plenty of insect repellent before venturing into the woods.* □ *Hand me the bug spray, will you? The mosquitoes are killing me!*

install   to put something in place and get it ready to work. □ *I installed a fan over the stove in the kitchen.* □ *Follow these instructions to install the database program.*

Instamatic™   a brand of camera manufactured by the Kodak company. □ *Where can I get film for my Instamatic?* □ *She put the Instamatic in her pocket.*

instrument panel   a panel containing a vehicle's controls and gauges. □ *The pilot checked everything on the instrument panel prior to takeoff.* □ *The truck's instrument panel lights up at night.*

insulation   a substance that protects a building or a person from the outside temperature or from an electrical current. □ *There's eight inches of fiberglass insulation in the attic.* □ *These gloves contain a special insulation. They'll keep your hands warm even when it's forty degrees below zero.*

interactive   requiring a choice or an action from the user or the audience. □ *There are interactive comic books on CD-ROM. They allow you to choose what will happen next.* □ *The children's museum has many interactive exhibits.*

interchange   a system of ramps at a highway intersection. (See also CLOVERLEAF.) □ *At the interchange, get onto I-70 West.* □ *It's eleven miles to the US 61 interchange.*

intercom   a device that can both transmit and receive sounds, especially voices. (Compare with PUBLIC ADDRESS SYSTEM.) □ *I spoke into the intercom at the front door of the apartment building.* □ *The boss made an announcement over the intercom.*

interfacing   a stiff material sewn or ironed into a garment to help it keep its shape. (See also FUSIBLE INTERFACING.) □ *Put a layer of interfacing behind the buttonholes, so that they will not stretch and sag.* □ *Cut a layer of interfacing to fit the shirt collar.*

interference   noise or disturbance in a television or radio signal. (See also SNOW.) □ *When I turn on the air conditioner, I get interference on the TV.* □ *The radio music was interrupted by bursts of interference.*

International Standard Book Number AND **ISBN**   an identification number for a book. □ *To order the book, you will need to know the International Standard Book Number.* □ *The ISBN is printed on the back cover of the book.*

internet   a system of connections between computers all over the world. (Often capitalized.) □ *For $25 a month, our service gives you access to the internet.* □ *The university library catalog is on the Internet, so I can dial it up on my computer at home and search for the books I want.*

intersection   a place where two or more roads cross. □ *Turn left at the second intersection.* □ *There is a traffic light at the intersection of Walnut and Eighth.*

iron   1. a heated device for pressing cloth. □ *I plugged in the iron and let it heat up.* □ *The iron has a steam attachment.* **2.** to use an IRON on something. □ *You'd better iron that shirt before you put it on.* □ *He ironed the linen tablecloth.*

ironing board   a flat board, usually with a tapered end, on which things can be IRONED. □ *I set up the ironing board and started ironing the clothes that had just come out of the dryer.* □ *You can adjust the height of the ironing board so that it is comfortable for you to use.*

ISBN   See INTERNATIONAL STANDARD BOOK NUMBER.

italics   a slanted typeface, used to draw attention to a word. □ *This sentence is printed in italics.* □ *She selected the word she wanted to emphasize, then chose "Italics" from the "Style" menu.*

Tt

J

jack **1.** an opening for connecting a microphone, head-phones, or a speaker to an electronic device that records or produces sound. □ *Where's the headphone jack on this CD player?* □ *The tape recorder has a built-in microphone, but you can attach an external microphone through this jack.* **2.** a device that raises a vehicle, usually so that a tire can be removed or repaired. (To *jack up* a vehicle is to raise it using a JACK.) □ *I fitted the jack under the bumper and jacked up the car.* □ *She found a jack and a tire iron in the trunk, along with the spare tire.*

jam fruit boiled in sugar to a thick consistency. (Compare with JELLY.) □ *I made jam from the strawberries in our garden.* □ *She spread the toast with raspberry jam.*

Jams™ a brand of short, very loose pants. □ *The kids wore brightly-colored Jams to the beach.* □ *I like these Jams. They're comfortable.*

jar opener a tool that helps unscrew the lid from a jar. □ *This rubber jar opener helps you get a grip on the jar lid.* □ *I can't get this lid off. Hand me the jar opener.*

Jell-O™ a brand of gelatin dessert. □ *He cut up bananas and mixed them into the lime Jell-O.* □ *She put the Jell-O into the refrigerator to set.*

jelly a clear, soft, sweet food made from fruit boiled with sugar and strained out. (Compare with JAM.) □ *I made a sandwich with peanut butter and jelly.* □ *The restaurant served each English muffin with a small packet of grape jelly.*

jelly roll pan a flat pan with sides about half an inch high, sometimes used to bake a flat cake that is rolled up to form a dessert. □ *I use this jelly roll pan for baking pizza.* □ *Spread the batter into a well-greased jelly roll pan.*

jersey **1.** a sweater or shirt made of knitted fabric, put on by pulling it over the head. □ *Children's striped jerseys are on sale this week.* □ *The wool jersey protected me from the cold wind.* **2.** a soft knitted fabric. □ *I bought two yards of cotton jersey.* □ *This pattern works best with jersey or other knits.*

jigger a measure equaling one and one-half ounces, used in mixing cocktails. □ *To make a daiquiri, combine six jiggers of rum, two jiggers of lime juice, and half a jigger of sugar syrup.* □ *How many jiggers of vermouth go into a martini?*

jigsaw a machine-operated saw with a very narrow blade that moves up and down. □ *I drilled a starter hole, then used the jigsaw to cut a circular opening in the middle of the board.* □ *This jigsaw is great for cutting curves.*

jimmies See SPRINKLES.

John Deere™ a brand of tractors and lawn mowers. □ *The farmer hooked up the cultivator to his John Deere.* □ *She rode the John Deere back and forth across the lawn.*

juicer a device that extracts the juice from a fruit. □ *I cut the grapefruit in half and squeezed it on the juicer.* □ *He placed the lemon in the juicer and pulled the lever down.*

julienne **1.** [of food] cut into thin strips. □ *The main course comes with a side dish of fried julienne potatoes.* □ *Add a half cup of julienne carrots.* **2.** to cut food into thin strips. □ *Julienne the vegetables.* □ *The food processor can slice, dice, or julienne.*

jump to transfer electric current from the battery of one vehicle to the battery of another by connecting them with cables. (Informal. See also JUMPER CABLE.) □ *My battery was dead. Fortunately, someone stopped and jumped it for me.* □ *They used the truck to jump the car battery.*

jumper a dress designed to be worn over a shirt. □ *The little girl wore a plaid jumper.* □ *This loose-fitting jumper is very comfortable.*

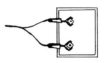

jumper cable   a pair of cables for connecting the positive and negative terminals of one vehicle's battery to those of another vehicle's battery. (See also JUMP.) □ *We can't jump this car. We don't have a jumper cable.* □ *Clip the black jumper cable to the negative terminal.*

junction box   a metal box that houses an electrical outlet, switch, or fixture. □ *I removed the switch plate and looked into the junction box.* □ *The ceiling light fits into this junction box.*

K

kebab See SHISH KEBAB.

kerf the width of a cut made by a saw. □ *Allow a ⅛-inch kerf when measuring the wood.* □ *This saw blade has a ¹/₁₆-inch kerf.*

kernel a seed, a grain, or a nut. □ *I removed the kernels from the corncob.* □ *I cracked the shell of the almond and removed the kernel.*

ketchup See CATSUP.

kettle a large, heavy pot. □ *I always use this kettle when I make soup.* □ *The beef stock was boiling away in the kettle.*

key **1.** a device, usually a specially-shaped piece of metal, that opens a lock. □ *This is my house key.* □ *I lost the key to the file cabinet.* **2.** a control on a typewriter, computer, telephone, or calculator that performs some type of action when pressed. (See also BUTTON, KNOB, SWITCH.) □ *Find the escape key on the computer keyboard.* □ *The "w" key on the typewriter doesn't work.*

keyboard a set of keys on a typewriter or computer. □ *His fingers flew over the computer keyboard as he typed.* □ *The layout of this keyboard is not familiar to me.*

keyless lock a lock that opens with a card or a code number instead of a key. □ *The hotel room door had a keyless lock.* □ *He slid his key card through the keyless lock.*

keypad the set of keys on a telephone or calculator. □ *Please enter your identification number using your telephone keypad.* □ *The keys on the calculator keypad are too small for me to use.*

kick pleat a pleat at the bottom of a skirt that allows the legs to move more freely. □ *The close-fitting skirt had a kick* *pleat at the back.* □ *Without the kick pleat, the skirt would be so tight at the knees that you could barely move.*

kickstand   a metal support for a bicycle or motorcycle that can be swung up and down with the foot. □ *I put the kickstand down and left the bike on the sidewalk.* □ *Put the kickstand back up before you start riding.*

k(ilo)byte   one thousand bytes. (Used to measure computer memory or files.) □ *This floppy holds 720 kilobytes.* □ *The file is 500 kbytes.*

king-size bed   a very large bed, roughly seven by eight feet. □ *All the rooms in this hotel feature king-size beds.* □ *I need a comforter that will fit my king-size bed.*

kitchen cabinet   a box or set of shelves with a door on the front, mounted on the wall of a kitchen. □ *I repainted the doors on the kitchen cabinets.* □ *The kitchen cabinets were full of pots, pans, and dishes.*

kitchen counter   a horizontal surface at roughly waist height, installed in a kitchen. □ *I collected all the ingredients for the stew on the kitchen counter.* □ *She set the toaster on the kitchen counter.*

(kitchen) range   an appliance with a set of gas or electric burners, usually with an oven underneath. (See also STOVE.) □ *The apartment was furnished with a refrigerator and an electric kitchen range.* □ *Several pots were simmering on the range.*

kitchen scissors AND **kitchen shears**   a heavy pair of SCISSORS used in the kitchen, for opening packages or cutting food. □ *Snip the tips of the artichoke leaves with kitchen scissors.* □ *He slit open the bag of flour with his kitchen shears.*

kitchen shears   See KITCHEN SCISSORS.

kitchen table   a table located in a kitchen. □ *We usually ate breakfast at the kitchen table.* □ *She kneaded the bread dough on the kitchen table.*

kitchen towel a towel used in a kitchen. □ *She dried the dishes with the kitchen towel.* □ *Wipe your hands on the kitchen towel.*

kitty litter See CAT LITTER.

Kleenex™ a brand of paper tissue. □ *Give me a Kleenex. I need to blow my nose.* □ *She wiped her eyes with a Kleenex.*

knead to push and squeeze something repeatedly with the hands. □ *Knead the dough until it becomes smooth and elastic.* □ *Knead the biscuit dough lightly.*

knee kicker a tool for stretching carpeting onto the nails or tacks that hold it to the floor. □ *Nail down two sides of the carpet, then use a knee kicker to stretch it onto the nails on the other two sides of the room.* □ *She pushed the knee kicker with her knee until the carpet caught on the tacks.*

knife block a block of wood with slots for holding knives. □ *The cleaver fits into the widest slot on the knife block.* □ *The knife block holds the knife handles at a convenient angle.*

knife sharpener a tool that grinds the edge of a knife until it is sharp. □ *She rolled the knife blade back and forth on the rolling knife sharpener.* □ *He inserted the blade into the electric knife sharpener.*

knob a usually round device that can be grasped, pulled, or turned. (See also BUTTON, DIAL, KEY, SWITCH.) □ *Turn the bottom knob clockwise to increase the volume on the TV.* □ *The glass door to the bookcase opened with a crystal knob.*

knot **1.** a tying together of long, slender things. □ *I tied a secure knot at the end of the rope.* □ *There were some stubborn knots in the girl's long hair.* **2.** a bunched-up area in the grain of wood. □ *This lumber is very poor quality. It's full of knots.* □ *The saw blade caught in a knot.* **3.** a unit of speed, used to measure the speed of boats and wind. (One KNOT is 1.15 miles per hour.) □ *There is a southwest wind blowing at six knots.* □ *The current was moving at fifteen knots.*

knothole   a hole in a board where a KNOT used to be. □ *I peeked through a knothole in the fence.* □ *He sanded the edges of the knothole.*

L

ladle   **1.** a tool with a small bowl on the end of a long handle, used for scooping up liquids. □ *She dipped a ladle into the kettle of soup.* □ *He poured lemonade out of the ladle into a glass.* **2.** to move liquid with a LADLE. □ *He ladled soup into the bowls.* □ *Ladle the pudding into custard cups.*

laminate   **1.** to put a layer of clear plastic on both sides of something. □ *I had my library card laminated so it wouldn't tear.* □ *This machine can laminate documents up to 11 by 14 inches.* **2.** a layer of plastic. □ *The workers put brightly colored laminate on the doors of the kitchen cupboards.* □ *The sturdy table has a top made of durable laminate.*

lampshade   a structure of translucent material, such as cloth or paper, placed over a lamp in order to reduce the glare of the light. □ *The lampshade had a fringe around the bottom.* □ *The lampshade in the baby's room was painted with frolicking animals.*

LAN   See LOCAL AREA NETWORK.

landing   a platform joining two FLIGHTS OF STAIRS. □ *She put her shopping bags down and rested for a while on the landing.* □ *He stood on the landing and looked down onto the floor below.*

lane   a strip along a road, wide enough for a line of cars to pass along. □ *Get into the right-hand lane.* □ *This is a two-lane road.*

lapel   the edges along the opening of a coat, just below the collar. (LAPELS are usually folded back.) □ *The sport coat had wide lapels.* □ *She put a flower into the buttonhole of her lapel.*

laptop (computer)   a portable computer, small enough to be held on the lap. (See also DESKTOP (COMPUTER), NOTEBOOK (COMPUTER), PALMTOP.) □ *This laptop computer has a*

120 megabyte hard drive. □ *I take my laptop with me on the commuter train, so that I can get some work done during the ride.*

lard   hog fat. □ *You can use either lard or vegetable shortening in this recipe.* □ *Deep fry the onion rings in lard.*

laser paper   paper that can be used in a LASER PRINTER. □ *Laser paper also works well in inkjet printers and plain-paper copy machines.* □ *One side of a piece of laser paper has a smoother texture than the other.*

laser printer   a computer printer that uses a laser to do fast, high-quality printing. □ *We have a laser printer at the office.* □ *The laser printer is out of toner.*

latch   a device that holds a door, lid, or flap in place. □ *Release the latch on the film door of the camera and remove the film canister.* □ *The door latch fit precisely into the hole in the faceplate.*

latex paint   a paint made with latex, a sticky, white liquid extracted from plants. (LATEX PAINT can be thinned and washed away with water, unlike oil-based paint, which has to be dissolved with PAINT THINNER.) □ *I chose a glossy-finish latex paint for the walls in the bedroom.* □ *She soaked the paint roller in water to remove the latex paint.*

launder   to wash cloth. □ *Those sheets need to be laundered.* □ *I gathered up all the dirty clothes and laundered them.*

laundry bag   a bag in which dirty clothes are collected. □ *When she went home to visit her mother, she always brought a full laundry bag.* □ *The laundry bag is overflowing. It's time to do some laundry.*

laundry basket   a large basket for carrying clothes to and from washing. □ *He put the clean, wet clothes from the washing machine into the laundry basket and carried them to the dryer.* □ *She piled the clean, dry, folded clothes into the laundry basket.*

laundry detergent   soap used to wash clothes. □ *I use a special, gentle laundry detergent for my wool clothes.* □ *He measured the laundry detergent into the washing machine.*

laundry hamper   See (CLOTHES) HAMPER.

laundry room   a room in which clothes are washed, usually containing a WASHING MACHINE, a DRYER, and a sink. □ *Is there a laundry room on the same floor as your apartment?* □ *I carried the laundry basket to the laundry room.*

lawn chair   a chair, often a folding chair, that can be used outdoors. □ *In the springtime, we put lawn chairs out on the patio.* □ *Many people brought lawn chairs to the outdoor concert.*

lawn mower   a machine that cuts grass. (LAWN MOWERS are either pushed by hand or driven by a motor.) □ *I pushed the lawn mower across the lawn.* □ *I pulled the cord to start up the lawn mower.*

laxative   a drug that helps the bowels release their contents. □ *The doctor prescribed a laxative for Bill's constipation.* □ *Jane takes a laxative every morning.*

layer cake   a cake made of cake layers with filling or frosting between them. □ *Dessert was chocolate layer cake.* □ *The lemon-flavored layer cake had strawberry jam between the layers.*

lazy susan   a round, rotating platform. □ *I keep all my spices on a lazy susan.* □ *The host arranged a number of dishes on the lazy susan, and we turned it to help ourselves to whatever we wanted.*

LCD   See LIQUID CRYSTAL DISPLAY.

leader   the first part of a roll or reel of film, usually left blank. □ *I fit the holes on the film leader to the sprockets on the film path of the camera.* □ *He fed the leader into the film projector.*

leaven   to add yeast or baking powder to dough or batter. □ *The bread was not leavened and came out quite flat.* □ *She leavened the batter with baking powder.*

leavening   yeast or baking powder used to create fermentation in doughs or batters. □ *If you fail to add the leavening, the cake will be flat.* □ *Too much leavening will ruin the batter.*

LED   See LIGHT EMITTING DIODE.

leggings   tight-fitting pants made of knitted material. □ *Leggings are so comfortable, and flatter any figure when worn with a long, loose-fitting top.* □ *She wore a T-shirt and leggings.*

lengthwise   from top to bottom. (Compare with CROSS-WISE.) □ *Split the carrots in half lengthwise.* □ *I folded the bedspread lengthwise.*

lens   a specially-shaped piece of glass or plastic that focuses light onto a surface, such as film in a camera or a person's eye. □ *I dropped my glasses, and one of the lenses broke.* □ *The photographer fitted a special lens onto the camera.*

lens cap   a cover for a camera LENS. □ *Take the lens cap off before you try to take a picture!* □ *Where's the lens cap for the video camera?*

letterhead   writing paper and envelopes printed with the name and address of a person or an organization. (Compare with STATIONERY.) □ *The secretary typed the letter on company letterhead.* □ *I am designing my own letterhead.*

letter-quality   [of printing] high quality, clear and sharp. □ *This dot-matrix printer can produce letter-quality printing.* □ *The price on the inkjet printer is reasonable, but is the printing letter-quality?*

levee   a structure of piled-up earth designed to hold back floodwater. (See also DIKE.) □ *They built a levee alongside the river.* □ *The rain continued to fall and the river to swell. More levees burst.*

level   **1.** perfectly horizontal. □ *That picture frame doesn't look level.* □ *I propped up the table leg so that the table would be level.* **2.** See (CARPENTER'S) LEVEL.

level control   a control that adjusts the strength of the electronic signal going into a sound recording device. □ *Say something into the microphone, so that I can set the level control.* □ *If the level control is not properly adjusted, the recording will be distorted.*

Levi's™   a brand of clothing, including blue jeans. □ *"These worn old Levi's are my favorite pair of pants," Sarah remarked as she hung them on the clothesline.* □ *"Where's your wallet?" Jim asked. "Must be in the pocket of the Levi's I was wearing yesterday," said Joe.*

LF   See LINE FEED.

license plate   a metal plate showing the license number of a car and the state that issued the LICENSE PLATE. (LICENSE PLATES are attached to either the back or both the front and back of a car.) □ *That car has Alaska license plates.* □ *I copied down the number from the car's license plate.*

lift bridge   a bridge in which a whole section moves up to let boats pass underneath. (Compare with DRAWBRIDGE.) □ *The lift bridge rose up between its two support towers.* □ *The bridge over the river is a lift bridge.*

light emitting diode AND **LED** a small electric device that lights up when electric current passes through it. (Many electronic devices have LED displays, which usually appear as lighted red characters on a dark background. Compare with LIQUID CRYSTAL DISPLAY.) □ *The calculator has a light emitting diode display.* □ *This LED lights up if you have given an incorrect password.*

lighter   a device that produces a small flame for lighting a cigarette, cigar, or pipe. □ *He flicked his lighter and lit the cigarette.* □ *JANE: Do you have a match? CHARLIE: No, but I've got a lighter.*

light meter   a device that measures the amount of light, used to figure out the correct exposure setting for a camera. □ *The photographer read the exposure time off the light meter.* □ *The camera has a built-in light meter.*

light rail   an electric-powered train system for local transportation. □ *The city council allocated money to develop a light rail system.* □ *You can go all the way out to the suburbs via light rail.*

line feed AND **LF**   a control on a computer printer that moves the paper ahead one line. (Compare with FORM FEED.) □ *She pressed LF until the top of the paper was aligned with the top of the print head.* □ *He used the line feed to move the paper ahead.*

line in jack   an opening for attaching a cable that feeds an audio or video signal into a recording device. □ *I am using this VCR to record the tape playing on that one, so I'll connect a cable from the "video out" jack on that one to this line in jack.* □ *To record a CD on tape, connect a line from the CD player to the line in jack on the tape recorder.*

lineman's pliers   a heavy pair of pliers used for gripping and cutting wire. □ *I cut the electric cable with lineman's pliers.* □ *I held the wire with lineman's pliers and guided it through the hole in the junction box.*

linen closet   a closet with shelves where sheets, towels, and table linens can be stored. □ *I got a clean towel out of the linen closet.* □ *The apartment has a small linen closet.*

lingerie   women's underwear and sleeping garments. □ *He bought some pretty lingerie for his wife.* □ *That store sells fancy silk and lace lingerie.*

linkage   a set of rods or bars that are linked together. □ *The throttle linkage leads from the accelerator pedal to the throttle.* □ *The joints in the choke linkage are not moving freely.*

linseed oil   oil extracted from flax seeds, used as a wood finish. □ *The carpenter rubbed linseed oil onto the surface of* *the finished table.* □ *Instead of using a varnish, I used lin-seed oil on the wooden chair.*

lint very small particles of cloth. □ *The jacket was covered with white lint.* □ *I shook the lint out of the bedspread.*

lintel a horizontal support across the top of a door, window, or fireplace. □ *There was a half-inch gap between the top of the door and the lintel.* □ *The wooden lintel above the window was crumbling away.*

lint screen AND **lint trap** a screen that catches the LINT from clothes in a DRYER. □ *The dryer is more efficient if you clean out the lint screen between loads.* □ *The cotton blanket left a thick layer of lint in the lint trap.*

lint trap See LINT SCREEN.

liqueur a sweet alcoholic liquor. □ *The ice cream was garnished with little cakes soaked in liqueur.* □ *The cocktail is flavored with coffee liqueur.*

liqueur glass See CORDIAL GLASS.

liquid crystal display AND **LCD** a panel in which characters are formed from darkened strips of liquid crystal material. (LCDs usually have black or blue characters on a green background. Compare with LIGHT EMITTING DIODE.) □ *It's hard for me to read the LCD on this digital watch.* □ *The laptop has a liquid crystal display screen.*

liquid measure a system of measures for liquids. (Note: Most U.S. measuring cups are LIQUID MEASURES, as are measurements given in recipes. Contrasts with DRY MEASURE.) □ *A liquid measure pint is smaller than a dry measure pint.* □ *The recipe calls for a quart of milk, liquid measure.*

Liquid Paper™ a brand of CORRECTION FLUID. □ *"Do you have some Liquid Paper? I made a mistake on this invoice,"* said Bill. □ *"Just cover up the typo with Liquid Paper,"* my boss advised.

live trap   a trap that captures but does not kill an animal. □ *I put a live trap in the backyard to see if I could catch the raccoon that's been getting into my garbage pails.* □ *There were three mice in the live trap in the kitchen. I took them out to the woods and released them.*

load bearing wall   a wall that supports the roof or an upper story. (Compare with PARTITION WALL.) □ *You can't knock out the wall between the living room and the kitchen. It's a load bearing wall.* □ *The building was not safe. There was a crack in one of the load bearing walls.*

loaf pan   a deep, rectangular pan, designed for baking a loaf of bread. □ *Grease two loaf pans.* □ *Pour the banana bread batter into a loaf pan.*

loam   spongy, porous soil. □ *My garden plants are thriving in the rich loam.* □ *I put in a layer of loam over the sandy soil in the backyard.*

lobby   a room just behind the entrance to a building or an office. (See also ENTRY(WAY), FOYER.) □ *I sat in the lobby of the doctor's office, reading a magazine.* □ *I'll meet you in the hotel lobby at noon.*

local area network AND **LAN**   a physically close group of computers that are connected electronically. □ *All the company's computers are linked in a LAN.* □ *The technician connected all the PCs in the office into a local area network.*

lock   **1.** a device that holds something shut until it is opened with a key or a code. □ *She had three separate locks on her front door.* □ *I bought a good, solid bicycle lock.* **2.** to fasten something with a LOCK. □ *Lock the file cabinet before you leave the office.* □ *I locked the car door.* **3.** a structure that allows boats and ships to pass between levels of a canal or river. □ *The boat waited in the lock while the water drained.* □ *The lock gates opened and let water flow into the lock, bringing the water level up again.*

(lock) cylinder   the part of a LOCK in which the key turns. □ *The locksmith changed the lock by removing the lock* *cylinder and putting in a different one.* □ *The key got stuck in the cylinder.*

locking pliers   a pair of pliers with jaws that can be fastened in place. (See also Vise-Grips™.) □ *I clamped the cable to the workbench with a pair of locking pliers.* □ *I got a good grip on the stubborn nut with my locking pliers.*

lock nut   a hexagonal metal nut with a layer of plastic inside or a LOCK WASHER attached. □ *I put the children's swing set together with lock nuts, which ought to hold no matter how hard they play on it.* □ *He worked the lock nut onto the end of the bolt.*

lockset   all the parts of a door LOCK, including a pair of doorknobs and the hardware for installing them. □ *A lockset for an interior door is different from an exterior one.* □ *The lockset can be opened with a key on one side, and by turning a button on the other.*

lock washer   a metal ring with teeth or a spiral structure, slipped over a bolt to prevent it from loosening. (See also WASHER.) □ *Place a lock washer on one side of the nut.* □ *I fastened the bolt with a nut and a lock washer.*

locomotive   a vehicle that houses a train engine and pulls or pushes the cars of a train. (See also ENGINE.) □ *The engineer backed up the locomotive until the train was alongside the station platform.* □ *They have an old steam locomotive at the history museum.*

logo   a symbol that represents a company or organization. □ *The Chrysler logo is a pentagon with a five-pointed star.* □ *The letterhead is printed with the company logo.*

long grain rice   rice with long grains. □ *I put a cup of long grain rice into the soup.* □ *You can use either long grain rice or short grain rice, whichever you prefer.*

long-life bulb   a light bulb that lasts a long time. □ *Long-life bulbs are expensive, but they cost less per hour than regular light bulbs.* □ *I put a long-life bulb in the reading lamp.*

longnose pliers AND **needlenose pliers** a pair of pliers with long, narrow, tapering jaws. □ *I held the wire in place with longnose pliers.* □ *He used the needlenose pliers to grip the thin nail.*

long playing (record) AND **LP** **1.** a record on which sound is recorded at 33⅓ revolutions per minute. □ *I don't have a CD player. All my music is on LPs.* □ *He put the long playing record on the turntable.* **2.** Long Play, a setting that passes videotape through a VCR at a fairly slow speed, so that 4 hours of material will fit onto one standard cassette. □ *This tape was recorded at LP.* □ *I recorded the program at Long Play.*

long-term parking parking where cars can be left for long periods of time. (Contrasts with SHORT-TERM PARKING.) □ *Long-term parking at the airport is $6 a day.* □ *A shuttle bus goes between long-term parking and the main terminal.*

loose-leaf paper unbound paper with holes punched in the edge so that it can be stored in a BINDER. □ *I took my class notes on loose-leaf paper and filed them away in three-ring binders at the end of the day.* □ *The draft of the memo was handwritten on loose-leaf paper.*

lotion a liquid to be rubbed on the skin. (See also OINT-MENT.) □ *This antiseptic lotion helps relieve the pain of sunburn.* □ *I put lotion on my dry, chapped hands.*

loudness control a control on a stereo system that increases the treble and bass at low levels of volume. □ *He adjusted the loudness control until the flute melody sounded crisp and clear.* □ *This button is the loudness control.*

louvers a set of flat, narrow pieces of rigid material that can be pivoted to stand at any angle. □ *She peeked out between the louvers of the Venetian blind.* □ *I opened the louvers on the furnace vent so that more hot air could flow into the room.*

love seat a piece of furniture with a seat and a back, big enough for two people to sit on. □ *I got a sofa and a matching love seat.* □ *He lay down on the love seat to watch TV.*

low beam [of headlights] on low power and aimed low. (Contrasts with HIGH BEAM.) □ *This button switches the lights from low beam to high beam.* □ *I put my lights on low beam so as not to blind the approaching driver.*

lower case small letters. (Contrasts with UPPER CASE.) □ *The poet e.e. cummings always typed the letters of his name in lower case.* □ *The first letter in this sentence is in upper case, and all the rest are lower case.*

LP See LONG PLAYING (RECORD).

luggage bags or cases for taking things on a trip. □ *I bought a set of matching luggage.* □ *The shoe repair shop also repairs luggage.*

luggage rack a rack for carrying LUGGAGE; part of a vehicle. □ *We strapped the suitcases onto the luggage rack on the roof of the car.* □ *There is a luggage rack above each seat on the train.*

luggage tag a card attached to a piece of LUGGAGE showing the name and address of the owner. □ *I put a luggage tag on each one of our suitcases.* □ *She had a brass luggage tag with her name engraved on it.*

lug hole a hole in a wheel that fits over a bolt on the end of the axle. □ *I matched up the lug holes with the bolts.* □ *The lug holes on the spare tire are too small to fit on these bolts.*

lug nut nuts that hold a car wheel onto the axle. □ *Loosen the lug nuts and remove the wheel.* □ *Make sure the lug nuts are evenly tightened.*

lukewarm slightly warm. □ *Put the yeast in lukewarm water.* □ *The soup had cooled to lukewarm.*

lumber   wood that is ready to be used in building. □ *I bought all the lumber I needed to make the bookshelves.* □ *What kind of lumber did you use to build the garage frame?*

lunch meat   spiced ground meat packed into a casing and cut in slices. (See also COLD CUTS.) □ *I had lunch meat, cheese, and lettuce in my sandwich.* □ *Bologna is a popular lunch meat.*

M

Mace™ a brand of chemical that disables the person it is sprayed on. (You may hear MACE used as a verb.) □ *"If you have to walk around downtown at night, you should carry a canister of Mace," said Phil.* □ *"The woman sprayed Mace at her attacker and was able to run away," said the newspaper story.*

machine bolt a bolt with threads part way up the shaft. □ *A machine bolt held the car seat to the frame of the car.* □ *She spun the nut onto the end of the machine bolt.*

machine screw a screw with a flat end, designed to go into a hole in metal. □ *You don't want to use that screw on wood. It's a machine screw.* □ *Thread the machine screw into the metal bracket.*

machine washable suitable for washing in a WASHING MACHINE. □ *Is this blouse machine washable?* □ *The silk dress was not machine washable. It had to be dry-cleaned.*

Mac(intosh)™ a brand of computer manufactured by Apple Computer Inc. (MAC™ is informal.) □ *"Will this program run on a Macintosh?" I asked the software salesperson.* □ *"Is that a Mac or an IBM?" Julie wanted to know.*

macro a combination of computer keystrokes that will perform some function, such as typing out a stored combination of characters. □ *I had to type the client's name so often that I set up a macro for it.* □ *The "Alt-X" macro automatically underlines the word you just typed.*

magazine **1.** a publication that contains a number of stories or articles and comes out at more or less regular periods. □ *I subscribe to a weekly news magazine.* □ *The literary magazine publishes stories, poems, and artwork.* **2.** a container that holds cartridges for an automatic pistol or rifle. □ *She slid a fresh magazine into her pistol.* □ *He pulled the lever that released the empty magazine.*

magnetron an electronic device that produces microwaves; part of a MICROWAVE (OVEN). □ *Replacing the magnetron turned out to cost almost as much as a new oven.* □ *He put a metal pan in the microwave, and the magnetron burned out.*

mag wheel a kind of decorative hubcap. □ *The sports car had mag wheels.* □ *I'm saving up for a set of mag wheels.*

mail box a box where mail is collected or delivered. □ *There's a mail box on my way to work. I'll drop the letter off there.* □ *I unlocked my mail box and took out the day's mail.*

mail drop a place from which mail is collected. □ *I put my outgoing letters in the mail drop at work.* □ *She put the package in the mail drop.*

mailer a container in which something can be mailed. □ *I need a mailer big enough to hold this manuscript.* □ *She put the cassette tape in the padded cassette mailer.*

mailing label a label on which a mailing address can be written or printed. □ *I printed out a mailing label for every person in the database.* □ *He stuck a mailing label on the package.*

mail merge a computer program that prints out a form letter for every name and address in a database. □ *I used the mail merge function of the word processor to send a thank-you letter to all the donors.* □ *I set up a form letter to use with the mail merge.*

mail order **1.** buying and selling by mail. □ *I run a mail order business that sells gourmet chocolates.* □ *I saw an ad for mail order health foods.* **2.** the process of buying and selling by mail. □ *There aren't many stores in our small town, so I get a lot of things by mail order.* □ *All the merchandise in this catalog is available either in our stores or by mail order.*

mail slot a slot through which mail is delivered. □ *A pile of mail had accumulated under the mail slot while I was* *away.* □ *I don't have a mail box. There's a mail slot in the front door.*

main   a pipe or passage that carries something to or from a number of branches. □ *I examined the heating duct all the way back to the furnace main, but I couldn't find the source of the noise.* □ *The water main burst and flooded the street.*

main dish   See ENTRÉE.

make-up   colored substances applied to the face. (See also COSMETICS.) □ *She wore too much make-up. It made her look like a clown.* □ *She applied her make-up—lipstick, mascara, and eyeliner.*

mandarin collar   a collar made of a stiff, narrow band of fabric. □ *The jacket had a mandarin collar.* □ *The mandarin collar fastened with a fancy gold button.*

manila envelope   an envelope made of stiff yellow or tan paper. □ *I put the report in a manila envelope and mailed it to my boss.* □ *I need a 10 × 13 inch manila envelope.*

manila folder   a folder made of stiff, pale tan paper. □ *I kept each year's bank statements in a separate manila folder.* □ *I bought a box of 500 manila folders.*

mansard roof   a roof that is flat on top with sides that curve down to the CORNICE. □ *The old house had a mansard roof.* □ *I liked the graceful lines of the mansard roof.*

mantel   a shelf above a FIREPLACE. □ *An antique clock sat on the mantel.* □ *The fireplace had a slab of marble for a mantel.*

manual   **1.** operated by hand. □ *He cranked the handle of the manual drill.* □ *Using the manual hedge clippers really developed her arm muscles.* **2.** See STANDARD. **3.** an instruction book. □ *MARY: How do you get this darn computer to print something? JANE: Let's check the manual.* □ *The manual for my VCR is hard to understand.*

manual typewriter   a typewriter in which the pressure of a finger on a key provides the power that pushes the type element against the page. (Compare with ELECTRIC TYPE-WRITER.) □ *The author wrote everything on a manual typewriter.* □ *After I use that manual typewriter, my fingers ache.*

manufacturer   a company that makes something. □ *If you find a defect in this product, please notify the manufacturer at the following address.* □ *I work for a clothing manufacturer.*

manure   animal dung, especially dung used as fertilizer. □ *I put a layer of manure on the seedlings in the garden.* □ *I cleaned the manure out of the horse's stall.*

maraschino cherry   a cherry preserved in a sweet syrup. □ *The ice cream sundae had a maraschino cherry on top.* □ *The drink was garnished with a maraschino cherry.*

margin   **1.** the blank area at the edge of a page. □ *Leave a 1½-inch margin at the bottom of the page.* □ *The left margin should be about an inch wide.* **2.** a control on a typewriter or word processor that determines where a line of printing will begin and end. □ *I set the margin a little further to the left.* □ *To set the margins, use "Page Setup" on the "Format" menu.*

margin release   a control on a typewriter that allows you to type beyond a set MARGIN. □ *I pushed the margin release so that I could type the rest of the sentence on the same line.* □ *Where's the margin release on this keyboard?*

marinade   a flavored liquid in which a food, usually meat, is soaked. □ *Let the chicken sit in the teriyaki marinade for several hours.* □ *This red wine marinade works well with beef.*

marinate   to soak something in a flavored liquid. □ *Marinate the tofu in the soy sauce mixture.* □ *The fish had been marinated in lemon juice.*

marmalade   a jam made of shredded fruit peel boiled in sugar. (Usually made with oranges.) □ *I spread marmalade on my toast.* □ *Try this lime marmalade.*

marshmallow   a soft candy made of gelatin, corn syrup, and sugar. □ *We toasted marshmallows over the campfire.* □ *I floated a marshmallow on each cup of hot cocoa.*

marshmallow cream AND **Marshmallow Fluff**™   a soft food made of whipped sugar, corn syrup, and gelatin. (MARSHMALLOW FLUFF™ is a brand name.) □ *When I was little, my favorite snack was graham crackers spread with marshmallow cream.* □ *"The topping on that pie isn't hard to make. It's just Marshmallow Fluff," said Lisa.*

Marshmallow Fluff™   See MARSHMALLOW CREAM.

masking tape   a tape made of tan paper, easy to remove. □ *I put the poster on the wall with masking tape.* □ *Before painting the wall, I covered the electrical outlet with masking tape, so that it wouldn't get painted.*

Masonite™   a brand of board made of pressed wood fiber. □ *"Is this tabletop Masonite or plywood?" Jill asked.* □ *"Put down a layer of Masonite before installing the tile floor," the home repair book advised.*

Mason jar   a wide-mouthed glass jar, often used for canning foods. □ *She gave me a Mason jar full of cherry preserves.* □ *I put the Mason jar in boiling water to sterilize it.*

masonry   construction with bricks or stone. □ *The contractor does both masonry and carpentry.* □ *The walls were masonry.*

maternity clothes   See MATERNITY WEAR.

maternity wear AND **maternity clothes**   clothing for a pregnant woman. □ *You'll find nursing bras in the maternity wear department.* □ *As soon as Lisa found out she was pregnant, she bought a whole wardrobe of maternity clothes.*

math coprocessor an electronic device designed to make arithmetical calculations. □ *There is an optional math co-processor available with this PC model.* □ *The CAD program requires a math coprocessor.*

matte not shiny. □ *This paint has a matte finish.* □ *She used a matte pink lipstick.*

mattress a pad for sleeping on. (A common kind of MATTRESS is made of a set of springs in a wooden frame, covered with a layer of cloth padding.) □ *I got a backache from sleeping on that soft mattress.* □ *My waterbed mattress sprang a leak, and I got soaked.*

mattress pad a layer of cloth put on top of a MATTRESS to protect it from stains. □ *How long has it been since you washed that mattress pad?* □ *The mattress pad fit onto the mattress with elastic loops.*

measuring tape a strip of flexible material marked with measurements such as inches or centimeters. □ *The tailor ran the measuring tape around my waist.* □ *I used a measuring tape to measure the circumference of the jar.*

meat grinder a device that chops meat into fine pieces. □ *She pushed the chunk of pork into the meat grinder.* □ *Put the beef through a meat grinder.*

meat thermometer a device that measures the temperature of cooking meat. □ *A meat thermometer has a long, pointed end that is driven into the meat.* □ *I looked into the oven and checked the meat thermometer.* □ *Place a meat thermometer in the breast of the turkey.*

mechanical pencil a pencil that pushes lead out by a mechanism such as a spring or a screw. □ *I put a new lead in my mechanical pencil.* □ *He twisted the mechanical pencil, and the lead retracted.*

median a strip of ground or pavement in the middle of a road, separating the two directions of traffic flow. □ *The* *median was planted with trees.* □ *I looked for a break in the median so that I could turn left.*

meg(abyte)   1,048,576 bytes of information. (Used to measure computer files, memories, or disk capacities. Abbreviated MG.) □ *This is a one megabyte floppy.* □ *How many megs is your hard drive?*

melon baller   a small scoop for cutting out ball-shaped pieces of melon or other foods. □ *I scooped out cantaloupe balls with the melon baller.* □ BILL: *How did you make the potato balls in the soup?* JANE: *I used a melon baller.*

melt   **1.** to cause something to become liquid. □ *Melt the butter in a small saucepan.* □ *Use a soldering iron to melt the solder.* **2.** to become liquid. □ *Oh, no! The ice cream melted!* □ *I left the candy bar in the hot sun, and it melted.*

menu   **1.** a list of things served by a restaurant. □ *He studied the menu before placing his order.* □ *The menu listed a number of tempting appetizers.* **2.** a list of actions that a computer program can perform. □ *To start up the word processor, choose "Word" on the main menu.* □ *Click on the word "File" to see the menu of things you can do with files.*

menu driven   [of a computer program] operated by choosing actions from a set of MENUS. □ *The computerized card catalog is menu driven.* □ *You don't need to know any special commands to use this database. It's completely menu driven.*

mercerized   [of yarn or thread] made shiny by a special treatment. □ *Look at the lovely sheen of this mercerized cotton.* □ *The sweater is made of mercerized yarn.*

Mercurochrome™   a brand of merbromin, an ANTISEPTIC. □ *"Put some Mercurochrome on that cut," said Grandpa.* □ *"Ouch! That Mercurochrome really stings!" said Nancy.*

metronome   a device that measures out equal intervals of time. (Usually used to measure out musical beats.) □ *The* *music teacher turned on the metronome and made the stu-dent play the piece again.* □ *I heard the regular clicking of the metronome.*

microcassette   a very small audio cassette. □ *The an-swering machine records messages on this microcassette.* □ *She dictated a letter onto the microcassette.*

(micro)chip   a small electronic device that performs a par-ticular function. □ *A microchip in the telephone can store up to twenty frequently called phone numbers.* □ *The VCR con-tains a memory chip.*

micrometer   a tool for making very fine measurements. □ *I measured the width of the steel plate with a micrometer.* □ *She checked the diameter of the ball bearing with a micrometer.*

microphone AND **mike**   a device that converts sound into electrical impulses, which can then be fed into an electron-ic amplifier or a recording device. (MIKE is informal.) □ *I plugged a microphone into the amplifier.* □ *Please speak di-rectly into the mike.*

microprocessor   a MICROCHIP that controls the running of programs in a computer. □ *What kind of microprocessor does that desktop have?* □ *That microprocessor is too slow to handle the programs I need to run.*

microwaveable   able to be cooked or used in a MI-CROWAVE (OVEN). (See also MICROWAVE SAFE.) □ *I bought a microwaveable frozen dinner.* □ *This plastic storage dish is microwaveable.*

microwave cart   a cart designed to support a MICROWAVE (OVEN). □ *I store all my microwaveable dishes in the cabi-net in the bottom of the microwave cart.* □ *When I don't need to use the microwave, I wheel the microwave cart out of the way.*

microwave (oven)   an oven that heats food using high en-ergy radio waves. (Compare with CONVECTION OVEN.) □ *It* *takes just one minute to heat up a cup of coffee in a microwave oven.* □ *I reheated the leftovers in the microwave.*

microwave safe [of dishes] able to be used in a MICROWAVE (OVEN). (See also MICROWAVEABLE.) □ *Is this coffee cup microwave safe?* □ *Put the instant cereal and the water in a microwave safe container.*

mike See MICROPHONE.

mike stand a rod that supports a MICROPHONE. □ *The singer adjusted the mike stand so that the microphone came up to her mouth.* □ *The performer had two microphones on the mike stand—one for his voice, and one for his guitar.*

milk of magnesia a drug that relieves acid stomach. (MILK OF MAGNESIA is an opaque white liquid resembling milk.) □ *I took a spoonful of milk of magnesia to settle my stomach.* □ *Jim takes a lot of milk of magnesia. I wonder if he's developing a stomach ulcer.*

(milk)shake a drink made of ice cream and milk blended together. (SHAKE is informal.) □ *I'd like a chocolate milkshake, please.* □ *Gimme a shake and an order of fries.*

mince to cut something into very small pieces. □ *Please mince two cloves of garlic.* □ *Mince the celery and add it to the soup.*

miniblind a window covering made of narrow horizontal slats that can be adjusted to any angle. (See also VENETIAN BLIND.) □ *I had blue miniblinds installed in the kitchen.* □ *She pulled up the miniblind, and light flooded into the room.*

misfire AND **miss** [of an engine] to fail to ignite fuel at the proper time. □ *The mechanic could not figure out why the engine was misfiring.* □ *The engine sounded ragged. Every so often, one of the cylinders would miss.*

miss See MISFIRE.

miter   to join two pieces at an angle. □ *Miter the edges of the door molding.* □ *She mitered the corners of the picture frame.*

miter box   a device that allows you to cut something at a precise angle. □ *The carpenter slid the length of molding into the miter box.* □ *Make the cuts with a miter box, so that the two boards will meet at the right angle.*

mitten   a covering for the hand, with one section for the thumb and another for all four fingers. □ *The skiers wore special mittens to keep their hands from freezing.* □ *It was hard to get my car key out of my pocket with my mittens on.*

mix   to combine things together. □ *Mix the flour, baking soda, and salt.* □ *He mixed a little yellow paint into the red paint.*

mixing bowl   a bowl in which foods can be mixed together. □ *Put two eggs in a small mixing bowl and beat them well.* □ *Measure six cups of flour into a large mixing bowl.*

mixing spoon   a large spoon used for mixing foods. □ *He beat the cake batter with a mixing spoon.* □ *She stirred the spaghetti sauce with a mixing spoon.*

Mixmaster™   a brand of electric mixer with a rotating bowl attached. □ *"Use a Mixmaster to whip the egg whites," said Jim.* □ *"I'll put the cake mix into the Mixmaster," Mary offered.*

mode   a way of operating. □ *In Insert mode, the word processor allows you to type in new characters without erasing the characters that were there before.* □ *In order to insert numbers into the spreadsheet, you must go into Data Entry mode.*

model   a particular kind of manufactured thing. □ MARY: *What model car is that?* JANE: *It's a 1985 Nissan Sentra.* □ *That TV is an older model. I'm afraid we don't have the parts to repair it.*

modem   a device that allows a computer to send and receive information over a telephone line. □ *I plugged the computer into the modem and dialed up the electronic bulletin board.* □ *This laptop has an internal modem.*

modular jack   an opening designed for a special plastic connector on a telephone wire. □ *I plugged the phone into the modular jack in the wall.* □ *There's a modular jack on one side of the computer. It connects to the internal modem.*

molding   a strip of decorative material. □ *He nailed a wooden molding all around where the wall met the floor.* □ *The car had fancy chrome moldings.*

Molly™ bolt   a brand of bolt with attached strips of metal that bend outward as the bolt is screwed in. (See also TOG-GLE BOLT.) □ *The instructions said, "Use Molly bolts to attach the shelf to the drywall."* □ *"A Molly bolt gives you a secure fastening to a thin surface," said the carpenter.*

monitor   a computer screen. □ *Does the price of the computer include the monitor?* □ *I have a color monitor for my PC.*

monkey wrench   a large wrench with smooth, parallel jaws. □ *I loosened the nut with a monkey wrench.* □ *I gripped the pipe fitting with a monkey wrench.*

mop   **1.** a tool with a long handle and absorbent material at one end, usually used for cleaning floors. □ *I pushed the damp mop across the dirty floor.* □ *Rinse out the mop before you put it away.* **2.** to use a MOP. □ *I mopped the bathroom floor.* □ *He mopped the standing water from the basement floor.*

mortar   **1.** a mixture of cement, lime, and sand, used to join bricks together. □ *He troweled mortar onto the brick.* □ *I mixed up a batch of mortar for repairing the back wall.* **2.** a deep bowl in which things are ground with a PESTLE. □ *I put a handful of dried spices into the mortar.* □ *She crushed the garlic with a mortar and pestle.*

mortise and tenon   a way of joining two pieces of wood, with projections on one piece fitting into openings in the other. □ *The corners of the drawer were joined with a mortise and tenon.* □ *The carpenter cut a mortise and tenon joint.*

motorcycle   a two-wheeled motor vehicle. □ *He rode through the neighborhood on his new motorcycle.* □ *Wear a helmet when you ride your motorcycle.*

motor home   a motor vehicle containing a living space, often including a toilet and a kitchen. (See also CAMPER.) □ *We don't like staying in strange hotels when we travel, so we bought a motor home.* □ *They had a big screen TV in their motor home.*

motor oil   oil used to lubricate a car or truck engine. □ *She put a quart of motor oil into the engine.* □ *Where can I dispose of used motor oil?*

mountain bike   a sturdy bicycle suitable for riding on steep and unpaved roads. □ *They rode their mountain bikes up the steep trail.* □ *I packed up my camping gear and rode off on my mountain bike.*

Mountain standard time AND **MST**   the time in the time zone that covers much of the Western United States. (See also CENTRAL STANDARD TIME, EASTERN STANDARD TIME, PACIFIC STANDARD TIME.) □ *It's 8:00 PM, MST.* □ *JANE: Is Dallas on Mountain standard time?* CHARLIE: *No, it's in the Central time zone.*

mouse   a hand-held device used to point at and select items on a computer screen. □ *This is a basic, two-button mouse.* □ *I plugged the mouse into the serial port.*

mousetrap   a device that catches mice. □ *I set a mousetrap under the sink.* □ *I checked the mousetrap in the basement. There was a mouse in it.*

mouthpiece   the MICROPHONE in a telephone receiver; the part that you hold to your mouth when speaking.

(Compare with EARPIECE, RECEIVER.) □ *The spy unscrewed the mouthpiece and inserted a small recording device in the ambassador's phone.* □ *She whispered into the mouthpiece.*

mouthwash   a substance for rinsing the inside of the mouth. □ *Jim really should use a mouthwash. He's got bad breath.* □ *The dentist gave me a fluoride mouthwash to help strengthen my tooth enamel.*

moving floor AND **moving walkway**   a moving belt that carries people. □ *It's a long walk from the ticket counter to the gate. Fortunately, there's a moving floor along most of the way.* □ *I stepped onto the moving walkway and gripped the handrail.*

moving walkway   See MOVING FLOOR.

MST   See MOUNTAIN STANDARD TIME.

mucilage   a liquid that sticks things together. □ *I dabbed mucilage across the top of the paper.* □ *He stuck the postcard into his postcard album with mucilage.*

mud flap AND **splash guard**   a piece of material that hangs behind a wheel to protect a vehicle from the mud and water that the wheel tosses up. □ *The mud flaps on the truck were decorated with funny sayings.* □ *I put splash guards on the rear wheels of my van.*

mud room   a small room just behind an outside door, where people can take off muddy shoes and wet coats before entering the house. □ *I store my garden tools in the mud room.* □ *Take those boots off in the mud room!*

muffin   a small, round, sweet bread, in the shape of a cupcake, often containing fruits or spices. (See also ENGLISH MUFFIN.) □ *I got up early and baked blueberry muffins.* □ *We had coffee and muffins for breakfast.*

muffin pan AND **muffin tin**   a pan with small, round depressions for baking MUFFINS. □ *Line a muffin pan with*

baking cups. □ *I greased the muffin tin before spooning in the muffin batter.*

muffin stand a stand with plates at three levels, used for holding and serving food. □ *She arranged the cookies on a muffin stand.* □ *Each tier of the muffin stand held a different kind of muffin.*

muffin tin See MUFFIN PAN.

muffler 1. a piece of cloth wrapped around the neck and face to keep them warm. (See also SCARF.) □ *Put on a muffler if you go out into that cold weather.* □ *I knitted Joe a muffler.* 2. a device that reduces the noise of a vehicle's exhaust. □ *The car was making a deafening noise. It needed a new muffler.* □ *The bracket that holds the muffler in place had rusted away, and the muffler was dragging on the ground behind the car.*

mug a large, heavy cup with a handle. □ *I poured myself a big mug of coffee.* □ *He ladled the tomato soup into a mug.*

mulch material that covers the ground and helps things grow. □ *These wood shavings make a good mulch.* □ *The gardener used a plastic mulch to keep the soil warm.*

mulching mower a lawn mower that makes the cut grass into MULCH. □ *My grass has been so much healthier since I got that mulching mower.* □ *Mary's mulching mower sure cuts down on the amount of time she has to spend on yard work.*

multimedia using still pictures, moving pictures, sound, and text. □ *We have a multimedia computer in our classroom.* □ *The multimedia CD-ROM encyclopedia includes short movies on many interesting subjects.*

multimeter a device that measures electric current, voltage, and resistance. □ *The technician tested the telephone components with a multimeter.* □ *I used the multimeter to measure the output voltage of the circuit.*

Murphy bed   a bed that folds into a closet or a space in a wall when not being used. □ *The Murphy bed is a great space-saver in this little apartment.* □ *There's a Murphy bed in the spare room.*

muslin   a kind of woven cotton cloth. □ *Use muslin for the back of the quilt.* □ *She embroidered flowers on the muslin kitchen towel.*

mute button   a button that turns the sound off or on. □ *I hit the mute button when the TV commercial came on.* □ *She pressed the mute button on the telephone while she asked her boss a question she didn't want the caller to hear.*

Muzak™   a brand of sound system that provides background music. (See also ELEVATOR MUSIC, PIPED MUSIC.) □ *"I'd like to get Muzak for my waiting room," said the dentist.* □ *"The conversation in the restaurant is so loud that you can hardly hear the Muzak," the waiter observed.*

muzzle   the open end of a gun. □ *Run the cleaning brush in through the muzzle of the gun.* □ *I felt the cold muzzle of a pistol press against my back.*

Mylar™   a brand of thin plastic sheeting, usually silver or clear. □ *"Why are your windows covered with Mylar?" Joe asked. Jane answered, "It reflects the hot sun and keeps the rooms cool."* □ *"Those shiny balloons are made of Mylar," said the store clerk. "Children love them."*

N

(nail) clipper   a device for cutting fingernails and toenails. □ *My nails are getting too long. Where's the nail clipper?* □ *This heavy-duty clipper is good for thick toenails.*

nail scissors   SCISSORS with a small, curved blade, used for cutting fingernails and toenails. □ *She trimmed her nails with nail scissors.* □ *I always take my nail scissors with me when I travel.*

nap   a fuzzy surface. □ *Fabrics with nap include corduroy, velvet, and velour.* □ *You will need to be very careful in laying out the pattern on a fabric with nap.*

napkin   a piece of material used to wipe the hands and mouth while eating. □ *I spread the napkin on my lap.* □ *The place mats had matching napkins.*

napkin holder   a device that holds a supply of NAPKINS. □ *I filled the wooden napkin holder with paper napkins.* □ *He set a napkin holder on the table for his guests to use.*

napkin ring   a decorative ring through which a NAPKIN can be placed. □ *Each place setting had a cloth napkin in a wooden napkin ring.* □ *These napkin rings are so cute! They're shaped like fish!*

Naugahyde™   a brand of plastic material resembling leather. □ *MARY: Is this a leather sofa? JANE: No, it's Naugahyde.* □ *"These chairs are so easy to clean," Jim said enthusiastically. "They're made of Naugahyde."*

needle   **1.** a thin, pointed piece of metal with a slit in one end, used for passing yarn or thread through material. □ *He threaded the needle and began to sew.* □ *I replaced the needle on my sewing machine.* **2.** a small, thin, pointed piece of metal that comes in contact with the groove on an LP record; part of a phonograph. (See also CARTRIDGE, STYLUS.) □ *Somebody bumped the record player, and the* *needle skipped.* □ *She carefully cleaned the dust off the needle.*

needlenose pliers   See LONGNOSE PLIERS.

negative   a piece of photographic film with an image in which dark areas appear light and light areas appear dark. (Photographs are printed by passing light through a NEGATIVE onto photographic paper.) □ *If you give me the negative for that picture, I can get some copies printed.* □ *Handle the negative carefully—don't get fingerprints on it.*

neutral   [of color] not bright, able to appear in combination with many other shades. □ *You can wear this neutral blouse with a skirt of almost any color.* □ *The living room was decorated in neutral tones.*

newel post   the post at the bottom of a stair rail. □ *She polished the wooden newel post.* □ *The children were in the habit of tossing their coats onto the newel post as they came in.*

new potato   a small, young potato. □ *I served a salad of new potatoes in vinaigrette dressing.* □ *The side dish was new potatoes garnished with dill.*

Nicad™ battery   a brand of battery that can be recharged. (See also RECHARGEABLE BATTERY.) □ *"I got a set of Nicad batteries for my Walkman," said Amy.* □ *"Put the Nicad batteries in the recharger and plug them in overnight," said the instruction sheet.*

900 number   a telephone number with an area code of 900. (900 NUMBERS are services that charge a fee, usually some amount of money per minute. Compare with 800 NUMBER.) □ *The time and temperature service is not a free call. It's a 900 number.* □ *The fortune-teller had a 900 number.*

non-dairy creamer   a substance that resembles cream, usually made from vegetable oils. □ *I put a few spoonfuls of non-dairy creamer into my coffee.* □ *My doctor says I shouldn't eat dairy products, so I use non-dairy creamer.*

non-stick   very smooth, not likely to have anything stick. □ *I have a set of non-stick saucepans.* □ *The loaf of bread popped right out of the non-stick loaf pan.*

non-stick cooking spray   an oil sprayed onto cooking dishes to keep food from sticking. □ *Line the muffin tin with baking cups, or use a non-stick cooking spray.* □ *This non-stick cooking spray adds very few calories to food.*

notebook (computer)   a small, light, portable computer. (See also DESKTOP (COMPUTER), LAPTOP (COMPUTER), PALM-TOP.) □ *I downloaded the information into my notebook computer.* □ *This notebook has 4 meg of RAM.*

notions   items other than cloth used in sewing garments, such as needles, thread, buttons, and decorations. □ CUS-TOMER: *Where can I find the zippers?* SALES CLERK: *In the sewing department, with all the other notions.* □ *On the back of the dress pattern, there is a list of the notions you will need.*

nozzle   a narrow tube out of which a gas or liquid can flow. □ *I opened up the nozzle on the garden hose until I got a good stream of water.* □ *He placed the nozzle of the gas pump into the gas tank of his car.*

num lock key   a key on a computer keyboard, labeled "Num Lock," that switches the functions of the numeric keys. (When the NUM LOCK KEY is engaged, the numeric keys will type out numbers; when the NUM LOCK KEY is disengaged, the numeric keys perform other functions, such as moving the cursor.) □ MARY: *I'm trying to move the cursor up, and I keep getting a bunch of 8's on the screen!* CHARLIE: *That's because the num lock key is on.* □ *I hit the num lock key and began entering numbers into the database.*

nut   a metal block with spiral grooves inside, used to fasten onto a BOLT. □ *Match up each bolt with a nut of the correct size.* □ *Place a washer on the bolt, then screw on the nut.*

nutcracker a device for cracking nutshells. □ *I put the walnut between the jaws of the nutcracker.* □ *She has a fancy nutcracker that looks like a little old man.*

nut pick a thin metal tool used to pry the nut meat out of a nutshell. □ *She set out a basket of nuts in the shell, with a nutcracker and several nut picks.* □ *I needed a nut pick to get the Brazil nut out of its shell.*

NutraSweet™ a brand of ARTIFICIAL SWEETENER. □ *"This low-calorie soft drink is made with NutraSweet," the advertisement read.* □ *"Is there NutraSweet in this Jell-O?" Linda asked me.*

nylon a synthetic material. □ *This fishing line is made of nylon.* □ *The nylon in his jacket helped keep the wind out.*

O

octane a flammable chemical contained in gasoline. (The higher the OCTANE rating of a fuel, the higher the fuel's quality.) □ *The mid-grade gas has an octane rating of 78.* □ *I only buy high-octane fuel for my car.*

odometer a device that measures distance traveled. □ *The car's odometer read 97,543 miles.* □ *I attached an odometer to my bicycle so that I could measure the distance I rode.*

office paper paper used for business correspondence. (Typical OFFICE PAPER is white, $8\frac{1}{2} \times 11$ inches.) □ *Is this office paper suitable for laser printers?* □ *I typed the letter on high-quality office paper.*

office supplies material used in an office, such as paper, envelopes, pens, typewriter ribbons, etc. (See also STATIONERY.) □ *The drugstore sells some office supplies.* □ *How much did the company spend on office supplies last year?*

off ramp See EXIT RAMP.

oil change the act of removing used motor oil from a vehicle's engine, putting new oil in, and replacing the oil filter. □ *The manufacturer recommends an oil change every 3,000 miles.* □ *I do my own oil changes, because it saves money.*

oil finish an oil applied to wood in order to protect it and make it look good. □ *Rather than using a stain or a varnish, I decided to use an oil finish on the wooden deck.* □ *I like the mellow look of an oil finish on fine furniture.*

oil pan a pan at the bottom of an engine, where motor oil gathers. □ *To drain out the oil, loosen the nut at the bottom of the oil pan.* □ *The car seems to be losing oil. There may be a leak in the oil pan.*

ointment a semi-liquid, medicinal substance applied to the skin. (See also LOTION.) □ *The nurse put an antibiotic* *ointment on the wound.* □ *I dabbed burn ointment on my burned finger.*

oleo margarine. (Old-fashioned.) □ *Would you rather have butter or oleo?* □ *Here's some oleo for your toast.*

omelet a round shape of cooked, beaten egg. □ *I had a ham and cheese omelet for breakfast.* □ *The omelet was filled with mushrooms and melted cheese.*

omelet pan a flat-bottomed pan for cooking OMELETS. (Some OMELET PANS are hinged in the middle so that the omelet can be folded in half easily.) □ *She poured the beaten eggs into the heated omelet pan.* □ *Grease an omelet pan and heat it over a low flame.*

one size fits all [of clothing where] only one size is made, and it fits people of many different sizes. □ *This handy straw hat will keep out the sun. One size fits all.* □ *Wool socks— one size fits all.*

on line [of a computer or computer accessory] ready and working, accepting incoming data. □ *I'll be able to take your order when our computers come back on line.* □ *MARY: The printer doesn't seem to be printing. JANE: Is it on line?*

online on a computer. □ *I subscribe to a computer service that includes an online encyclopedia.* □ *Jim belongs to an online chat group.*

on/off switch a switch that turns a machine on or off. □ *The on/off switch is located at the rear left of the computer.* □ *Where's the on/off switch on the radio?*

on ramp See ENTRANCE RAMP.

open-end wrench a wrench with fixed, open jaws. (Contrasts with BOX-END WRENCH.) □ *I can't fit a box-end wrench into that space. I'll have to use an open-end wrench.* □ *This open-end wrench is specially made for working on bicycles.*

open-face sandwich a sandwich made of one slice of bread with filling placed on top. □ *These open-face* *sandwiches are simple to make. Just grate cheese onto the bread and broil for a few minutes.* ☐ *I ordered the open-face avocado sandwich on sourdough bread.*

operating system   a computer program that communicates directly with the computer hardware, controlling the screen, the disk drives, the memory, etc. ☐ *What operating system does your computer use?* ☐ *This program is designed to run under the MS-DOS operating system.*

organic   grown without chemical fertilizers or pesticides. ☐ *The health food store sells organic fruits and vegetables.* ☐ *These bath towels are made of organic cotton.*

O-ring   a thin, circular piece of rubber or plastic, used to seal spaces in some pieces of plumbing. ☐ *There is an O-ring at the bottom of the faucet handle.* ☐ *Use a screwdriver to pry out the old O-ring.*

OS/2™   a computer operating system designed and manufactured by IBM Corporation. ☐ *MARY: Are you running DOS on your PC? CHARLIE: No, OS/2.* ☐ *The first sentence in the software manual is, "This program is designed to run under the OS/2 operating system."*

OTC   See OVER THE COUNTER.

ottoman   a large, padded footstool. ☐ *I pulled an ottoman up to the armchair.* ☐ *The cat was curled up on the ottoman.*

outboard motor   a motor mounted outside the hull of a boat. (Contrasts with INBOARD MOTOR.) ☐ *He has a little fishing boat with an outboard motor.* ☐ *She pulled on the cord to start the outboard motor.*

outdoor grill   See (BARBECUE) GRILL.

outerwear   coats and jackets. (An advertising term.) ☐ *Outerwear is on sale this week.* ☐ *We sell rugged outerwear for outdoor people.*

oven mitt   a mitten-shaped pad that protects the hand from hot surfaces. (Compare with POT HOLDER.) □ *Put on an oven mitt before you take that muffin tin out of the oven.* □ *She put on an oven mitt and removed the pot lid.*

ovenproof   [of dishes] suitable for heating in an oven. □ *This serving dish is ovenproof and microwave safe.* □ *I kept the food warm on an ovenproof plate.*

oven rack   a wire rack that supports pans and dishes inside an oven. □ *Put the oven rack in the middle of the oven.* □ *The oven rack was covered with spilled, baked-on food.*

oven thermometer   a device for measuring the temperature inside an oven. □ *The oven thermometer showed that the back of the oven was ten degrees hotter than the front.* □ *I checked the oven thermometer to make sure the oven was the correct temperature.*

overhaul   **1.** to repair something. □ *I had my old sewing machine overhauled.* □ *How much will it cost to overhaul the computer?* **2.** a repair job. □ *The garage gave the car engine a thorough overhaul.* □ *The printer overhaul will take five to ten working days.*

overload   too large a load. □ *An electrical overload caused the fuse to blow.* □ *There's a system overload—too many people trying to use the computer.*

overpass   a place where one road passes over another. (Compare with UNDERPASS.) □ *Turn left and go under the freeway overpass.* □ *Traffic was stalled on the overpass.*

over the counter AND **OTC**   [of drugs that are] sold without a prescription. □ *Is this cough syrup available over the counter?* □ *There are several OTC asthma remedies available.*

owner's manual   a book of instructions for a machine. □ *Be sure to read the owner's manual before trying to operate* *the VCR.* ☐ *The owner's manual lists authorized repair centers for the coffee maker.*

Oxford cloth   a medium-weight woven cloth. ☐ *This shirt is made of durable Oxford cloth.* ☐ *This Oxford cloth is sixty percent cotton, forty percent polyester.*

P

PA   See PUBLIC ADDRESS SYSTEM.

Pacific standard time AND **PST**   the time in the time zone that covers the West Coast of the United States. (See also CENTRAL STANDARD TIME, EASTERN STANDARD TIME, MOUNTAIN STANDARD TIME.) □ *The show will air at 11 PM Eastern, 8 PM Pacific standard time.* □ *It's 10:45, PST.*

packing material   See EXCELSIOR.

packing tape   strong tape used to seal packages. □ *She taped down the box flaps with packing tape.* □ *The boxes were sealed with clear packing tape.*

padding   a layer of soft material placed between carpeting and the floor. □ *The price of the carpet includes padding and installation.* □ *How many square yards of padding will you need?*

padlock   a lock with a U-shaped latch. □ *I put a padlock through the hasp on the storage locker.* □ *He locked his bicycle with a padlock and a chain.*

pager   a device that alerts you when someone is trying to get in touch with you. (See also BEEPER.) □ *Here's the phone number for my pager.* □ *He's out of the office, but we can contact him via his pager.*

pain killer   See ANALGESIC.

pain reliever   See ANALGESIC.

paint remover   a substance that dissolves and removes paint from wood. □ *Spread paint remover over the painted surface.* □ *Use eye protection when using this paint remover. It is a strong chemical.*

paint roller a handle with a removable, rolling cylindrical brush. □ *I rinsed the paint roller under the hose.* □ *She painted the wall with a paint roller.*

paint thinner a substance that dissolves oil-based paint. □ *Clean the paintbrush in paint thinner.* □ *The paint was drying out, so I added a little paint thinner.*

pallet a movable platform on which things can be stacked and stored. □ *The forklift moved the pallet loaded with boxes.* □ *The warehouse workers stacked the pallet with cases of machine parts.*

palmtop a portable computer, small enough to hold in the hand. (See also DESKTOP (COMPUTER), LAPTOP (COMPUTER), NOTEBOOK (COMPUTER).) □ *I have the names and addresses of my clients stored in my palmtop.* □ *I uploaded the information from my palmtop into my desktop PC.*

pancake AND **flapjack; hotcake, griddle cake** a thin round of batter cooked on a frying pan. (FLAPJACK, HOTCAKE, and GRIDDLE CAKE are folksy.) □ *I made pancakes for a special weekend breakfast treat.* □ *She made up a recipe of buttermilk flapjacks.* □ *He covered the stack of hotcakes with maple syrup.* □ *Our griddle cakes are famous in these parts.*

pancake syrup sweet syrup for pouring onto PANCAKES. □ *The waitress brought three different kinds of pancake syrup.* □ *This pancake syrup contains real maple sugar.*

pancake turner a tool with a handle and a flat blade, used for turning and lifting food. (See also SPATULA.) □ *She flipped the hamburgers with a pancake turner.* □ *I slid a pancake turner under the cooking pancake.*

panel a flat structure or piece of material. □ *Remove the front panel from the air conditioner unit.* □ *The printer controls are located on a side panel.*

pan fry to fry something in shallow oil. (Compare with DEEP FRY.) □ *We pan fried the fish we had caught that day.* □ *He pan fried the hamburgers.*

panier   one of a pair of containers attached over the back wheel of a bicycle or motorcycle. □ *I put my schoolbooks in the bicycle paniers.* □ *I packed everything I needed for the trip in the paniers.*

pantyhose   a pair of thin stockings that fit the body close-ly from the waist to the toes. □ *I bought a pair of sheer pantyhose.* □ *She pulled on her pantyhose.*

paper bail   a rod that holds paper against the PLATEN in a typewriter or computer printer. □ *Pull the paper bail to-ward you and remove the paper.* □ *He let the paper bail snap back against the page.*

paper clip   a device made of wire bent into two loops, used to hold papers together. □ *He fastened the envelope to the letter with a paper clip.* □ *The pages were held together with a paper clip.*

paper cup   a disposable drinking cup made of paper. □ *I bought a supply of paper cups for the party.* □ *At the store, they were giving out fruit juice samples in paper cups.*

paper napkin   a napkin made of paper. □ *We took paper napkins on the picnic.* □ *I use paper napkins, except for for-mal meals.*

paper plate   a plate made of paper. □ *I used paper plates for the big dinner, so I wouldn't have to wash dishes after-wards.* □ *The campers threw their paper plates into the bonfire.*

paper towel   a towel made of paper. □ *I mopped up the spill with a paper towel.* □ *He wiped off the counter with a paper towel.*

parallel cable AND **Centronics™ cable**   a computer cable that can transmit more than one bit of information at a time. (CENTRONICS™ is a brand name. Compare with SERIAL CABLE.) □ *Use a parallel cable to connect the laser printer to the parallel port.* □ *"I need a Centronics cable with a 25-pin connector,"* I said to the clerk in the computer store.

207

parallel parking   **1.** a parking arrangement in which cars are parked parallel to the curb and directly in front of or behind each other. (Compare with DIAGONAL PARKING.) □ *Parallel parking is permitted along both sides of the street.* □ *There is parallel parking available in front of the store.* **2.** the process of positioning a car parallel to the curb and in front of or behind other parked cars. □ *I'm no good at parallel parking.* □ *I practiced parallel parking at the curb in front of my house.*

parallel port   a place on a computer for connecting a parallel cable, a kind of cable that can communicate with printers and a number of other devices. (Compare with SERIAL PORT.) □ *This laptop has a serial port and a parallel port.* □ *You can connect an external hard drive to the parallel port.*

paramedic   a person trained to give emergency medical care. □ *She's choking! Call a paramedic!* □ *The paramedics got out of the ambulance and ran to the injured woman.*

paring knife   a knife with a short blade. □ *She peeled the apple with a paring knife.* □ *Use the paring knife to slice the cheese.*

parity   a property of information in a computer signal. (PARITY can be even, odd, or none.) □ *For a terminal to receive data properly, it must be set to the same parity as the incoming signal.* □ *Set your communications software to 7 data bits, 1 stop bit, even parity.*

parking brake   See EMERGENCY BRAKE.

parking lights   a set of small lights at the four corners of a car, often used while parking at night. □ *Turn this knob one click to turn on the parking lights. Two clicks turns on the headlights.* □ *It is illegal to drive at night with only your parking lights on.*

parking lot   an area where cars can be parked. □ *The grocery store has a large parking lot.* □ *Please park your car in the parking lot behind the theater.*

parking meter   a coin-operated device that measures out the amount of time you may park your car in a parking space. □ *I parked the car and put a quarter in the parking meter.* □ *There's twenty minutes left on this parking meter.*

parking ramp   a multi-level structure where cars may be parked. (Regional.) □ *There's a parking ramp just half a block from my office.* □ *The elevator takes you from the hotel parking ramp to the hotel lobby.*

parquetry   the joining of flat wooden shapes into a pattern on a floor or a piece of furniture. □ *The floor was parquetry.* □ *Just look at the fine parquetry on this tabletop.*

particle board AND **chipboard**   a board made of wood chips pressed together. □ *I used particle board for the kitchen cabinets.* □ *The shelves were just cheap chipboard things.*

partition wall   an interior wall that does not support the roof or the floor above it. (Compare with LOAD BEARING WALL.) □ *I built a partition wall between the living room and the dining area.* □ *This is a partition wall and can be removed without weakening the structure of the building.*

passenger seat   the front car seat that is not the driver's seat. □ *I got into the passenger seat, and Jim drove.* □ *The passenger seat can be adjusted separately from the driver's seat.*

passenger side   the side of the car opposite the side where the driver sits. □ *The driver's side door on my car froze shut, so I have to get in from the passenger side.* □ *This car has an airbag on the passenger side.*

password   a code that gives you access to something, such as a computer or a building. (See also PERSONAL IDENTIFICATION NUMBER.) □ *Type in your user name and password.* □ *You need a special password to open the lock on the door.*

pasta   dough shapes, such as noodles, spaghetti, and macaroni. □ *There are several kinds of pasta on the menu.* □ *I boiled up some pasta for a quick dinner.*

paste   **1.** a thick adhesive. □ *The children spread paste on the construction paper.* □ *This paste is non-toxic.* **2.** to stick things together, especially with PASTE. □ *She pasted a sign to the door.* □ *I pasted wrapping paper onto the box.* **3.** to put a piece of text into a computer file. (See also CUT.) □ *This word processor makes it very easy to cut and paste.* □ *Press the right mouse button to paste to that location.*

pastry   **1.** sweet foods made of rich dough that is baked or fried. □ *A marble slab is useful for making pastry.* □ *That bakery makes the best pastry in town.* **2.** a piece of PASTRY. □ *I had an apricot pastry with my coffee.* □ *I bought a few pastries to take home.*

pastry bag   a paper or plastic bag with a PASTRY TIP a one end, used for squeezing PASTRY dough into fancy shapes. (See also DECORATING BAG.) □ *The chef scooped the dough into the pastry bag.* □ *Use a pastry bag with a large, star-shaped tip to pipe the dough into a ring.*

pastry blender   a tool with U-shaped blades attached to a handle, used for mixing shortening into flour for PASTRY dough. □ *Cut in the butter with a pastry blender.* □ *Cut the shortening into the flour with a pastry blender, until the mixture resembles coarse crumbs.*

pastry board AND **pastry marble**   a flat piece of marble for kneading or rolling PASTRY dough. (Dough does not stick to the cool marble.) □ *Roll out the dough on a pastry board.* □ *Sprinkle a pastry marble with flour.*

pastry brush   a flat brush for applying liquid to the surface of a dough. □ *Using a pastry brush, glaze the dough with melted butter.* □ *She dipped the pastry brush in milk and whisked it across the rolls.*

pastry cloth   a plastic cloth on which PASTRY can be kneaded or rolled. □ *The pastry cloth is marked with circles of different diameters, so that you can roll a pie crust to the right size.* □ *Dust the pastry cloth with flour.*

pastry marble   See PASTRY BOARD.

pastry tip   a metal or plastic cone with a specially shaped opening at the small end; used with a PASTRY BAG. (See also ICING TIP.) ☐ *Use a large, round pastry tip to shape the dough.* ☐ *Use a pastry bag with a fluted pastry tip.*

patch pocket   a pocket formed by sewing a piece of cloth onto a garment. ☐ *These shorts have two sideseam pockets and a patch pocket in back.* ☐ *I sewed a patch pocket onto the skirt.*

pattern   a guide for the shape of something. ☐ *The woodworking book includes patterns for a basic chair and table.* ☐ *I pinned the dress pattern to the cloth.*

patty   a portion of food molded into a flat shape. ☐ *I fried the salmon patties in vegetable oil.* ☐ *I would like a hamburger patty without the bun.*

pause button   a control that causes a machine to stop temporarily. ☐ *I pushed the pause button on the VCR so that the tape would stop while I got up to get something to drink.* ☐ *The phone rang. I pushed the pause button on the CD player and went to answer the phone.*

pay phone   a telephone that requires you to pay for a call with coins or a credit card. ☐ *I looked around for the nearest pay phone.* ☐ *I slid my credit card through the slot on the pay phone and picked up the receiver.*

PC   See PERSONAL COMPUTER.

peanut butter   a food made of peanuts ground into a paste. ☐ *This brand of peanut butter has no added sugar.* ☐ *I spread peanut butter on a slice of whole wheat bread.*

peat   partially decomposed plant material. ☐ *The gardener worked some peat into the soil.* ☐ *The soil here is mostly peat. It needs to be drained before plants will grow well.*

peat moss   a soft, stringy moss. ☐ *You can work peat moss into alkaline soil to lower the pH.* ☐ *The flowers were arranged in baskets full of peat moss.*

peat pot a plant pot made of pressed moss. □ *The seedlings are grown in peat pots. You can plant them in the garden, pot and all.* □ *Start the seeds in peat pots.*

peck eight quarts, DRY MEASURE. □ *I bought a peck of apples.* □ *Squashes are four dollars a peck.*

pedal **1.** a structure designed to be pushed by the foot. □ *The bicycle seat was so high, I could barely reach the pedals.* □ *The harder you push on the pedal of the sewing machine, the faster it will stitch.* **2.** to crank something by pushing on PEDALS. □ *The cyclists pedaled up the hill.* □ *I spent half an hour pedaling the exercise machine.*

pedestal a base or support for something. □ *The bronze statue stood on a marble pedestal.* □ *The figurine was displayed on a tall pedestal.*

pedestrian a person traveling on foot. □ *Pedestrians have the right of way.* □ *The sidewalk was crowded with pedestrians.*

pedestrian walkway a structure that allows people to walk over or under a road. (See also FOOTBRIDGE.) □ *A pedestrian walkway led from the parking lot to the zoo.* □ *A pedestrian walkway was built under the busy street.*

peekhole See PEEPHOLE.

peel **1.** the outer layer of a fruit. □ *The orange had a thick peel.* □ *The candy is made with lemon peel.* **2.** to remove the outer layer of a fruit or vegetable. □ *Peel the eggplant and soak it in salt water.* □ *Peel and core six medium-sized apples.*

peephole AND **peekhole** a small hole for looking through, especially for looking through a door to see the person outside. □ *By law, every apartment door must have a peephole.* □ *I looked out the peekhole to see who was knocking.*

peg a short, round piece of rigid material such as wood or metal. □ *Hang your coat on the peg by the door.* □ *The boards were held together with wooden pegs instead of nails.*

pegboard   a sheet of pressed wood with a holes drilled in it in a grid pattern. □ *I hang hooks from the pegboard on the kitchen wall, and I hang my pots and pans from the hooks.* □ *I have my tools organized on a pegboard in the garage.*

pellet   a small metal ball fired from a shotgun. □ *One pellet hit the deer in the leg.* □ *A shotgun cartridge contains pellets.*

pencil sharpener   a device that grinds a pencil to a point. □ *I broke my lead. Do you have a pencil sharpener?* □ *He cranked the handle of the pencil sharpener.*

Pendaflex™   a brand of hanging file folders. □ *"I need legal size Pendaflex folders to fit my filing cabinet," the lawyer said to the supply room clerk.* □ *"The filing system uses different colored Pendaflex folders for different kinds of documents," the secretary explained.*

penny loafers   low-heeled leather shoes without laces. (PENNY LOAFERS are decorated with a leather band with an opening into which a penny can fit.) □ *Are penny loafers acceptable office wear?* □ *I polished my penny loafers.*

peppercorn   a dried berry from a pepper bush. □ *I filled the pepper grinder with peppercorns.* □ *I bought a mix of red and black peppercorns.*

pepper grinder AND **pepper mill**   a device that grinds peppercorns. □ *I cranked the pepper grinder over my soup.* □ *She turned the handle of the pepper mill.*

pepper mill   See PEPPER GRINDER.

Pepto-Bismol™   a brand of medicine for upset stomach. □ CHARLIE: *My stomach hurts.* MARY: *Do you need some Pepto-Bismol?* □ *"If your little girl's sick to her stomach, try some Pepto-Bismol," my friend advised.*

percolator   a device that brews coffee by passing boiling water through ground coffee beans. □ *I put the percolator on the stove.* □ *He measured coffee into the percolator.*

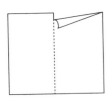

perennial a plant that lives for a number of years. (Compare with ANNUAL.) ☐ *Asparagus is a perennial.* ☐ CHARLIE: *Are chives an annual or a perennial?* JANE: *A perennial.*

perforated pierced with a line of small holes. ☐ *The pages of the spiral notebook are perforated at the edge, so that you can tear them out easily.* ☐ *The computer paper is perforated between sheets.*

periodical a publication that comes out at intervals; a newspaper or magazine. (Formal.) ☐ *He subscribed to a number of scholarly periodicals.* ☐ *Where is the periodicals section of the library?*

peripheral a device for getting information into or out of a computer. (Keyboards, screens, printers, modems, and computer mouses are all PERIPHERALS.) ☐ *You can add peripherals to this computer system through the serial port.* ☐ *Go to the "Setup" menu to set up communications between the program and your peripherals.*

permanent press [of cloth that has] the quality of resisting wrinkles and not requiring ironing. ☐ MARY: *Do you need to iron that shirt?* JANE: *No. It's permanent press.* ☐ *This jacket is made of easy care, permanent press polyester.*

Perma-Prest™ a brand of PERMANENT PRESS clothing. ☐ *"This Perma-Prest suit travels well," Jim remarked.* ☐ *"I bought some Perma-Prest pants on sale," said Mary.*

personal computer AND **PC** a computer small and inexpensive enough for home use. ☐ *We went shopping for a new PC.* ☐ *This program is designed to run on a personal computer.*

personal identification number AND **PIN** a four-digit code number that gives you access to a bank or credit account of some kind. (See also PASSWORD.) ☐ *Put your ATM card in the slot to the left, and then enter your personal identification number on the keypad.* ☐ *I charged the phone call to my home number by keying in my phone number and PIN.*

personal organizer   a folder containing a calendar, address book, and other items that record someone's schedule or appointments. □ *I made a note of the meeting in my personal organizer.* □ *I have a special place in my personal organizer to store the business cards people give me.*

pesticide   a substance that kills insects or rodents. (See also INSECTICIDE, INSECT REPELLENT.) □ *I sprayed the garage with pesticide.* □ *Does this pesticide kill roaches?*

pestle   a cylindrical object used to grind or crush things in a MORTAR. □ *I ground the chalk with a mortar and pestle.* □ *She crushed the garlic under the pestle.*

Peter Pan collar   a small collar with round ends, usually used on clothing for women and girls. □ *The little girl wore a cute pink blouse with a Peter Pan collar.* □ *I think this bow tie goes well with the Peter Pan collar on the blouse.*

petroleum jelly   an ointment made of petroleum. □ *I put a little petroleum jelly on the baby's rash.* □ *She dabbed petroleum jelly onto her cold sore.*

pH   a measure of acidity or alkalinity. (A pH lower than 7 is acid; a pH higher than 7 is alkaline.) □ *I tested the soil pH in the garden.* □ *Many plants, such as onions, parsnips, and celery, require a low soil pH.*

pharmacy   a place where prescription drugs are dispensed. (See also DRUGSTORE.) □ *The pharmacy is in the back of the drugstore.* □ *I picked up my prescription at the pharmacy.*

Phillips head   a screw head with two slots at right angles to each other. (Compare with SLOTTED HEAD.) □ *The case is attached with two Phillips head screws.* □ *I need a Phillips head screwdriver.*

phone card   a plastic card that allows you to pay for a call from a pay telephone. □ *I bought a $10 phone card so that I could make calls while I was on the road.* □ *This pay phone doesn't take this kind of phone card.*

phonograph   a device that can play audio recordings on vinyl disks. (Formal.) □ *This cable connects the phonograph to the amplifier.* □ *I put another record on the phonograph.*

photocell   a device that detects light. □ *The burglar alarm uses a ray of light and a photocell to detect movement.* □ *The light meter contains a photocell.*

photocopier AND **copy machine**   a machine that makes copies of papers. (COPY MACHINE is informal.) □ *Several people were waiting in line to use the copy machine at the library.* □ *This photocopier can make up to sixty copies a minute.*

piano bench   a backless seat for sitting at a piano. □ *The piano bench has a hinged lid, and you can store sheet music inside.* □ *She pulled the piano bench up to the piano.*

piano hammer   a small, wooden, felt-covered hammer that strikes a piano string when the PIANO KEY is pressed. □ *The link between the key and the piano hammer was broken, so that's why the key didn't make any sound.* □ *I lifted the piano cover so that I could watch the piano hammers striking the keys.*

piano key   one of the flat, black or white levers on the front of a piano. □ *The surface of the piano keys is ivory.* □ *She pressed the piano key and listened to the note.*

piano string   one of a set of wires stretched inside the frame of a piano, which makes a musical sound when struck by a PIANO HAMMER. □ *The piano tuner adjusted the piano strings until each one was in tune.* □ *I bounced a ball on the piano strings, just to see what it would sound like.*

picket fence   a fence with narrow vertical boards, or pickets, nailed along the rails. □ *The yard was surrounded by a white picket fence.* □ *The picket fence needs painting.*

pickle   **1.** a vegetable or fruit preserved in salt, vinegar, and spices. □ *The grilled cheese sandwich comes with a pickle.* □ *I munched the okra pickle.* **2.** to preserve something in salt, vinegar, and spices. □ *I pickled the beets from the garden.* □ *These cucumbers are just the right size for pickling.*

pie   a food item with a filling in a PIE CRUST. (A typical PIE is shallow and round in shape.) □ *Try some of this lemon meringue pie.* □ *For cheese and onion pie, you will need a pound of cheese and four large onions.*

pie crust   a layer of dough for a PIE. (Compare with PIE SHELL.) □ *Line the pie tin with pie crust.* □ *Pour the cherry pie filling into a baked pie crust.*

pie filling   a food mixture, usually sweet, used to fill a PIE CRUST. □ *I used cherry pie filling from a can.* □ *You'll need a double boiler to make chocolate pie filling.*

pie pan AND **pie plate; pie tin**   a flat-bottomed, round, shallow pan or plate for baking PIES. □ *Line an 8-inch pie pan with shortbread pie crust.* □ *If you are using a glass pie plate, you will need to adjust the oven temperature.* □ *I don't quite have enough pie crust to cover this pie tin.*

pie plate   See PIE PAN.

pier   **1.** a post that supports a building or a bridge. □ *Is this house built on piers or a concrete slab?* □ *The construction workers reinforced the bridge piers.* **2.** a structure that extends out into a body of water. □ *I walked along the pier.* □ *They tied the boat to the pier.*

pie server   See CAKE SERVER.

pie shell   a PIE CRUST already formed. (Compare with PIE CRUST.) □ *I bought a frozen pie shell.* □ *Have a pre-baked pie shell ready.*

pie tin   See PIE PAN.

pile   a surface of short, soft, fur-like fibers. □ *The soft rug had a deep pile.* □ *She felt the luxurious pile of the velvet upholstery.*

pillow sham   a decorative cover for a pillow. □ *I got pillow shams to match my bedspread.* □ *She put the pillows in ruffled pillow shams.*

pilot light   a small flame that lights a gas burner. □ *Now I see why the stove burner didn't light. The pilot light is out.* □ *I had to relight the pilot light on the hot water heater.*

PIN   See PERSONAL IDENTIFICATION NUMBER.

pinch   a small amount, just as much as you can hold between your forefinger and thumb. □ *Add a pinch of salt.* □ *Just put in a pinch of oregano.*

pinch bar   See CROWBAR.

pin cushion   a small cushion for storing pins. □ *I stuck the needle into the pin cushion.* □ *I have a pin cushion that clips onto my wrist. It's very handy.*

pink   to make a zigzag cut with PINKING SHEARS. □ *Pink the raw edges of the seam.* □ *The tailor pinked the edges of the fabric squares.*

pinking shears   a pair of SCISSORS that make a cut with a zigzag edge. □ *If you cut the cloth with pinking shears, the edges won't fray so easily.* □ *She trimmed the patch with pinking shears.*

pipe   **1.** hollow cylindrical material. □ *I'll need two feet of copper pipe.* □ *What kind of pipe do I need to put in a new sink?* **2.** a piece of hollow cylindrical material. □ *There's a leak in one of the pipes in the ceiling.* □ *I threaded the fitting onto the end of the pipe.* **3.** a tube with a bowl at one end, used for smoking. □ *He packed tobacco into his pipe.* □ *Jim used to smoke cigarettes, but now he smokes a pipe.* **4.** to put dough or frosting through a pastry tube. □ *Pipe the pastry dough into six-inch lengths.* □ *The cake decorator piped a line of pink frosting around the edge of the cake.*

piped music   music transmitted by wire into some public place. (See also ELEVATOR MUSIC, MUZAK™.) □ *The piped* *music in the doctor's office was coming from my favorite radio station.* □ *The office workers objected to the piped music in the office.*

pipkin   a small saucepan. □ *She boiled the egg in a pipkin.* □ *I poured melted butter out of the pipkin.*

(piston) displacement   the volume left in an engine cylinder when the piston has moved to the bottom. (If the engine has more than one cylinder, its PISTON DISPLACEMENT is the sum of the displacements of all the cylinders.) □ *Power saws are rated according to their piston displacement.* □ *The sedan has a 3.3-liter engine displacement.*

pit   **1.** the hard seed in the middle of some fruits, such as cherries, peaches, and avocadoes. □ *We ate the cherries, spitting the pits on the ground.* □ *I planted the avocado pit in my garden.* **2.** to remove the PIT from a fruit. □ *I pitted the cherries with a paper clip.* □ *Pit the peaches and slice them.*

pita (bread)   a flat, round bread, popular in many Middle Eastern countries. □ *The dip was served with wedges of pita bread.* □ *I made a sandwich with the pita.*

pitch   the angle of a roof. □ *In this climate, you need a pretty steep pitch, to make sure the snow will slide off the roof.* □ *The pitch of the roof was not sufficient to drain off the rainwater.*

pitched roof   a roof built at an angle. □ *It was a nice-looking cottage with a pitched roof.* □ *The garage originally had a flat roof, but I built a pitched roof on it.*

pitcher   a container with a handle and a spout, used for pouring liquid. □ *I made a pitcher of lemonade.* □ *Pass the milk pitcher, please.*

pitchfork   a tool with a long handle and several sharp prongs at the end. □ *I scooped up the manure with a pitchfork.* □ *They stacked up the hay with pitchforks.*

pivot **1.** a pin that fastens two things together so that one or both of them can swing. (See also HINGE, SWIVEL.) ☐ *The two blades of the scissors are joined by a pivot.* ☐ *This bolt on the bicycle brake arm acts as a pivot.* **2.** to turn or swing as if on a PIVOT. ☐ *He pivoted on his chair.* ☐ *The tone arm on the phonograph can pivot up and down as well as side to side.*

pizza a food item with various items, usually including tomato sauce and cheese, baked on a crust of yeast dough. ☐ *After the movie, we went out for pizza.* ☐ *I'd like a medium thin crust pizza with pepperoni and black olives.*

pizza cutter See PIZZA WHEEL.

pizza wheel AND **pizza cutter** a tool with a rolling, round blade in a handle, used for cutting flat foods, such as PIZZA. ☐ *She rolled the pizza wheel across the pizza.* ☐ *I used a pizza cutter to cut the tortillas in half.*

placket a band of fabric that reinforces a garment opening with buttons and buttonholes. ☐ *The blouse has a six-button placket.* ☐ *Mark the positions for the buttonholes on the placket.*

plain text [of a computer file] without special formatting. (See also AMERICAN STANDARD CODE FOR INFORMATION INTERCHANGE.) ☐ *If you save this document as a plain text file, you will lose all the underlining and special paragraph formats.* ☐ *You can edit a plain text file with any word processing program.*

plane **1.** a winged flying vehicle; an airplane. (Informal.) ☐ *What time does your plane leave?* ☐ *Mary flew to Charleston in her private plane.* **2.** a tool that cuts a horizontal surface. ☐ *The carpenter used a plane to smooth the board.* ☐ *I adjusted the blade in the plane until it just touched the surface of the wood.* **3.** to cut something with a PLANE. ☐ *Plane that board until it's perfectly flat.* ☐ *I planed the edge of the door until it would fit in the door frame.*

plank   a thick wood board. □ *The children used an old plank as a bridge over the creek.* □ *I nailed a plank across the top of the wall frame.*

planter   a container for a plant or plants. □ *She had a planter full of begonias on her front stoop.* □ *I got the cutest handmade clay planter at the craft sale.*

plant food   a chemical mixture that nourishes plants. □ *Just add this liquid plant food to the water when you water your houseplants, and watch them grow!* □ *The gardener worked plant food into the soil.*

Plastic Wood™   a brand of plastic for filling holes in wood. □ *"Fill the knothole with Plastic Wood, let it dry, and sand it smooth," Jane suggested.* □ *"You can mend the chipped tabletop with Plastic Wood," Mark told me.*

plastic wrap   a thin sheet of clear plastic used to wrap and store food. □ *I wrapped the leftover chicken in plastic wrap and put it in the fridge.* □ *Cover the top of the bowl with plastic wrap.*

platen   a rubber or plastic cylinder that rolls paper through a typewriter or a copy machine. □ *The paper bail holds the paper against the platen.* □ *The technician cleaned lint and ink off the platen.*

platter   a large, heavy serving plate. □ *I put the roast on a platter.* □ *The waitress brought a platter full of appetizers.*

playback   the playing of recorded material, especially a video cassette. □ *Follow these steps for VCR playback.* □ *To interrupt playback, press the pause button.*

pleat   **1.** a fold sewed into a piece of cloth. □ *Mark the positions where you want the pleats on the finished garment.* □ *There are pleats at the corners of the slipcover.* **2.** to sew a fold into a piece of cloth. □ *Pleat the fabric into a decorative ruffle.* □ *This sewing machine attachment pleats fabric automatically.*

Plexiglas™   a brand of clear plastic that does not break easily. □ *"These windows are Plexiglas. They shouldn't break," said the landlord.* □ *"The shower door is made of Plexiglas," Mary said. "It's very safe."*

pliable   able to bend or change shape. □ *Knead the plastic clay until it becomes soft and pliable.* □ *The brass wire is quite pliable.*

pliers   a tool with hinged metal jaws, used for gripping. □ *I used the pliers to bend the thick wire.* □ *He gripped the bolt with a pair of pliers.*

plumb   perfectly vertical. □ *The door frame isn't plumb, so the door doesn't hang right.* □ *They adjusted the partition wall until it was plumb.*

plumb bob   a weight at the end of a PLUMB LINE, used to determine if something is straight up and down. □ *The plumb bob indicated that the bookcase was not straight.* □ *I marked the position of the plumb bob on the floor.*

(plumber's) auger AND **(plumber's) snake**   a tool for drilling a clog out of a drain or a pipe. □ *If a chemical drain opener doesn't work, try an auger.* □ *He worked the plumber's snake down into the drain.* □ *She cranked the snake till it worked through the clog.*

plumber's friend   See PLUNGER.

plumber's helper   See PLUNGER.

(plumber's) snake   See (PLUMBER'S) AUGER.

plumb line   a cord with a weight at the end, used to determine if something is straight up and down. □ *They adjusted the wall frame until it came into line with the plumb line.* □ *I used a plumb line to mark a vertical line on the wall.*

plunger AND **plumber's friend; plumber's helper**   a handle with a large suction cup on one end, used to remove clogs from pipes. □ MARY: *The toilet's stopped up.* TOM: *I'll get the plunger.* □ *I worked on the sink drain with a plumber's friend.* □ *I keep a plumber's helper handy in the bathroom.*

plus size   a clothing size for large women. □ *Our store specializes in plus sizes.* □ *Do you have this outfit in a plus size?*

plywood   material made of thin sheets of wood glued in layers. □ *I built a simple table out of plywood.* □ *I used plywood for the kitchen cabinets, because it was cheap.*

poach   to cook something in a hot liquid. □ *Poach the eggs in boiling water and vinegar.* □ *He poached the fish in vegetable broth.*

point and shoot   **1.** [of a camera that is] able to adjust the focus and exposure automatically. (Informal. See also AUTO FOCUS.) □ *Even I can take pictures with this point and shoot camera.* □ CHARLIE: *Is that a point and shoot camera?* JANE: *No. I have to focus it manually.* **2.** [of a computer program] allowing the selection of something, such as a file name, but placing the CURSOR on the choice (pointing) and clicking (shooting). □ *My program is point and shoot, so it is easy to work.* □ *This program is not point and shoot. You have to type in the whole file name.*

poker   a heavy, pointed metal rod, used to stir burning logs or coals in a fireplace. □ *He pushed the log into place with the poker.* □ *She used the poker to stir up the embers until they flamed up.*

Polaroid™   a brand of camera that produces instant pictures. (You may hear POLAROID™ used to refer to pictures taken with a POLAROID™ camera.) □ *"I like to take my Polaroid camera on vacation,"* Jim said. *"That way, I can see right away how the pictures turned out."* □ *"Does this store carry Polaroid film?"* the customer asked.

polish   **1.** to make something shiny by rubbing it. □ *I polished the wooden tabletop.* □ *She polished the silver teapot.*

2. a substance that is applied to something to make it shiny. □ *This copper polish is great for my copper bottomed pots.* □ *She wore red nail polish.*

political map a map that shows political boundaries, such as those of countries, states, and cities. □ *I looked at a political map of Canada and noted the capital city of each province.* □ *The new political map showed the post-war borders of the country.*

polo shirt a knitted sports shirt with a collar that folds over. □ *I put on a polo shirt and some shorts.* □ CHARLIE: *How formal is this restaurant?* JANE: *Don't worry. You can wear your polo shirt.*

polyester a synthetic material. □ *These polyester pants are too hot to wear in the summer.* □ *This polyester shirt never needs ironing.*

polyurethane a synthetic varnish. □ *I used a high-gloss polyurethane to finish the cabinet I built.* □ *The floor has a polyurethane finish.*

polyvinyl chloride pipe AND **PVC pipe** a kind of plastic pipe. □ *The waste pipes in this building are all made of PVC pipe.* □ *I screwed the polyvinyl chloride pipe into the plastic fitting.*

pontoon bridge a bridge supported by floating structures. □ *There's a temporary pontoon bridge across the river.* □ *The pontoon bridge sank when one of the pontoons developed a leak.*

pop See SODA (POP).

popcorn corn that puffs open when heated, or puffed corn. □ *We ate popcorn while we watched the movie.* □ *I measured popcorn into the popcorn popper.*

popcorn popper a device that heats POPCORN until it pops. □ *Put a couple of tablespoons of oil in the popcorn* *popper, then add the popcorn.* □ *Hot, fluffy popcorn poured out of the hot-air popcorn popper.*

popover   a small, hollow MUFFIN made with egg batter. □ *I made popovers for breakfast.* □ *She opened the popover and spread it with butter.*

Popsicle™   a brand of frozen confection, made of sweet liquid frozen onto a stick. □ *"Daddy! Can I have a quarter for a Popsicle?" Jimmy begged.* □ *"When we were kids, we lived on Popsicles all summer long," Andy sighed.*

popsicle stick   a flat, round-ended wooden stick, such as those on which POPSICLES™ are frozen. □ *She built a lampshade out of popsicle sticks.* □ *I stuck a popsicle stick into the bottom of the apple and dunked the apple in melted caramel.*

porch   a platform attached to the ground level of a house, usually at a doorway. (See also BALCONY, GALLERY, VERANDA.) □ *I sat on the back porch and watched the children play in the yard.* □ *There's a screened-in porch on the front of the house.*

porous   able to absorb liquid; full of small holes. □ *This is good, porous soil. Plants will grow well here.* □ *This glue is for use only on porous materials.*

portable generator   an easily movable device for generating electricity. □ *When we go camping, we use a portable generator to run the TV.* □ *The electricity was out, so we hooked up the portable generator.*

Portacrib™   a brand of folding, portable crib. □ *"We brought a Portacrib for the baby in case she gets sleepy during the party," Ellen explained.* □ *"When I take my children to visit at my mother's house, I bring the Portacrib along," said Rick.*

portico   a small roof, supported by columns, in front of a building. □ *The mansion had a portico on the east side.* □ *I took shelter in the portico of the courthouse.*

postage meter   a machine that measures out postage for letters and packages. □ *I weighed the letter on the postage meter.* □ *The secretary took the postage meter to the post office and paid for the postage the company had used that month.*

postage scale   a device that weighs letters and packages and tells you how much it will cost to send them by mail. □ *According to the postage scale, I will need two air mail stamps for this letter.* □ *I weighed the package on my postage scale.*

post-consumer   used. (Describes the content of recycled material.) □ *This paper is 30% recycled, 10% post-consumer content.* □ *The bench was made of 50% post-consumer plastic.*

post hole   a cylindrical hole in the ground. (A *post hole digger* is a tool for making POST HOLES.) □ *I set the fence post into the post hole.* □ *They made a set of post holes along one side of the property.*

(potato) chips   thin, fried slices of potato. □ *All the sandwiches on the menu come with potato chips and a pickle.* □ *I had a soda and some chips for a snack.*

potato masher   a tool for mashing boiled potatoes and other soft foods. □ *I peeled the potatoes and mashed them with a potato masher.* □ *Use a potato masher to pulp the avocadoes.*

potato peeler   a device with a blade for cutting the peel off potatoes or other fruits and vegetables. □ *I peeled the potato with a potato peeler.* □ *Scrape the carrots with a potato peeler.*

potentiometer   an electrical control that can be adjusted continuously along a scale. □ *The volume control on this stereo is a potentiometer.* □ *The electrician replaced the potentiometer on the radio.*

pot holder AND **hot pad**   a pad used to protect the hand when touching a hot cooking utensil. (Compare with OVEN

MITT.) □ *She used a pot holder to grasp the handle of the saucepan.* □ *He got a hot pad for each hand when he reached into the oven for the cookie sheet.*

pot pie   a pie with a filling that is savory, not sweet. □ *We had chicken pot pie for dinner.* □ *I heated up the frozen beef pot pie in the microwave.*

potpourri   a mixture of sweet-smelling, dried plant material, such as flowers and wood chips. □ *I put some potpourri in a little dish on top of a candle, and as it heated up, the smell filled the room.* □ *I keep a little cloth bag of potpourri in my chest of drawers, to keep my clothes smelling sweet.*

pot roast   a piece of meat cooked in a pot with liquid. □ *We had pot roast for dinner.* □ *Brown the pot roast first, then put it in the pot with some stock.*

potty   a TOILET. (Usually used by adults when speaking to small children.) □ *Do you need to go to the potty?* □ *You'd better use the potty before we go.*

poultry   **1.** fowl raised for food. □ *Do you keep any poultry on your farm?* □ *We feed the poultry on dried corn and table scraps.* **2.** meat from fowl raised for food. □ *I don't eat red meat, but I do eat poultry.* □ *How are the prices on poultry at the grocery store?*

poultry seasoning   a mixture of spices for flavoring POULTRY. □ *Sprinkle a little poultry seasoning on the chicken before you bake it.* □ *I put some poultry seasoning into the breading on my fried chicken.*

pound cake   a rich, dense cake made with eggs and butter. (A traditional POUND CAKE recipe calls for a pound of eggs, a pound of butter, a pound of sugar, and a pound of flour.) □ *Dessert was pound cake with strawberries.* □ *We had coffee and pound cake.*

pour spout   a pointed opening for pouring liquid out of a package. □ *The bottle of laundry soap has a convenient pour spout.* □ *I folded out the pour spout on the milk carton.*

powdered milk   milk with all the water removed. (See also CONDENSED MILK, EVAPORATED MILK.) ☐ *I keep a box of powdered milk on hand in case we run out of milk.* ☐ *I use powdered milk for baking instead of whole milk.*

powdered sugar AND **confectioner's sugar**   very finely ground sugar. (Compare with GRANULATED SUGAR.) ☐ *She dusted the cookies with powdered sugar.* ☐ *Use confectioner's sugar to make the frosting.*

power brakes   car or truck brakes with a device that helps apply pressure, so that the driver does not have to press the brake pedal very hard in order to apply the brakes. ☐ *The car has power steering and power brakes.* ☐ *There's a problem in the vacuum hose in the power brakes.*

power cord   a wire or set of wires that carries power to a device. ☐ *Plug the power cord into the socket in the back of the laptop.* ☐ *The vacuum cleaner has a long power cord, so that you can move it around an entire room.*

power drill   a drill rotated by electric power. ☐ *I use the screwdriver tip on the power drill to put screws into wood.* ☐ *Turn the chuck key to secure the bit in the power drill.*

power saw   a saw moved by electric power. ☐ *I used the power saw to cut the lumber to the right size.* ☐ *He ran the power saw across the board.*

power steering   a steering system with a hydraulic device that helps move a vehicle's wheels. ☐ *This car is easy to steer. It has power steering.* ☐ *I checked the power steering for leaks.*

power tool   a tool powered by electricity. ☐ *I do a lot of woodworking, so I have a number of power tools.* ☐ *The wood shop at school taught the children how to use power tools.*

power train   a mechanism that transfers power from an engine to an axle. ☐ *The differential is part of a car's power* train. ☐ *The mechanic checked the various components of the power train.*

preheat   to bring an oven to the required temperature before putting in the food to be cooked. ☐ *Preheat the oven to 350 degrees.* ☐ *Preheat the oven while you put your ingredients together.*

prepared food   food that has been cooked, seasoned, or mixed. ☐ *It's much more expensive to buy prepared food than to cook it yourself.* ☐ *I'm on a low-salt diet, so I have to check the salt content of prepared foods like breakfast cereals and canned soup.*

(prepared) mustard   a mixture of ground mustard seeds and water. (Compare with DRY MUSTARD.) ☐ *Add a tablespoon of prepared mustard.* ☐ *I spread mustard on the hamburger bun.*

preservative   a chemical added to food to keep it from spoiling. ☐ *This whole-grain bread contains no preservatives.* ☐ *A preservative has been added to the packaging of this breakfast cereal.*

preserves   large pieces of fruit preserved by boiling in sugar syrup. ☐ *I spread apricot preserves on the toast.* ☐ *Dessert was vanilla ice cream topped with cherry preserves.*

pre-shrunk   already washed, so as not to shrink in further washing. ☐ *CUSTOMER: These jeans fit OK now, but what if they shrink? SALES CLERK: They're pre-shrunk.* ☐ *This denim shirt is made of pre-shrunk fabric.*

press   to apply heat and pressure to cloth in order to remove wrinkles. ☐ *I had the suit pressed at the dry cleaner's.* ☐ *You'd better press those pants before you wear them.*

press cloth   a cloth placed between an IRON and the item being ironed, in order to protect the item. ☐ *I dampened the press cloth and spread it over the silk blouse.* ☐ *Use a press cloth when you iron this linen tablecloth.*

pressed cookie   a cookie shaped by squeezing dough through a COOKIE PRESS or a COOKIE GUN. (See also BAR (COOKIE), DROP COOKIE.) □ *For a Christmas treat, Mom made pressed cookies in the shape of stars and Christmas trees.* □ *The dough for pressed cookies is rather soft.*

presser foot   a device that holds cloth flat underneath the needle of a sewing machine. □ *Lift the presser foot, cut the threads, and remove the cloth from the sewing machine.* □ *This lever moves the presser foot up and down.*

pressure cooker   a cooking pot with a tight-fitting lid, so that food inside is cooked quickly, at high pressure. □ *I boiled potatoes in the pressure cooker.* □ *Be very careful when taking the lid off the pressure cooker.*

prewash   a substance applied to cloth before washing, in order to remove stains. (See also STAIN REMOVER.) □ *Apply the prewash directly to the stain.* □ *I sprayed some prewash onto the shirt collar.*

prick   to make a small hole in something with a pointed instrument. □ *Prick the potatoes with a fork before baking them.* □ *I pricked a decorative pattern in the pie crust.*

prime a pump   to put liquid into a pump in order to get it started. □ *I moistened the nozzle of the spray bottle in order to prime the pump.* □ *You'll need to prime the pump in the garden. Here's some water.*

prime rib   beef ribs. □ *The restaurant is famous for their prime rib.* □ *Prime rib should be cooked for a long time at low temperatures.*

printer   a device that prints information from computer files onto paper. □ *I need an IBM compatible printer.* □ *All the computers in our office are hooked up to a single printer.*

print head   the part of a PRINTER that presses against the page to form the characters. □ *Align the top of the page with the print head.* □ *The print quality is blurred. It looks like you will need to replace the print head.*

printout a set of pages on which information from a computer is printed. □ *The doctor gave me a printout showing my blood cholesterol levels.* □ *A printout of the entire database would be several hundred pages long.*

probe a long, thin device used to examine something. □ *The mechanic clipped a probe to the car's exhaust pipe.* □ *The dental hygienist examined my gums with a curved probe.*

produce fruits and vegetables. □ *The grocery store on the corner always has nice, fresh produce.* □ *We bought some produce from a roadside stand out in the country.*

projection TV a device that projects a television picture onto a large screen. (See also BIG SCREEN TV.) □ *The sports bar has a projection TV. It's a great place to go to watch a football game.* □ *I rented a projection TV and invited my friends over to watch videos.*

prong a thin, pointed, rigid structure. □ *The prongs on the printer plug fit into brackets in the parallel port on the computer.* □ *Place the hole in the page over the metal prong in the binder.*

proof of purchase something, often a printed certificate, that proves that you bought a particular item. □ *To get the $5 rebate, send in your proof of purchase and a cash register receipt.* □ *Send in ten proofs of purchase from this cereal, and we will send you this plastic model rocket!*

propane torch a device that burns propane to produce a controllable flame. □ *The plumber soldered the pipes together with a propane torch.* □ *You should wear eye protection when you use a propane torch.*

protective goggles a plastic device worn to protect the eyes. □ *Wear protective goggles when you use the power saw.* □ *The students in the chemistry lab all wore protective goggles.*

protocol a procedure for transferring data from one computer to another. □ *Your computer must use the same* *communications protocol as the computer from which you wish to download information.* □ *This communications program uses the XMODEM protocol.*

prune **1.** a dried plum. □ *The pastry filling contains prunes, sugar, and brandy.* □ *I had a few prunes for a snack.* **2.** to cut branches or shoots from a plant. □ *You'll need to prune the rosebushes if you want them to bloom.* □ *I pruned the apple tree.*

pruning shears a large, heavy pair of blades used to PRUNE plants. □ *She trimmed the hedge with pruning shears.* □ *I got the pruning shears sharpened at the hardware store.*

prybar a flat tool with one end bent, used to pry flat things. □ *She pulled the molding from the wall with a prybar.* □ *I worked the prybar under the lid of the crate.*

PST See PACIFIC STANDARD TIME.

P-trap a pipe bent in a U-shape, used to prevent sewer gas from going up into a sink or toilet. □ *I opened the plug at the bottom of the P-trap and let the water out.* □ *The P-trap under the kitchen sink rusted through.*

public address system AND **PA** a device that amplifies sound and broadcasts it through a set of speakers. (Compare with INTERCOM.) □ *The principal addressed the school over the PA.* □ *A public address system was set up at the fairground.*

pudding a soft, usually sweet food made with thickened milk. □ *I made chocolate pudding for dessert.* □ *Stir the pudding constantly over low heat.*

pull-down menu a computer menu that is only visible when you use a mouse or the keyboard to select it. □ *A pull-down menu lists the type of fonts available.* □ *Click the left mouse button on the menu bar to see the pull-down menu.*

pulley a wheel with a grooved edge. (A rope or chain can be passed over the PULLEY, fitting into the groove, and a load at one end of the rope or chain can then be raised by pulling on the other end.) ☐ *They raised the iron beam by a pulley in the ceiling.* ☐ *The clothesline ran on a pulley.*

pull-out sofa   See SOFA BED.

pullover   a sweater put on by pulling it over the head. (Compare with CARDIGAN. See also SLIPOVER.) ☐ *I put on a wool pullover.* ☐ *She was knitting a pullover.*

pulp   **1.** a mushy, fibrous substance. ☐ *Paper is made from wood pulp.* ☐ *The hail storm crushed my flowers to a pulp.* **2.** the soft, fibrous part of some fruits or vegetables. ☐ *Cut off the tops of the tomatoes and scoop out the pulp.* ☐ *Chop up the squash pulp and boil it.*

pumpernickel   a sourdough bread made with rye flour. ☐ *I bought a loaf of pumpernickel.* ☐ *He spread cream cheese on a piece of pumpernickel.*

pumpkin pie spice   a mixture of spices for flavoring pumpkin pie, usually including cinnamon, nutmeg, and cloves. ☐ *Add a tablespoon of pumpkin pie spice to the mashed pumpkin.* ☐ *I put a dash of pumpkin pie spice in the hot apple cider.*

pumps   low-cut shoes worn on formal occasions. ☐ *These black pumps go with most of my dresses.* ☐ *I polished my white pumps.*

punch   **1.** a device for making holes in something. ☐ *I put the stack of papers in the paper punch.* ☐ *She used a punch to make decorative holes in the leather belt.* **2.** a drink made of a number of ingredients, often including liquor. ☐ *We have fruit punch for the children, and rum punch for the grown-ups.* ☐ *I poured ginger ale into the strawberry punch.*

push mower   a LAWN MOWER operated by pushing it across the grass. ☐ *By the time I finished mowing the lawn with the push mower, I was exhausted.* ☐ *When he finished with the push mower, he used a rake to gather up the grass clippings.*

push pin   a pin designed to be pushed into a surface with the fingers. (See also THUMB TACK.) ☐ *I put the postcard on the bulletin board with a push pin.* ☐ *She hung up the poster with push pins.*

putty   a flexible, somewhat sticky material used to fill gaps and cracks. ☐ *Putty held the window in place.* ☐ *I worked putty into the gap in the door frame.*

putty knife   a knife with a flat, dull blade, used for working with PUTTY and other pliable substances. ☐ *She worked the putty into the window frame with a putty knife.* ☐ *I spread spackling into the nail hole with a putty knife.*

PVC pipe   See POLYVINYL CHLORIDE PIPE.

Q

Q-Tip™   a brand of COTTON SWAB. □ *"Is it safe for me to clean the baby's ears with a Q-Tip?" the young mother asked her doctor.* □ *"Use a Q-Tip to put ointment on the wound," suggested the nurse.*

quarter   **1.** a coin worth twenty-five cents. □ *The washing machine takes three quarters.* □ *Can you give me four quarters for this dollar bill?* **2.** to cut something into four equal pieces. □ *Quarter the potatoes lengthwise.* □ *I quartered the sandwiches.*

queen-size bed   a large bed, roughly seven by seven and a half feet. □ *The hotel room has one queen-size bed.* □ *The queen-size bed took up most of the small bedroom.*

quick bread   a bread leavened with baking powder or baking soda, not requiring rising time, as a yeast bread does. □ *I have a recipe for banana quick bread.* □ *Pour the quick bread batter into a greased loaf pan.*

quilt   **1.** a padded blanket with the layers sewed together. □ *The quilt keeps the bed warm on even the chilliest nights.* □ *My grandmother made this patchwork quilt.* **2.** to sew the layers of a blanket together, especially with decorative stitching patterns. □ *The club gets together every week to quilt.* □ *After piecing the top of the patchwork quilt, I basted it to the padding and the backing and began to quilt it.*

quilted   with layers sewed together. □ *I have a quilted jacket.* □ *The bathrobe was made of quilted fabric.*

quoin   a decorative stone or brick at the corner of a wall. □ *The red brick wall had limestone quoins.* □ *We used a different size of brick for the quoin.*

R

rabbit ears   a pair of antennas in a V shape. ☐ *I adjusted the rabbit ears on the TV until the picture cleared.* ☐ *Pull out both of the rabbit ears on the radio.*

racing bike   a light bicycle with U-shaped handles and narrow tires, designed for riding in races. ☐ *The athlete rode a racing bike around the track.* ☐ *She bought a special seat for her racing bike.*

rack and pinion   a gear system with a round gear rolling along a flat one. (Many cars have steering systems based on a RACK AND PINION.) ☐ *This model has rack and pinion steering.* ☐ *I like the smooth feel of the rack and pinion steering.*

rack of lamb   lamb ribs. ☐ *I served roast rack of lamb to my dinner guests.* ☐ *I checked the prices on rack of lamb at the meat counter.*

radar detector   a device that alerts you if a police radar is being used nearby. ☐ *The radar detector showed that everything was clear. The truck driver sped up.* ☐ *The radar detector is picking up something. Looks like there's a speed trap up ahead.*

radial tire   a tire with belts of strong cloth or metal passing across the tire from rim to rim. ☐ *The radial tires are more expensive, but they should last longer.* ☐ *The used car has a good, solid set of radial tires.*

radiator   **1.** a set of looped pipes through which steam or hot water passes, heating a room. (See also CONVECTOR.) ☐ *I bled the air out of the radiator.* ☐ *The boiler is working, but the radiator isn't warming up.* **2.** a device that gives off the heat from an engine into the outside air. ☐ *I checked the fluid level in the radiator.* ☐ *There's a leak in the hose leading into the radiator.*

radiator core   the tubes inside a car or truck RADIATOR. ☐ *The radiator core had rusted out and needed to be replaced.* ☐ *The mechanic flushed the fluid out of the radiator core.*

radiator grille   a set of openings at the front of a car, through which hot air from the RADIATOR can escape. ☐ *She polished the gleaming chrome on the radiator grille.* ☐ *The name of the car manufacturer was molded into the radiator grille.*

rafter   a wood or metal beam supporting a roof. ☐ *I nailed roofing material onto the rafters.* ☐ *The swing hung from a rafter in the cabin.*

raglan sleeve   a sleeve attached by a straight diagonal seam from the neck to the underarm. ☐ *The cotton dress has raglan sleeves.* ☐ *Raglan sleeves are easy to sew.*

Raid™   a brand of INSECTICIDE. ☐ *"Ick! There's a roach! Give me the Raid!" hollered Bill.* ☐ *"I'll put a good dose of Raid under the sink," said Jim.*

railroad crossing   a place where railroad tracks cross a road. ☐ *The school bus stopped at the railroad crossing.* ☐ *The lights at the railroad crossing were flashing.*

raised bed   a tall-sided container for dirt, in which plants can be grown. ☐ *I'm growing vegetables in raised beds.* ☐ *There was a raised bed full of petunias in the front yard.*

rake   **1.** a tool for gathering leaves, grass clippings, etc., from a wide area into a pile. ☐ BILL: *Where do you keep your rake?* SALLY: *In the tool shed.* ☐ *I see the leaves are falling. It's time to get out my rake.* **2.** to use a RAKE on something. ☐ *Joe is outside, raking the lawn.* ☐ *After I mow the grass, I rake up the grass clippings.*

RAM   See RANDOM ACCESS MEMORY.

ramekin   a small, cylindrical, ceramic bowl. ☐ *Pour the beaten egg into a greased ramekin.* ☐ *She served individual ramekins of chocolate custard.*

ranch (dressing)   a salad dressing made with BUTTERMILK and seasonings. □ *I put ranch dressing on my salad.* □ *What kind of dressing would you like? We have French, Thousand Island, Italian, and ranch.*

rancid   [of fat] spoiled. □ *This butter is rancid.* □ *The food was ruined by cooking it in rancid oil.*

random access memory AND **RAM**   a kind of computer memory which can both take in and give out information. (Compare with READ-ONLY MEMORY.) □ *How many meg of RAM does this machine have?* □ *This program requires 640 kilobytes of random access memory.*

range   See (KITCHEN) RANGE.

range finder   a device that determines the distance between a camera and the object being photographed. □ *I looked at the range finder so that I would know what aperture setting to use.* □ *The photographer peered through the range finder.*

range hood   a structure above a (KITCHEN) RANGE that usually contains a light and a fan to remove heat and smoke. □ *I cleaned the grease off the range hood.* □ *Turn on the fan in the range hood.*

rapid transit   a fast public transportation system, such as a SUBWAY or elevated railway. □ *You can take rapid transit from the airport to downtown.* □ *I always commute via rapid transit.*

rasp   a tool for scraping wood. □ *The carpenter worked the rasp along the grain of the wood.* □ *Use a rasp to round off the corner of the board.*

ratchet   **1.** a device with a toothed wheel that can be moved in only one direction. (A RATCHET in the handle of a wrench or screwdriver makes it easier to turn nuts or screws.) □ *Use a ratchet screwdriver to get the job done quickly.* □ *The ratchet wrench made it easy to loosen the stubborn nut.* **2.** to move something using a RATCHET. □ *I* positioned the jack under the car bumper and ratcheted the car up. ☐ I ratcheted the bolt into place.

ravel [for cloth] to come apart. ☐ The fabric was raveling at the edges. ☐ The knit shirt raveled at the seams.

raw sugar sugar from which the molasses has not been removed. ☐ I like to use raw sugar in my baking. ☐ He spooned raw sugar into his coffee.

rayon a synthetic material. ☐ This jacket is made of rayon. ☐ This fabric is thirty percent rayon, seventy percent polyester.

razor a tool with a blade for cutting off hair close to the skin. ☐ He shaved his face with a double-bladed razor. ☐ I need a new blade for my razor.

read-only memory AND **ROM** a kind of computer memory which stores information but does not allow you to put information in. (Compare with RANDOM ACCESS MEMORY.) ☐ The encyclopedia was published as a ROM disk. ☐ The computer's startup instructions are stored in read-only memory.

rearview mirror a mirror on a vehicle that allows you to see what is behind you. ☐ I looked in the rearview mirror before changing lanes. ☐ He adjusted the rearview mirror.

rear window defogger See REAR WINDOW DEFROSTER.

rear window defroster AND **rear window defogger** a device that heats the rear window of a car in order to remove frost and condensation. ☐ The rear window is fogging up. Turn on the rear window defroster. ☐ The rear window cleared as the rear window defogger heated up.

rebate a portion of the price of something returned to you after you buy it. ☐ To receive your $5 rebate on this toaster, simply send your cash register receipt to the following address. ☐ The car dealer is offering a $600 rebate on all of last year's models.

reboot to restart a computer. (See also BOOT (UP).) □ *CHARLIE: I can't get the computer to respond. MARY: You may have to reboot it.* □ *Press Control-Alt-Del to reboot.*

receipt a document that shows you paid for something. □ *All returned merchandise must be accompanied by a receipt.* □ *I made sure the receipt showed the correct total.*

receiver AND **handset** the part of a telephone that is held to the mouth and ear when speaking. (Compare with EARPIECE, MOUTHPIECE.) □ *I picked up the receiver and listened for a dial tone.* □ *Place the handset back in the cradle.*

rechargeable battery an electric battery that can store electric current from a wall outlet. (See also NICAD™ BATTERY.) □ *The clock runs on rechargeable batteries.* □ *Plug in the rechargeable batteries for at least four hours.*

recliner (chair) a chair that can be set in a reclined, horizontal position. □ *Pull the lever toward you to put the recliner chair in the reclined position.* □ *We all chipped in to buy Grandma a recliner.*

record **1.** a long-playing vinyl disc that contains music or other sounds. □ *I put a record on the turntable.* □ *What record is that song on?* **2.** to store sound or pictures on an electronic medium, such as audiotape or videotape. □ *I want to record that TV program.* □ *I recorded a new message for my answering machine.*

recycle to use old materials to make new things. □ *Do they recycle newsprint in your neighborhood?* □ *These plastic milk jugs can be recycled.*

recycling bin a container for things that are to be RECYCLED. □ *Put the glass jars in the blue recycling bin.* □ *I took the recycling bins out to the curb to be collected.*

redial to dial a number again. □ *This button will redial the phone.* □ *The modem has an automatic redial feature.*

red meat   meat from a mammal. ☐ *I eat fish and poultry, but not red meat.* ☐ *The doctor warned me to limit the amount of red meat I eat.*

refinish   to remove the old surface of wood and put on a new one. ☐ *I refinished the old desk.* ☐ *The hardwood floor needs to be refinished.*

reflector   a plastic device that reflects light. ☐ *My headlights picked up a red bicycle reflector.* ☐ *These running shoes have reflectors on the heels.*

refrigerant   a fluid that absorbs and releases heat easily. ☐ *I had to put new refrigerant in my car's air conditioner.* ☐ *The refrigerant passes through the cooling coil.*

refrigerator AND **icebox**   a device that keeps food cool. ☐ *Put the milk in the refrigerator.* ☐ *The leftovers are in a yellow plastic bowl in the icebox.*

refrigerator cookie   a cookie made of dough that must be chilled before it is shaped. ☐ *Jill made a batch of refrigerator cookies.* ☐ *I made the dough for the refrigerator cookies today. I'll bake them tomorrow.*

relief map   a map that shows where land is high or low. (Compare with TOPO(GRAPHIC) MAP.) ☐ *Can you find the Andes mountains on this relief map?* ☐ *The relief map shows a low-lying area near the river.*

relish   a mixture of finely chopped, strongly flavored food, used to flavor or contrast with a main dish. ☐ *I would like some pickle relish for my hamburger, please.* ☐ *The catfish comes with a side of corn relish.*

remote (control)   a device that can control something else from a distance. ☐ *The model car is operated through this remote control.* ☐ *Hand me the remote for the VCR.*

reservoir   a space where a fluid is stored. ☐ *A window on the back of the steam iron lets you see how much water is in the reservoir.* ☐ *Fill the coffee decanter with the desired*

241

amount of water, and pour it into the reservoir of the coffee maker.

reset   to return a machine to the way it was before. ☐ *Reset the tape counter to zero.* ☐ *Reset the computer by pressing the "Reset" button.*

resin   a hard, clear glue. ☐ *Glue the paneling to the door with a waterproof resin.* ☐ *There are a number of resins that will bond with plastic.*

resolution   the level of detail visible on a screen or in a piece of printing. ☐ *Just look at the high resolution graphics available with this computer program.* ☐ *The low resolution of the printer made the printout hard to read.*

retaining wall   a wall that holds back a slope of earth. ☐ *There was a brick retaining wall at the bottom of the hill.* ☐ *A cement retaining wall ran alongside the highway.*

return address   the address of the person sending something. ☐ *Make sure to put your return address on the envelope.* ☐ *Type the return address at the top of the page.*

return duct   a passageway along which air moves from a room back to a furnace or an air-conditioning unit. ☐ *Clean the dust and dirt from the floor register leading to the return duct.* ☐ *Is this a supply duct or a return duct?*

reupholster   to remove the old cloth or leather covering from a piece of furniture and attach a new fabric. ☐ *I'm having the old easy chair reupholstered.* ☐ *He reupholstered the sofa in gray velvet.*

reverse   a gear that moves a vehicle backwards. ☐ *Put the car in reverse.* ☐ *When the truck is in reverse, a warning beep will sound, alerting people who may be behind it.*

rewind   **1.** to move audiotape or videotape quickly backward through a machine. ☐ *Make sure to rewind the movie after you are done watching it.* ☐ *The tape player will automatically rewind when it reaches the end of the tape.* **2.** a button which makes audiotape or videotape move quickly backward through a machine. (Contrasts with FAST-FORWARD.) □ *I pushed the rewind by mistake. I meant to push "play."* □ *The rewind is the button with the arrow pointing left.*

RGB [of a computer MONITOR, displaying images] in red, green, and blue. □ *This computer comes with an RGB monitor.* □ *You can hook up an RGB monitor to the laptop through this port.*

ribbon **1.** a thin strip of decorative material. □ *She tied a velvet ribbon in her hair.* □ *I put a red ribbon on the gift box.* **2.** a thin strip of material with ink in it, used in a typewriter or computer printer. □ *The typewriter needs a new ribbon. The old one is too faint.* □ *What kind of ribbon does that printer use?*

ribbon cable a wide, flat electrical cable with a number of wires running parallel to one another. □ *This ribbon cable is a Centronics parallel cable.* □ *A ribbon cable led from the modem to the terminal.*

rice **1.** a grain. □ *The sweet and sour shrimp comes with steamed rice.* □ *I added cooked rice to the soup.* **2.** to push a soft food through a RICER or other device with small holes. □ *Rice the potatoes, then add the flour and salt.* □ *The cook riced the cooked squash.*

ricer a tool that presses soft foods through small holes. □ *Put the boiled chestnuts through a potato ricer.* □ *She peeled the potatoes and pressed them through a ricer.*

rice vinegar vinegar made from fermented RICE WINE. □ *The salad dressing is made with rice vinegar.* □ *Rice vinegar is an ingredient in much Japanese cooking.*

rice wine wine made from RICE. □ *I added rice wine to the teriyaki sauce.* □ *He heated up a little rice wine for his guests.*

riding mower a gas-powered LAWN MOWER designed for a person to ride on. □ *Our backyard is big enough that it's* *convenient to use a riding mower.* □ *I put some gas in the riding mower so it would be all ready for next time.*

rifle   a gun with a spiral groove cut on the inside of a long barrel. (The groove makes the bullet spin, which makes it go further. Compare with SHOTGUN.) □ *What kind of ammunition do you use in your rifle?* □ *I'm taking my rifle to the practice range today.*

rim   the edge of a wheel, where the tire is attached. □ *The bicycle wheel is wobbling because there's a big dent in the rim.* □ *The tool pulled the tire off the rim.*

rind   the outer layer of a fruit or vegetable. □ *Grate the lemon rind.* □ *We ate the watermelon right down to the rind.*

ring mold   a deep, ring-shaped pan, used to shape food. □ *Put the Jell-O into a ring mold.* □ *Bake the rice custard in a ring mold.*

rinse   **1.** to clean something with a liquid, usually water. □ *Rinse the vegetables before chopping them.* □ *Work the shampoo into a full lather, then rinse the hair.* **2.** a liquid for cleaning something. □ *My dentist gave me a fluoride rinse to strengthen my tooth enamel.* □ *This henna rinse will bring out the color of your hair.*

riser   the vertical part of a step. □ *Nail the tread onto the riser.* □ *Make sure the riser is not too high.*

roadbed   the surface on which a road or a railroad is built. □ *The workers built up the roadbed over the dip in the ground.* □ *The asphalt cracked over the uneven roadbed.*

roast   **1.** to cook something in an oven or in a fire. □ *Roast the lamb for two hours at 300 degrees.* □ *We roasted ears of corn in the hot coals.* **2.** a piece of meat that has been ROASTED. □ *Will you carve the roast, please?* □ *I'm making a pork roast for lunch.*

roaster   a deep, covered pan for roasting meat in an oven. □ *Put the turkey in a roaster.* □ *I made gravy from the drippings in the roaster.*

roll   **1.** a small, specially shaped piece of baked bread dough. □ *The salads on our menu are served with fresh-baked rolls.* □ *I just love those crescent rolls you make.* **2.** something wound into a spiral. (See also COIL.) □ *I bought a roll of stamps.* □ *Each roll of wallpaper contains fifteen feet.*

rolled oats   oats that have been flattened by a roller. □ *Add 2/3 cup of rolled oats.* □ *This granola is made from whole, rolled oats.*

roller   See CURLER.

rolling boil   See FULL BOIL.

rolling pin   a cylindrical tool used to flatten dough. □ *Roll out the cookie dough with a rolling pin.* □ *Dust the rolling pin with flour.*

Rolodex™   a brand of rotating card file that can be turned to show the card you want. □ *"Let me write your name and phone number in my Rolodex," said the agent.* □ *"File that business card in your Rolodex," the boss advised.*

ROM   See READ-ONLY MEMORY.

root directory   the highest-level DIRECTORY on a computer disk. □ *There are four sub-directories under the root directory.* □ *The program is stored in the root directory.*

rotary beater   an EGG BEATER with a crank that is turned by hand. □ *It took forever to whip the egg whites with that rotary beater.* □ *I used a rotary beater to beat the cake mix.*

rotary cutter   a tool with a handle and a circular, rolling blade. □ *She used a rotary cutter to cut out the clothing pattern.* □ *The rotary cutter can cut through several layers of fabric.*

rotary dial   a round telephone dial that must be rotated for each digit. □ *A phone with a rotary dial will not work on a Touch Tone phone line.* □ *If you are calling from a phone with a rotary dial, please stay on the line. Someone will assist you shortly.*

rotisserie   a device that cooks food by slowly turning it over an open flame. (See also SPIT.) □ *I put a couple of chickens on the rotisserie.* □ *The cook basted the leg of lamb on the rotisserie.*

rotor   **1.** the disc that presses a brake pad against a wheel in a DISC BRAKE. □ *The rotors are fine, but the brake pads need to be replaced.* □ *The mechanic adjusted the rotors so that they would not drag against the wheel.* **2.** a rotating device that delivers current to each spark plug of an engine in turn; part of a DISTRIBUTOR. □ *The rotor was stuck in one position.* □ *Is the rotor delivering the correct voltage to the spark plug?*

round   meat from the hind thigh of a cow. □ *He ordered the grilled round.* □ *You can use ground round in this recipe.*

rounded   [of a measuring device that is] a little more than full. □ *Add a rounded teaspoonful of sugar.* □ *I put in a couple of rounded spoonfuls of cornstarch.*

roundhouse   a round building where LOCOMOTIVES are serviced. □ *The old stone roundhouse was turned into a shopping center.* □ *The train track in the middle of the roundhouse could rotate, so that a locomotive could go in or out of any of the bays.*

round trip   a trip from and back to the same place. □ *The round trip to Farmersville is twenty miles.* □ *This ticket is good for a round trip.*

rubber cement   an adhesive with a texture-like rubber. □ *I spread rubber cement on the paper.* □ *The picture is attached with rubber cement. It can easily be pulled off.*

(rubber) lid grip   a flat piece of rubber with a rough surface, used to grip the lid of a jar and twist it off. □ *I can't get* *this jar lid off. I need the rubber lid grip.* □ *I tried every-thing to open the jar. Finally, the lid grip worked.*

rubber scraper AND **rubber spatula** a tool with a flat rubber blade on a handle, used for scraping food from curved surfaces. □ *I used a rubber scraper to get every last bit of cake batter out of the bowl.* □ *She got the last of the peanut butter out of the jar with a rubber spatula.*

rubber spatula See RUBBER SCRAPER.

rubbing alcohol isopropyl alcohol. □ *I disinfected the cut with rubbing alcohol.* □ *The nurse massaged the patient with rubbing alcohol.*

ruffle a decorative band of PLEATED fabric. □ *A white ruf-fle ran around the edge of the bedspread.* □ *There was a ruffle at the neck of the blouse.*

rump roast a piece of meat from the hind end of a cow. □ *I put the rump roast in the oven at 350 degrees.* □ *This rump roast will make a good meal.*

run the depth, from front to back, of a stair TREAD. □ *These steps have a run of fifteen inches.* □ *The carpenter measured the run of the stairs.*

rung a step on a ladder. □ *I climbed up the ladder one rung at a time.* □ *The wooden rungs were old and creaky.*

runner **1.** a strip of cloth or carpeting used to protect a surface. □ *The embroidered linen table runner looked love-ly.* □ *The stair runner needs to be taken down and cleaned.* **2.** a plant shoot that can develop roots and grow into a new plant. □ *The spider plant is putting out several runners.* □ *By the end of the summer, the strawberry runners had grown into sturdy new plants.*

runway a usually paved strip of land where airplanes take off and land. □ *The plane gathered speed as it moved down the runway.* □ *I saw the plane touch down on the runway.*

rush bottom(ed)   having a seat made of the woven stems of rushes from plants. □ *Just look at this antique rush bottomed chair!* □ *Rush bottom furniture repaired here.*

rust inhibitor   a substance added to a car or truck radiator to keep it from rusting inside. □ *I put in some rust inhibitor along with the coolant.* □ *What brand of rust inhibitor does the manufacturer recommend?*

rust remover   a substance that removes rust from metal. □ *The bicycle frame could use some rust remover.* □ *I sprayed rust remover on the metal chair.*

rye bread   bread made with rye flour. □ *I have a delicious recipe for Swedish rye bread.* □ *Would you like that sandwich on white, wheat, or rye?*

S

saber saw a hand-held, electric-powered saw with a short, thin blade that moves up and down. □ *I cut an opening in the board with a saber saw.* □ *The saber saw cut through the metal plate.*

saddle the seat of a bicycle. □ *This saddle is too wide for me.* □ *Try raising the saddle on that bike.*

safety a latch that keeps an automatic weapon from firing accidentally. □ *Cock the pistol and engage the safety.* □ *The safety is on, so the gun won't fire, even if you pull the trigger.*

safety belt AND **seat belt** a strip of strong cloth designed to hold a person in a vehicle seat during a crash. □ *Please fasten your safety belts.* □ *I got in the car and put on my seat belt.*

safety rail a bar that can be grasped to keep you from falling. □ *I had a safety rail installed in the bathtub.* □ *The wind blew hard, but I held onto the safety rail at the edge of the observation platform.*

safety valve a VALVE that opens if pressure is too great. □ *There is a safety valve near the top of the furnace.* □ *I removed the defective safety valve from the hot water heater.*

(salad) dressing a mixture of liquids and seasonings used to flavor a salad. □ *CHARLIE: What's in this salad dressing? MARY: It's just oil and vinegar.* □ *What kind of dressing would you like? We have bleu cheese, Thousand Island, ranch, and creamy Italian.*

salad spinner a device that cleans and dries leafy vegetables by spinning them. □ *I put several lettuce leaves in the salad spinner.* □ *Wash the spinach leaves in a salad spinner.*

salsa a spicy sauce made of chopped vegetables. (Spanish.) □ *We had chips and salsa for an appetizer.* □ *The bean burrito is served with green chile salsa.*

saltine (cracker) a thin piece of crisp, baked wheat dough, covered with salt. □ *I ate saltine crackers with my soup.* □ *JANE: What kind of crackers would you like? TOM: Saltines, please.*

salt shaker a container with holes in the top, used for holding and dispensing salt. □ *Pass me the salt shaker.* □ *I need to put more salt in the salt shaker.*

salt substitute a substance that tastes like salt but does not have the same effects on the body. □ *Because I have high blood pressure, I have to use salt substitute instead of salt.* □ *He sprinkled salt substitute on his potato.*

sander an electric-powered device for smoothing wood with SANDPAPER. □ *The sander made it easy to get the old paint off the door.* □ *I put a new belt on the sander.*

sanding block a block that can be covered with SANDPAPER. □ *I put a new sheet of sandpaper on the sanding block.* □ *The sanding block has a curved shape that's easy to hold.*

sandpaper thick paper with a layer of sand glued to one side. □ *Smooth the surface of the board with sandpaper.* □ *I cut a piece of sandpaper to fit the sanding block.*

sanitary napkin AND **feminine napkin; sanitary pad** a pad for absorbing menstrual blood. (FEMININE NAPKIN is a euphemism.) □ *It's getting near that time of the month. I'd better get a box of sanitary napkins.* □ *These feminine napkins are form-fitting to be extra comfortable.* □ *Do not flush sanitary pads down the toilet.*

sanitary pad See SANITARY NAPKIN.

Sanka™ a brand of decaffeinated instant coffee. □ *I told the waiter, "I'll have a cup of Sanka, please."* □ *WAITER: Would you like some coffee? CUSTOMER: Do you have Sanka?*

sash   **1.** a band of cloth tied around the body. □ *The dress has a pink silk sash.* □ *The mayor wore a satin sash across his chest.* **2.** a frame in which window glass is set. □ *Raise the sash and let in some air.* □ *There are four panes in each sash.*

sash bar   a wood or metal bar passing across a window SASH. □ *The sash bars separated the sash into four panes.* □ *One of the sash bars was rotted and mildewed.*

satin finish   [of paint] having a somewhat shiny surface. □ *They painted the walls with satin finish paint.* □ *This is a one-coat, satin finish enamel.*

saucepan   a deep pan with a long handle. □ *This non-stick saucepan is great for cooking rice.* □ *Fry the onions in a saucepan.*

saucer   a small plate, designed to hold a cup. □ *She set her teacup on the saucer.* □ *The saucer caught the spilled coffee.*

sauna   a STEAM bath. □ *The apartment building has a swimming pool and a sauna.* □ *Let's have a sauna after we work out.*

sauté   to cook something quickly in hot oil. □ *Sauté the chopped onions.* □ *The chef sautéed the peppers.*

sauté pan   a wide, flat-bottomed pan with straight sides and a long handle, used to SAUTÉ food. □ *The chef tossed the vegetables in the sauté pan.* □ *Heat the olive oil in a sauté pan.*

sawhorse   a wooden structure with four legs supporting a horizontal beam. □ *I set the board across a pair of sawhorses.* □ *The barrier consisted of sawhorses with a chain strung between them.*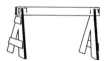

scald   to heat milk just to the boiling point. □ *Scald the milk and let it cool.* □ *After scalding the milk, sprinkle in one package of dry yeast.*

scan to search for a station on a radio or a track on an audio-tape or videotape. □ *Push that button to scan. If you find a station you want to listen to, push the button again to stop the scanning.* □ *Scan the tape until you find the song you want.*

scanner **1.** a device for reading a BAR CODE. □ *The cashier passed the box of cereal over the scanner, and the price appeared on the cash register.* □ *I gave my library books to the librarian, and she put them through the scanner to check them out to me.* **2.** a device that translates an image, such as a printed picture, into a computer file. □ *I put the photograph in the scanner and scanned it into the computer.* □ *If I had a scanner, I could put all kinds of images into my desktop publishing projects.*

scant not quite full. □ *Add a scant half cup of flour.* □ *The recipe calls for a scant tablespoon of molasses.*

scarf **1.** a piece of decorative cloth. □ *She tied a scarf over her hair to protect it from the wind.* □ *This hand-painted silk scarf is long enough to be worn as a belt.* **2.** a piece of thick cloth worn around the face and neck to keep them warm. (See also MUFFLER.) □ *The long, knitted scarf hung nearly to my knees.* □ *He tucked the ends of the scarf inside his coat collar.*

scissors a pair of blades joined by a hinge and having looped handles. (See also SHEARS.) □ *I used scissors to cut the cardboard.* □ *She snipped off the end of the thread with a sharp pair of scissors.*

scoop **1.** a tool with a handle and a cup or shovel-like blade on one end. □ *There's a plastic scoop in the flour canister.* □ *I used a scoop to get the candy out of the bulk bin.* **2.** to move something with a SCOOP or similar tool. □ *I scooped cornmeal out of the box.* □ *She scooped some dog food into the dog's bowl.*

scoop neck a garment neck with a deep, round opening. (See also BOAT NECK, CREW NECK, V NECK.) □ *The tank top has a scoop neck.* □ *The graceful scoop neck of the dress is edged with lace.*

scope See TELESCOPIC SIGHT.

scorch to heat something until it turns brown. □ *The iron is too hot. It will scorch the cloth.* □ *I left the pot on the burner too long, and it got scorched.*

score to make a straight, shallow cut in something. □ *Score the cardboard along the fold line.* □ *I scored the ice on the windshield with the blade of my scraper.*

Scotchgard™ a brand of chemical that protects cloth. (You may hear this word used as a verb.) □ *"This carpet is treated with Scotchgard," said the label.* □ *"I sprayed Scotchgard on my raincoat, and now the water just rolls off," said Linda.*

Scotch™ tape a brand of clear adhesive tape. □ *"Use Scotch tape to attach the picture to the page," said the instructions.* □ *"I need a piece of Scotch tape," Martha said, holding out her hand.*

scouring pad a piece of abrasive material, used for cleaning. □ *Is this scouring pad safe to use on non-stick pans?* □ *I scrubbed away at the layer of burned cheese with a heavy-duty scouring pad.*

scrambled eggs eggs that have been stirred while cooking. □ *I had toast and scrambled eggs for breakfast.* □ *I put grated cheese into my scrambled eggs.*

scratching post a post covered with rough material for a cat to scratch. □ *My stupid cat sharpens his claws on everything except the scratching post.* □ *The scratching post is covered with carpeting and has a little bell on top.*

screw a small metal cylinder with a wide head and a spiral groove along it, used as a fastener. □ *I loosened the screws that held the switch plate in place.* □ *There's a screw loose on the door hinge.*

screwdriver a tool for turning a SCREW. □ *I need a Phillips head screwdriver, please.* □ *Turn the screwdriver counterclockwise.*

scroll **1.** to move the cursor up or down on a computer screen. □ *Scroll down a few pages more.* □ *I used the "up"-arrow key to scroll back up through the file.* **2.** [for material] to move up or down on a computer screen. □ *How do you stop the file from scrolling so fast?* □ *The "Scroll Lock" key will stop it from scrolling.*

scroll saw a saw with a thin blade held in a U-shaped metal frame. □ *Use a scroll saw to cut a design in the edge of the board.* □ *I put a plastic-cutting blade in the scroll saw*

scroll work fancy patterns cut in wood. □ *Just look at the scroll work on the back of that chair.* □ *The balcony railing was ornamented with scroll work.*

scrubber a tool, such as a sponge or SCOURING PAD, for rubbing or scraping dirt off something. □ *I put a little dishwashing soap on the scrubber.* □ *This scrubber is specially designed for cleaning bathroom porcelain.*

scrub brush a brush for cleaning. □ *I used a scrub brush to get the soap deposits off the bathroom tiles.* □ *I have a long-handled scrub brush for cleaning pots and pans.*

seal **1.** to close something so tightly that nothing can get through. □ *Seal the edge of the tub with silicone caulk.* □ *I sealed the jars of preserves with a layer of wax.* **2.** the filling up of a gap. (See also GASKET.) □ *The rubber gasket forms a tight seal.* □ *The seal between the pipes has broken. There's a leak.* **3.** something that fills a gap. □ *Remove the plastic seal from the faucet assembly.* □ *Pry out the rubber O-ring seal.*

sealant a substance used to fill a joint or a crack in concrete. □ *Spread the sealant into the joint between the concrete slabs.* □ *The construction workers filled the cracks in the road with sealant.*

sealer a substance that forms a protective cover on something. □ *I put blacktop sealer on my new asphalt driveway.* □ *Use a waterproof sealer on your wooden deck.*

seam   a line of sewing that joins pieces of cloth. □ *There is a seam along the outside of the pants leg.* □ *A curved seam helps to shape the garment.*

seam allowance   the distance between the edge of a piece of cloth and the place where a SEAM is to be sewn. □ *This pattern has a ⅜-inch seam allowance.* □ *Mark the seam allowance on your pattern pieces.*

seam binding   a strip of fabric sewn over the raw edges of a SEAM to keep them from raveling. □ *Use a seam binding in a matching color.* □ *Press the seam binding to fit the curved edge.*

seam ripper   a tool for ripping out a line of stitching. □ *I quickly dismantled the garment with a seam ripper.* □ *Use a seam ripper to remove that badly stitched seam.*

sear   to cook something over high heat, burning the surface. □ *Put the prime rib in a 450-degree oven for ten minutes. The high heat will sear the meat, locking the juices in.* □ *Sear the chile peppers, then wrap them in moist towels. The skins will then come off easily.*

season   **1.** to add something flavorful to a food. □ *Season the meat with rosemary, salt, and pepper.* □ *The soup was seasoned with garlic oil.* **2.** to dry out lumber so that it can be used. □ *Those boards will warp if they haven't been seasoned.* □ *This wood was seasoned in a dry oven.*

seasoned salt   a mixture of salt and spices. □ *I sprinkled seasoned salt on my salad.* □ *Put a little seasoned salt on the French fries.*

seasoning   a flavorful substance, such as a SPICE. □ *What kind of seasoning did you put in this casserole? It's delicious!* □ *Oregano and basil are popular seasonings in Italian cooking.*

seat belt   See SAFETY BELT.

sedan   a car with front and back seats and either two or four doors. □ *Come in and test-drive this luxury sedan.* □ *This model is available as a sedan or a station wagon.*

sedative AND **tranquilizer**   a drug that makes you calm. ☐ *The doctor prescribed a sedative to stop the patient's fits of hysteria.* ☐ *The nurse gave the nervous woman a tranquilizer.*

sediment   fine particles of something that do not dissolve in a liquid and fall to the bottom of a container. ☐ *There is a brown sediment in this glass of water.* ☐ *A sediment had formed in the container of paint thinner.*

seeder   a device that spreads seeds over the ground. ☐ *I filled the seeder with grass seeds and pushed it over the lawn.* ☐ *She used the seeder to plant a large bed of prairie flowers.*

selector   a control that allows you to choose one of several options. ☐ *Move the temperature selector to "cold."* ☐ *Adjust the speed selector on the record player to match the disc you want to play.*

self-cleaning oven   an oven that can be set to a very high temperature in order to get rid of grease and spilled food inside it. ☐ *This self-cleaning electric oven also has a built-in timer.* ☐ *I set the self-cleaning oven to "clean."*

self-defrosting   removing frost and ice automatically. ☐ *Is this freezer self-defrosting?* ☐ *The self-defrosting freezer compartment has an optional ice maker attachment.*

self-healing   able to join cuts and cracks back together. ☐ *This cutting surface is made of self-healing plastic.* ☐ *To cut out patterns, I use a rotary cutter and a self-healing cutting mat.*

self-rising flour   a mixture of flour and baking powder. ☐ *The pancakes require two cups of self-rising flour.* ☐ *If you use self-rising flour, omit the baking powder listed in the recipe.*

self-seeding   dropping its own seeds; not needing a person to plant the seeds. ☐ *Are these herbs self-seeding?* ☐ *I thought I would try a self-seeding grass for the backyard.*

self-serve   See SELF-SERVICE.

self-service AND **self-serve**   requiring customers to get or do something themselves. (SELF-SERVE is informal. Contrasts with FULL SERVICE.) □ *I pulled up to the self-service gas pump.* □ *The restaurant has a self-serve soft drink machine.*

self-stick   See SELF-STICKING.

self-sticking AND **self-stick**   not needing to be moistened in order to stick to something. □ *New self-sticking stamps are available at your local post office.* □ *I peeled the protective paper from the self-stick envelope and pressed the flap down.*

self-timer   See AUTO TIMER.

selvage   a lengthwise edge of a woven piece of cloth. □ *Put the edge of the pattern up against the selvage.* □ *The arrow on the pattern piece should be placed parallel to the selvage.*

semisweet chocolate   a mixture of chocolate and sugar. □ *Use a twelve-ounce bag of semisweet chocolate chips.* □ *Melt two ounces of semisweet chocolate in the top of a double boiler.*

sensor   a device that detects something. □ *The sensor on the dashboard tells you that the exhaust system needs an overhaul.* □ *A sensor on the camera tells you if you need to use the flash.*

separates   garments that can be worn in different combinations. □ *There's a sale on knit separates at the department store.* □ *Instead of buying a dress, I got a number of separates—a blouse, a skirt, and a pair of slacks.*

septic system   a system for removing toilet waste from a building, treating it, and allowing it to drain into the ground. (See also CESSPOOL, SEPTIC TANK.) □ *We hired a contractor* *to install a septic system for our country house.* □ *The building is too far away from the town sewer lines. We'll have to install a septic system.*

septic tank   an underground tank for collecting and treating SEWAGE. (See also CESSPOOL, SEPTIC SYSTEM.) □ *A cast iron pipe leads from the house out to the septic tank.* □ *I added chemicals to the septic tank to speed up the sewage decomposition.*

serial cable   a computer cable that transmits information one bit at a time. (Compare with PARALLEL CABLE.) □ *The mouse is connected by a serial cable.* □ *You can use either a serial cable or a parallel cable to hook up the printer.*

serial number   a unique identification number. □ *The insurance card shows the serial number of my car.* □ *I copied down the computer's serial number.*

serial port   a place where a serial computer cable can be plugged in. (Compare with PARALLEL PORT.) □ *The laptop has both a parallel and a serial port.* □ *Plug the mouse into the serial port.*

serrated   having small points or teeth along the edge. □ *Use a serrated knife to slice the bread.* □ *The serrated butcher knife cut cleanly through the roast.*

service   to repair or maintain something. □ *We service all makes and models of IBM-compatible PCs.* □ *Where do you usually have your car serviced?*

service panel   an electrical panel where electricity from outside power lines is connected to the circuits in the building. □ *We checked the circuit breakers on the service panel.* □ *The hot wire is connected to a terminal on the service panel.*

service station   a business that sells gasoline and repairs cars. (See also GAS STATION.) □ *My car engine's making a funny sound. I'll have to take it to the service station.* □ *I got my oil changed at the service station.*

serving   a portion of food. □ *This yogurt has 150 calories per serving.* □ *I had several servings of the tuna casserole.*

set   [for an adhesive] to become solid. □ *It takes an hour for the glue to set.* □ *Keep the pieces of wood clamped together while the glue sets.*

set-in sleeve   a sleeve cut out separately and sewn onto a garment. □ *The shirt has set-in sleeves.* □ *The set-in sleeves have double-stitched seams.*

set screw   a screw that holds something in place. □ *The set screw on the lock cylinder is loose, and the cylinder is wiggling from side to side.* □ *Fasten the set screw into the hole on the light fixture.*

78   a phonograph disc designed to be played at 78 revolutions per minute. (78s were popular in the first half of the 20th century but are no longer made.) □ *I have a set of 78s of John Phillip Sousa marches.* □ *This is a tape recording of an old 78.*

sewage   waste water, urine, and feces. □ *The septic tank treats the sewage before letting it drain into the ground.* □ *This pipe carries sewage out of the building.*

sewing gauge   a small ruler with a sliding pointer, used to measure hems, seam allowances, and buttonholes. □ *Using a sewing gauge, I marked a 2-inch hem all the way around the bottom of the skirt.* □ *I marked the size of the button on the sewing gauge.*

shaft   a long, thin cylindrical structure. □ *The golf club has a metal shaft.* □ *The piston rotates this shaft.*

shakes   pieces of wood split from a log and used to cover a roof or the outside wall of a building. □ *The cabin walls were covered with cedar shakes.* □ *I need to replace some of the shakes on the roof.*

shampoo   soap for washing hair. □ *This shampoo has a strawberry scent.* □ *I worked the shampoo into my hair.*

shank   a straight part of something. □ *The shank of the bolt is half an inch in diameter.* □ *The screwdriver has a steel shank.*

shank button   a button sewed on by a metal loop on the bottom. □ *Is there a special technique for sewing on a shank button?* □ *I need a shank button to match the others on my coat.*

sharpener   a device for making something sharp. □ *I put the knife blade in the electric knife sharpener.* □ *This sharpener is especially for eyebrow pencils.*

sharpening steel   a long steel cylinder across which knives are drawn in order to sharpen them. □ *He sharpened the carving knife on the sharpening steel.* □ *The chef used a sharpening steel to keep her knives razor sharp.*

shaving cream   a foam applied to the skin in order to make it easier to shave. □ *He lathered his face with shaving cream.* □ *The shaving cream has a nice, fresh scent.*

shawl collar   a collar made of a wide band of fabric folded outward. □ *I like the shawl collar on that coat.* □ *The silk blouse has a shawl collar.*

shears   a pair of long blades joined by a hinge. (See also SCISSORS.) □ *I cut the fabric with my sewing shears.* □ *I used shears to trim Jill's hair.*

sheath   **1.** a close-fitting cover for something. □ *I put the knife in its plastic sheath.* □ *The pipe passes through an insulating sheath.* **2.** a close-fitting dress. □ *She wore a black silk sheath.* □ *The sheath fitted her exquisitely.*

sheer   easy to see through. □ *The blouse was made of sheer fabric.* □ *She wore a pair of sheer stockings.*

Sheetrock™   a brand of DRYWALL. □ *"The interior walls are made of Sheetrock," said the contractor.* □ *"Screw the Sheetrock to the wooden studs," Nancy told me.*

shelf paper   paper for covering shelves. ☐ *I put plastic-coated shelf paper on the kitchen shelves.* ☐ *I protected the bookshelves with shelf paper.*

shell   **1.** a thin, hard, outer covering. ☐ *The oysters were served in their shells.* ☐ *I peeled the shell off the egg.* **2.** to remove the SHELL from something. ☐ *Shell the peanuts.* ☐ *She quickly shelled the shrimp.* **3.** a women's close-fitting, short-sleeved, or sleeveless shirt. ☐ *This silk shell is perfect for wearing with a summer suit.* ☐ *She wore a tailored skirt and a sleeveless shell.* **4.** a computer program that makes it easier for you to communicate with the OPERATING SYSTEM program. ☐ *CHARLIE: What shell are you running? JANE: C Shell.* ☐ *You can modify the shell to respond to commands that you create.*

shellac   a glossy liquid used as a furniture finish. ☐ *When I dropped the box onto the table, the brittle shellac on the tabletop cracked.* ☐ *I wiped the chair with alcohol to remove the old shellac.*

shift key   a key on a computer or typewriter keyboard that, when engaged, makes a letter key type a capital letter or symbol. ☐ *To type a dollar sign, hold down the shift key and press the number 4.* ☐ *To see the Help menu, hold down the shift key and press F1.*

shim   a thin wedge of material used to fill a gap. ☐ *I put a shim between the girder and the floor joist to stop the squeak in the floor.* ☐ *He slipped a shim under the table leg to get the table level.*

shingle   a small, rectangular piece of building material. (Rows of SHINGLES are typically used to cover a roof.) ☐ *The roof of the cottage was made of stone shingles.* ☐ *The brick house had a roof of wooden shingles.*

shirt cardboard   a piece of cardboard around which a shirt can be folded to keep it neat. ☐ *I took the new shirt out of the package and removed the shirt cardboard.* ☐ *When I got my shirts back from the cleaners, they were folded around shirt cardboards.*

shirt tail   the part of a shirt that hangs below the waist in back. ☐ *His shirt tail was coming out from the top of his pants.* ☐ *Tuck in your shirt tail.*

shish kebab AND **kebab**   chunks of meat and vegetables skewered on a long stick and cooked on a grill. (KEBAB is informal.) ☐ *We had shish kebabs at the cookout.* ☐ *What would you like on your kebab—beef, chicken, or shrimp?*

shock absorber   a device that absorbs the bounces and shocks of traveling over a rough road. ☐ *The car bounces a lot even on smooth roads. It probably needs new shock absorbers.* ☐ *Where are the shock absorbers mounted on this model?*

shop vac   a heavy-duty vacuum cleaner that can be used to clean a workshop. (See also WET VAC.) ☐ *This shop vac is strong enough to pick up nuts and bolts.* ☐ *I cleaned up the sawdust with the shop vac.*

short circuit   a fault in an electric circuit that occurs when parts of the circuit touch each other. ☐ *The short circuit blew a fuse.* ☐ *There's a short circuit in this lamp somewhere.*

shortening   fat, such as butter or vegetable fat. (See also CRISCO™.) ☐ *This recipe calls for a cup and a half of shortening.* ☐ *Melt the shortening in a saucepan.*

short ribs   a cut of beef containing the ends of the ribs. ☐ *I put the short ribs on the grill.* ☐ *She ordered barbecued short ribs.*

short-term parking   parking where cars can be left for short periods of time. (Contrasts with LONG-TERM PARKING.) ☐ *When I went to the airport to pick up Bill, I left the car in short-term parking.* ☐ *Short-term parking is $1.50 an hour.*

shortwave radio   **1.** a kind of radio transmission that can travel long distances. ☐ *I communicate with my friend in Venezuela by shortwave radio.* ☐ *This radio picks up AM, FM, and shortwave radio.* **2.** a device that can receive

SHORTWAVE RADIO transmissions. □ *I listened to a BBC program on my shortwave radio.* □ *I picked up a faint signal on my shortwave radio.*

shot glass   a small glass that can hold one drink of hard liquor. □ *The bartender poured whiskey into the shot glass.* □ *Jim handed me a shot glass of tequila.*

shotgun   a gun with one or two long barrels that are smooth on the inside. (Compare with RIFLE.) □ *I loaded up my double-barreled shotgun.* □ *He dropped another cartridge into the shotgun.*

shovel   **1.** a tool with a long handle and a cupped blade, used for digging or moving loose material. (See also SPADE.) □ *I dug a hole with the shovel.* □ *She used a shovel to get the ashes out of the fireplace.* **2.** to move material with a SHOVEL or as if with a SHOVEL. □ *They shoveled gravel out of the truck onto the parking lot.* □ *We shoveled the trash out of the basement.*

shower curtain   a sheet of cloth or plastic that keeps water from a shower from spraying outside the bathtub. □ *I bought a yellow shower curtain to match the yellow bath mat.* □ *I pulled the shower curtain across as I got in the shower.*

shower head   a device perforated with a number of holes and attached to a water pipe. (Water from the pipe passes through the holes and comes out in a fine spray.) □ *I removed the shower head and cleaned out the lime deposits.* □ *He had a special shower head with an adjustable spray pattern.*

shower rod   a rod for hanging a SHOWER CURTAIN. □ *I slipped the plastic rings over the shower rod and hung the shower curtain from them.* □ *Kids, don't hang off the shower rod! It'll come down!*

shred   to cut something into fine, short strips. □ *Add two cups of cheddar cheese, coarsely shredded.* □ *Shred the carrots in the food processor.*

shrink-wrap   a layer of clear plastic surrounding something. (The plastic is heated and shrunk to fit the object it surrounds.) ☐ *The book was covered in shrink-wrap.* ☐ *I cut open the shrink-wrap and opened the box.*

shrub   a small, woody plant; a bush. ☐ *I planted flowering shrubs along either side of the walkway.* ☐ *The gardener pruned the shrubs.*

shuck   to remove the outer covering of something. ☐ *If you shuck this corn for me, we'll have corn on the cob tonight.* ☐ *We sat on the beach, shucking the oysters we had gathered that day.*

shut-off valve   a device that can start or stop the flow of something into a pipe. ☐ *I turned the shut-off valve on the radiator to keep the room from heating up any more.* ☐ *Before you try to repair the sink, cut off the water supply at the shut-off valve.*

shutter   **1.** a wooden panel that can swing to cover a window. ☐ *I closed the shutters to keep out the light and heat.* ☐ *They put up the shutters to protect the windows from the hail.* **2.** the part of a camera that can be opened to let light from the lens onto the film. ☐ *This setting allows you to operate the shutter manually. It will remain open for as long as you hold the shutter lever.* ☐ *I heard the snap of a camera shutter.*

shutter release   a control that opens a camera SHUTTER. ☐ *This big red button is the shutter release.* ☐ *When you have the picture composed, push the shutter release.*

sideboard   a piece of furniture on which dishes of food can be placed to make room on the table. (See also BUFFET.) ☐ *I set the roast on the sideboard.* ☐ *Help yourself to any of the dishes on the sideboard.*

side dish   a food served in small portions to accompany the ENTRÉE. ☐ *We had fried chicken with a side dish of* *green beans. □ The menu allows you to choose from a number of side dishes.*

side mirror   a mirror attached to the side of a vehicle, allowing the driver to see what is behind and to the side. □ *I checked the side mirror. There was no one in the left lane. □ The truck has side mirrors on both sides.*

side panel   a narrow side of a box. □ *See nutrition information on the side panel. □ I read the instructions on the side panel of the box of detergent.*

side rail   See BED RAIL.

sideseam pocket   a pocket placed in the seam on the side of a garment. □ *The skirt has two sideseam pockets. □ I put a sideseam pocket in my favorite dress.*

sidewall   the part of a tire between the tread and the rim of the wheel. □ *The tires had white sidewalls. □ The sidewall has pulled away from the wheel rim.*

siding   protective material attached to the outside wall of a building. □ *I had aluminum siding put on the house. □ The wooden siding on the barn was starting to rot away.*

sieve   a device with a bottom of fine mesh, used to sift powdery substances. □ *I shook the flour through the sieve. □ Use a sieve to sift the rocks out of the soil.*

sight   a device that helps you aim a gun. □ *I got the ducks in my sight. □ He peered along the sight at the distant target.*

signal   See (TURN) SIGNAL.

signature block   the typed or printed name and title of a person, appearing below a signature at the bottom of a letter. □ *The secretary typed the boss' signature block at the bottom of the letter. □ Put the signature block at the left margin.*

silencer   a device that muffles the firing of a gun. □ *No one heard the fatal shot. The murderer had used a silencer.* □ *I bought a silencer for my handgun.*

silicone   a rubbery substance used to seal gaps. □ *I used silicone to caulk around the edge of the bathtub.* □ *I patched my rain boots with silicone.*

silver   See SILVERWARE.

silver plate   **1.** metal with a thin coating of silver. □ *The tea service was silver plate.* □ *The silver was beginning to wear off the silver plate serving tray.* **2.** utensils made of metal with a thin coating of silver. □ *I have sterling silverware for special occasions and a set of silver plate for everyday use.* □ *I polished the silver plate and put it away.*

silver polish   a substance for cleaning and shining silver. □ *I rubbed silver polish onto the silver teapot.* □ *She cleaned her silver jewelry with silver polish.*

silverware AND **silver**   forks, spoons, and knives made of silver. (SILVERWARE is also sometimes used for any forks, spoons, and knives used for eating. See also CUTLERY, FLATWARE.) □ *I put silverware at each place setting.* □ *She brought out her best silver for the honored guest.*

simmer   **1.** to keep a liquid just hot enough to bubble. □ *Simmer the soup for five minutes.* □ *The spaghetti sauce was simmering on the stove.* **2.** to cook something in a liquid just hot enough to bubble. □ *Simmer the scallops in butter.* □ *Let the pasta simmer for twenty minutes.*

single lens reflex AND **SLR**   [of a camera] having a mirror that reflects the image from the lens into the viewfinder. □ *I like to use this SLR for close-up shots.* □ *This single lens reflex comes with a zoom lens and flash attachment.*

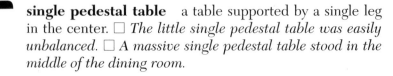

single pedestal table   a table supported by a single leg in the center. □ *The little single pedestal table was easily unbalanced.* □ *A massive single pedestal table stood in the middle of the dining room.*

sink   a large, bowl-shaped structure for holding water. □ *I cleaned the bathroom sink.* □ *The kitchen sink was full of dirty dishes.*

sink strainer   a device that fits into a SINK drain and strains out solid matter, such as food particles or hair. □ *I emptied the sink strainer into the garbage.* □ *The sink strainer caught the ring before it could go down the drain.*

siphon   **1.** a tube used to move liquid from one container to another. □ *I put the end of the siphon into the gas tank.* □ *She used a siphon to empty the clogged sink.* **2.** to move liquid with a SIPHON. □ *I siphoned gas out of the tank.* □ *Siphon a little oil into the plastic jug.*

sirloin   a cut of beef from the side of the animal near the pelvis. □ *Jane treated me to an excellent sirloin.* □ *We had grilled sirloin for dinner.*

sissy bar   a U-shaped bar on the back of a motorcycle for a passenger to rest against or hold onto. (Slang. A *sissy* is a coward.) □ *I grabbed the sissy bar as the motorcycle sped around the curb.* □ *If you're going to ride with me on my motorcycle, maybe I should have a sissy bar installed.*

six-cylinder   [of an engine] having six cylinders and pistons. □ *This six-cylinder engine gives excellent mileage, without sacrificing power.* □ *Is your car a four-cylinder or a six-cylinder?*

six pack   six containers packaged together. (Commonly used to refer to a package of six cans of beer.) □ *I bought a few six packs for the party.* □ *The pudding cups are sold in convenient six packs.*

sizing   a substance applied to a wall to make it easier to apply wallpaper. □ *How many gallons of sizing will I need for a room this size?* □ *Scrape the old paper from the wall, then apply a coat of sizing.*

skewer   **1.** a long, thin, rigid object, often used in cooking pieces of food. □ *Put the chunks of meat on a skewer, then*

cook them on the grill. □ *The vegetables were cooked on a wooden skewer.* **2.** to run a SKEWER or other thin, rigid object through something. □ *I skewered the shrimp on my fork.* □ *Skewer the slices of fruit with a toothpick.*

skillet a flat-bottomed pan with a long handle. (Compare with FRYING PAN, GRIDDLE.) □ *I fried the potato pancakes in a cast-iron skillet.* □ *Heat some oil in a skillet.*

skim **1.** to remove fat from a liquid. □ *Skim the grease from the beef stock.* □ *I skimmed the cream from the pail of fresh milk.* **2.** [of milk] having all the fat removed. □ *I poured skim milk on my cereal.* □ *This cheese is made with skim milk.*

ski rack a structure for holding skis; part of a vehicle. □ *The station wagon has a ski rack on the roof.* □ *We secured our skis on the ski rack.*

slab **1.** a flat, rectangular object. □ *A few slabs of wood served as a walkway up to the house.* □ *The monument was carved out of a granite slab.* **2.** a concrete surface that supports a building. □ *This house has no basement. It's built on a slab.* □ *The construction workers poured a slab for the new house.*

slash pocket a pocket attached to an opening cut into a garment. □ *There are two slash pockets in the front of the skirt.* □ *The coat has slash pockets that snap closed.*

slat a narrow, flat piece of rigid material. □ *She peered between the slats of the Venetian blind.* □ *I nailed the broken fence slat back in place.*

sleeper sofa See SOFA BED.

sleeve **1.** the part of a garment that covers the arm. □ *He wore a shirt with short sleeves.* □ *The sleeves of the sweater were much too long. They covered up most of my hand!* **2.** a protective, surrounding cover. □ *The wire passes through this plastic sleeve.* □ *I slipped the LP into its paper sleeve.*

sleeve cap   the top of the SLEEVE, where it joins the body of the garment. □ *Ease the sleeve cap into the armhole.* □ *The puffed sleeve cap should stand up above the shoulder.*

slice   **1.** to cut something into thin pieces. □ *I sliced the ham.* □ *Slice the carrots lengthwise.* **2.** a thin section of something. □ *I put a slice of roast beef on my sandwich.* □ *Would you like a slice of cheese?*

slide   a transparent photographic image. □ *I took a lot of slides on our trip to Italy.* □ *The lecturer showed slides of the architectural styles she was discussing.*

slide projector   a device for projecting transparent pictures or SLIDES onto a screen or other surface. □ *I got out the slide projector and showed everyone my vacation slides.* □ *He turned the focus knob on the slide projector until the picture on the opposite wall was clear and sharp.*

slide tray   a device that holds a number of SLIDES or transparent pictures. □ *I put the slide tray into the slide projector.* □ *The professor brought in a slide tray of pictures of great art.*

slip   **1.** an undergarment shaped like a dress. □ *Put on a slip under that sheer silk dress!* □ *Her slip was hanging out underneath the hem of her skirt.* **2.** a section from a plant that can be grown into a new plant. □ *Jim gave me a slip from his begonia.* □ *I rooted the coleus slip in a glass of water.*

slipcover   a cloth or plastic cover for a piece of furniture. □ *I had a slipcover made for the old chair.* □ *A clear plastic slipcover protected the sofa.*

slipover   a garment that pulls on and off over the head. (See also PULLOVER.) □ *There's no fastening on the dress. It's a slipover.* □ *He drew on a slipover sweater as the evening grew chilly.*

sliver   **1.** to cut something into very thin, small pieces. □ *Use half a cup of slivered almonds.* □ *Sliver the green onions* *with a sharp knife.* **2.** a very thin piece. □ MARY: *Would you like a piece of pie?* JANE: *Oh, just cut me a sliver.* □ *I garnished each plate with a few slivers of carrot.* **3.** a small, thin, sharp object. □ *I got a sliver in my finger.* □ *I worked the sliver out with a needle.*

slo mo   See SLOW MOTION.

sloppy Joe   a round bun covered with a sauce of ground beef, tomatoes, and seasonings. □ *Come on over to my house for dinner. I'm making sloppy Joes.* □ *The kids love to make sloppy Joes when we go camping.*

slotted head   [of a screw] having a head with a single groove in it. (Compare with PHILLIPS HEAD.) □ CHARLIE: *What kind of screw is it?* MARY: *It's a slotted head screw.* □ *I put the slotted head screwdriver attachment onto the power drill.*

slotted spoon   a spoon with several long, narrow holes in the bottom. □ *Lift the potatoes out of the boiling water with a slotted spoon.* □ *I used the slotted spoon to get the hard-boiled eggs out of the pot.*

slow motion AND **slow mo**   a slowed down speed. (SLOW MO is slang.) □ *The sports announcer said, "Let's see that play again in slow motion."* □ *Push this button on the remote to see the video in slow mo.*

SLP   See SUPER LONG PLAY.

SLR   See SINGLE LENS REFLEX.

slug   **1.** a BULLET. (Slang.) □ *The police officer took a slug in the shoulder.* □ *I fired several slugs, but missed every time.* **2.** a small, slimy, soft-bodied animal that eats plants. □ *I found slugs on my tomato plants.* □ *A slug was crawling up the basement wall.* **3.** a piece of metal shaped like a coin, used to cheat a coin-operated machine. □ *The soft drink machine was full of slugs.* □ *He was caught trying to feed a slug into a parking meter.*

smoke alarm AND **smoke detector** a device that will sound a warning if there is smoke in the air. □ *I checked the battery in the smoke alarm.* □ *The smoke detector saved our lives. It woke us up in time to get out of the burning house.*

smoke detector See SMOKE ALARM.

smokestack a hollow structure through which smoke escapes from a train LOCOMOTIVE or a building. □ *The factory smokestack had the company name painted on it.* □ *White smoke billowed out of the smokestack on the locomotive.*

smooth bore [of a gun barrel] having a smooth inside surface. □ *CHARLIE: Is that a rifle? JANE: No, it's a smooth bore shotgun.* □ *We saw a display of early smooth bore pistols.*

snap a metal clothing fastener that makes a snapping sound when pressed closed or pulled open. □ *I sewed a snap on the jacket collar.* □ *The dress is fastened with snaps in the back.*

sneakers casual or sports shoes with flexible soles. (See also TENNIS SHOES.) □ *I wear my old sneakers when I go out to work in the garden.* □ *I can't believe you paid ninety dollars for a pair of sneakers!*

snooze button a button that delays the alarm on an ALARM CLOCK. □ *My alarm clock rang. I hit the snooze button.* □ *She pushed the snooze button six times this morning and wound up being late for work.*

snow **1.** small ice crystals that fall from clouds. □ *The ground was covered with snow.* □ *I shoveled the snow off the front walk.* **2.** small, flashing spots in a TV picture. (Informal. See also INTERFERENCE.) □ *When I tune in to channel 5, all I get is snow.* □ *I adjusted the TV antenna until I got rid of the snow.*

snowblower a machine that clears SNOW away by blowing it to one side. □ *Now that we live in Minnesota, we need* *a snowblower.* □ *She pushed her snowblower up and down the driveway.*

snowmobile   a one- or two-person vehicle for traveling over SNOW. □ *Every winter weekend, Joe likes to ride through the woods on his snowmobile.* □ *The snowmobile sped down the snowy trail.*

snow pants   a pair of padded, WATERPROOF pants that keep the wearer warm and dry in the SNOW. □ *Put on your snow pants before you go out to play in the snow.* □ *The children all wore snow pants and parkas.*

snowplow   a truck equipped with a plow that can clear SNOW from roads or sidewalks. □ *The snowplows were out the minute that the snow stopped, and the roads were clear within an hour.* □ *I need a snowplow to clear my driveway.*

snow shovel   a shovel with a wide, flat blade, for moving SNOW. □ *I used a snow shovel to clear the front walk.* □ *I had to get the snow shovel to get the snow off the car.*

snow tire   a tire with a deep tread, designed to give a good grip on SNOW or ice. □ *It's November—time to put the snow tires on the car.* □ *I bought a set of snow tires for the truck.*

socket   an opening into which something fits tightly. (Most often used to describe openings for light bulbs or electric plugs.) □ *I screwed a new bulb into the socket.* □ *Is there a socket where I can plug this in?*

socket wrench   a tool with a heavy handle onto which metal sockets of different sizes can fit. (The SOCKETS fit onto nuts and bolts of different sizes. By pushing or pulling the handle, you can tighten or loosen the nuts.) □ *The mechanic used a socket wrench to remove the stubborn bolt.* □ *I put a ³/₈-inch socket on the socket wrench.*

sod   grass and the dirt held by the grass roots. □ *I had sod put in to cover the front yard.* □ *She put new sod over the spot where the grass had been torn up.*

soda (pop) AND **pop**   a carbonated SOFT DRINK. (Regional.) □ *Would you like some soda pop with your lunch?* □ *I bought a soda from the vending machine.* □ *What kinds of pop do you have?*

sofa bed AND **pull-out sofa; sleeper sofa**   a sofa that un-folds into a bed. □ *Come and visit sometime. I have a sofa bed.* □ *The pull-out sofa needs a new mattress.* □ *This love seat is a sleeper sofa with a double mattress.*

soffit   the underside of an overhanging structure, such as the lower edge of a roof. □ *We put in a vinyl soffit so we wouldn't have to keep repainting the wood.* □ *Be careful when painting the kitchen soffit that the paint doesn't drip down onto the cabinet doors.*

soft boiled   [of eggs] boiled until the white is firm but the yolk is still somewhat liquid. (Compare with HARD BOILED.) □ *I had a soft boiled egg and toast for breakfast.* □ *She used a spoon to scoop the soft boiled egg from its shell.*

soft drink   a non-alcoholic drink, usually carbonated and sweetened. □ *The waiter listed the soft drinks served at the restaurant.* □ *Do you have any soft drinks without caffeine?*

soften   **1.** to make something soft or let it become soft. □ *Soften eight ounces of butter.* □ *Soften the putty by rolling it between your hands.* **2.** [for a substance] to become soft. □ *The vinyl LP softened in the hot sun.* □ *The stiff cloth soft-ened as I ironed it.*

software   a set of instructions given to a computer; a com-puter program or programs. (Contrasts with HARDWARE.) □ *This word processing software is really easy to use.* □ *This seems to be a problem with the software, not the hardware. You will need a programmer to fix it.*

soft water   water that is free of unwanted chemicals such as iron and sulfur. (Contrasts with HARD WATER.) □ *We have a good water supply in our town. We get soft water out of the tap.* □ *It's so much easier to get things clean in soft water.*

solar panel   a device that gathers energy from the sun and uses it to heat or cool a building or a water supply. □ *I installed solar panels on the south side of the house.* □ *The cabin is heated by those solar panels out back.*

solder   a soft metal wire that can be melted onto something in order to hold it in place. □ *I fixed the wire onto the metal plate with solder.* □ *A line of solder joined the two pipes.*

solenoid   a device constructed of a coil of wire with a magnet inside. □ *The mechanic replaced a solenoid in the car's ignition system.* □ *The solenoid on the dishwasher is malfunctioning.*

soleplate   the flat metal surface of an iron. □ *This soleplate on this model has a non-stick coating.* □ *The soleplate is stained with a sticky, brown substance.*

solvent   a substance that dissolves something. □ CHARLIE: *What solvent should I use to clean this latex paint?* TOM: *Warm water.* □ *Alcohol is a useful solvent.*

SOS™ pad   a brand of metal SCOURING PAD. □ *I tried everything to get the burned food off the bottom of the pot. Finally, an SOS pad got it off.* □ *I rubbed at the saucepan with an SOS pad.*

soufflé   a food item made of whipped, baked eggs and other ingredients. □ *The soufflé was so light, it just melted in your mouth.* □ *I made a cheese soufflé for the dinner party.*

sound card   a device that makes a computer able to play and record sound. □ *Does this PC come with a sound card?* □ *I put a sound card in the expansion slot.*

soup spoon   a spoon with a wide bowl, used for eating soup. □ *Waiter? May I have a soup spoon for my soup? This teaspoon is too small.* □ *I got a set of soup spoons in my silver pattern.*

sour cream   cream to which a bacteria culture has been added. □ *Each baked potato was topped with sour cream.* □

Sour cream in the batter makes this poppy-seed cake nice and rich.

sourdough   a dough that has been allowed to ferment with natural yeasts. □ *This sourdough bread is delicious.* □ *The restaurant is famous for their crusty sourdough rolls.*

soy sauce   a sauce made from fermented soybeans. □ *I seasoned the stir fry with soy sauce.* □ *The chicken was marinated in soy sauce, sugar, and rice wine.*

SP   See STANDARD PLAY.

space bar   a wide key on a typewriter or computer keyboard that moves the carriage or the cursor forward by one blank space. □ *Press the space bar to see the next page.* □ *I pressed the space bar until the carriage was lined up beneath the left-hand edge of the previous line.*

spackling   material for filling small holes in interior walls. □ *I used a putty knife to fill the nail hole with spackling.* □ *I repaired the wall with spackling before I painted it.*

spade   a digging tool with a long handle and a flat blade coming to a point. (See also SHOVEL.) □ *I turned over the earth in the garden plot with a spade.* □ *He stepped on the edge of the spade, driving it into the hard-packed dirt.*

spading fork   a tool with several flat TINES on one end, used for moving dirt. □ *I softened up the ground with a spading fork.* □ *Use a spading fork to work any big clods out of the soil.*

spaghetti pot   a large, tall pot. □ *Bring six quarts of water to boil in a spaghetti pot.* □ *I like to use this spaghetti pot for making soup.*

Spam™   a brand of processed meat. □ *I made a Spam sandwich.* □ *Cut the Spam into strips and fry it.*

spanner   a flat, open-end wrench. (In British English, SPANNER means any wrench.) □ *This spanner fits around* *the nut at the bottom of the sink drain.* □ *I got a set of span-ners for bicycle repairs.*

spare (tire) an extra car wheel and tire. (SPARE is infor-mal.) □ *Make sure your spare tire has plenty of air in it.* □ *In just a few minutes, we had removed the flat tire and put on the spare.*

spark plug a device that creates an electric spark in an engine cylinder, thus igniting the fuel. □ *The mechanic rec-ommended replacing my spark plugs.* □ *This tool measures the gap at the end of a spark plug.*

spatula **1.** a kitchen tool with a flat blade, used for lifting and moving flat food items. (Regional. See also PANCAKE TURN-ER.) □ *I slid the spatula under the potato pancake on the skil-let.* □ *He turned the hamburgers with a spatula.* **2.** See RUBBER SCRAPER. **3.** a knife with a flat, blunt, round-tipped blade, used for spreading soft foods. □ *Use a spatula to spread frosting on the cake.* □ *I smoothed the batter with a spatula.*

speaker a device that turns an electronic signal into sound. □ *The car stereo had such powerful speakers that people for blocks around could hear it.* □ *I connected the speakers to the stereo amplifier.*

speaker phone a telephone that transmits sound through an open SPEAKER, so that you do not have to hold a receiver in order to use it. □ *I'm going to put this call on the speaker phone, so that everyone in the room can participate in the conversation.* □ *I talked on the speaker phone while I rocked the baby.*

speaker wire wire for connecting a SPEAKER to a stereo system. □ *Place the copper half of the speaker wire in the red plastic clip on the speaker.* □ *There seems to be a short in the speaker wire.*

specifications requirements. □ *This computer meets the specifications necessary to run the software package.* □ *This power cord is designed for use with appliances that meet the following specifications.*

speed dial   a function that dials an entire telephone number when a special combination of keys is pressed. ☐ *Does this phone have speed dial?* ☐ *I have my sister's number in my speed dial. If I want to call her, I just press *5.*

speedometer   a device that measures how fast a vehicle is traveling. ☐ *My speedometer says I'm going 35 miles per hour.* ☐ *The speedometer shows both miles and kilometers per hour.*

spell checker   a computer program that corrects spelling. ☐ *I ran the spell checker on my document.* ☐ *Use the word processor's spell checker if you're not sure you've spelled the word correctly.*

spice   a flavorful seed, root, or bark. (See also HERB.) ☐ *I added some spices to the spaghetti sauce.* ☐ *Black pepper is a popular spice.*

spice grinder   a device that grinds SPICES. ☐ *I put the whole cloves into my electric spice grinder.* ☐ *I cranked the cinnamon bark in the spice grinder.*

spice rack   a holder for bottles of SPICES and HERBS. ☐ *JANE: Do you have any tarragon? MARY: Look in the spice rack.* ☐ *I put the cardamon back on the spice rack.*

spillway   a surface down which excess water can flow. (Part of a dam.) ☐ *In the heavy rain, a constant flow went over the spillway.* ☐ *The workers repaired a crack in the spillway.*

spin cycle   part of the process of washing clothes in a WASHING MACHINE, in which the clothes are spun in order to remove water. ☐ *This light indicates that the washing machine is on the spin cycle.* ☐ *The clothes unbalanced the machine in the middle of the spin cycle.*

spindle   a thin cylinder that holds something and allows it to turn. ☐ *The hole in the middle of the record fits onto the spindle on the turntable.* ☐ *The film cartridge snaps onto a spindle inside the film compartment.*

spine   the bound edge of a book. □ *The title is printed on the spine.* □ *Be careful when you open the book. Don't crack the spine.*

spit   a rod for turning food over a source of heat. (See also ROTISSERIE.) □ *They put a whole lamb on the spit and roasted it over an open fire.* □ *I turned the chicken on the spit in the charcoal grill.*

splashboard   See BACKSPLASH.

splash guard   See MUD FLAP.

splitter   a device that splits an electronic signal so that it can travel along two wires. □ *I used a splitter to put the signal into both speakers.* □ *The technician attached the wire to the socket on one side of the splitter.*

spoiler   a horizontal bar across the back of a vehicle that helps keep the rear of the vehicle from slipping when traveling at high speeds. □ *The sports car had tinted windows, mag wheels, and a spoiler.* □ *There was a spoiler mounted on the rear of the race car.*

spoke   one of a set of thin wire or metal rods that connect the hub of a wheel to the rim. □ *I replaced the bent spoke in my bicycle wheel.* □ *The wheel stopped turning when something got caught in the spokes.*

sponge   a piece of flexible material filled with small holes, used to absorb liquid. □ *I mopped up the spill with a sponge.* □ *I worked soap into the sponge.*

sponge cake   a light cake with a texture like a SPONGE. □ *I baked a chocolate sponge cake.* □ *She had a piece of sponge cake for dessert.*

sponge mop   a mop with a SPONGE at the end. □ *I cleaned the floor with a sponge mop.* □ *He plunged the sponge mop into the bucket of sudsy water.*

spool   **1.** a cylinder on which something, especially thread, is wound. □ *I need a spool of black thread.* □ *Place the spool* *on this spindle on top of the sewing machine.* **2.** to put a computer file in line to be printed. □ *Now spooling your file to printer 1.* □ *The printer is currently busy. Your file will be spooled and printed when the printer is available.*

spoon **1.** a utensil with a bowl-shaped structure on a long handle. □ *Here's a spoon for your soup.* □ *I stirred the sauce with a spoon.* **2.** to use a SPOON to put something somewhere. □ *Spoon the batter into a muffin tin.* □ *I spooned strained peas into the baby's mouth.*

spork a spoon with points like a fork at the end of the bowl. (Informal. SPORK is a combination of SPOON and FORK.) □ *I served the green beans with a spork.* □ *Try this spork for eating your grapefruit.*

sport coat AND **sports jacket** a tailored jacket for informal wear. □ *He wore a navy blue sport coat and beige pants.* □ *You can't wear that sports jacket to a formal dinner!*

sports car a car designed to go at high speeds. □ *He drove up in a red sports car.* □ *That sports car seems very expensive and not very practical.*

sports jacket See SPORT COAT.

spout a narrow opening for liquid to pour out. □ *Syrup trickled out the spout of the pitcher.* □ *I turned the hot-water tap, and hot water rushed out the spout.*

spread **1.** to apply a soft substance to cover a flat surface. □ *Spread butter on the toast.* □ *I spread the paint onto the wall.* **2.** a soft food that can be easily SPREAD. □ *This cream cheese spread makes tasty sandwiches.* □ *Instead of margarine, I use a low-fat spread.*

spreadsheet a chart giving information in rows and columns. (There are a number of computer programs for making SPREADSHEETS.) □ *This spreadsheet shows how much we spent each month for housing, food, clothing, and entertainment.* □ *I learned how to set up a spreadsheet in my computer.*

sprig   a small section of a branch or stalk. □ *The dish was garnished with sprigs of parsley.* □ *I put a sprig of blossoming cherry into a vase.*

springform mold   See SPRINGFORM PAN.

springform pan AND **springform mold**   a round pan with sides attached by a spring. (When the spring is released, the sides can be removed, making it easy to remove the contents of the pan.) □ *Use a springform pan for this cheesecake recipe.* □ *I made the fruit tart in a springform mold.*

sprinkle   to drop small amounts of a liquid or powder all over a surface. □ *Sprinkle the top of the loaf with poppy seeds.* □ *I sprinkled plant food onto the houseplant.*

sprinkler   a device that sprays water onto something. □ *I turned on the sprinklers to water the lawn.* □ *The fire alarm sounded, and the sprinklers in the ceiling began to spray.*

sprinkles AND **jimmies**   small candies used to decorate cakes or cookies. □ *The chocolate cupcakes were decorated with blue sprinkles.* □ *I sprinkled jimmies onto the cutout cookies.*

sprocket   a small projection designed to fit through a hole. (As the SPROCKET moves, it moves the object with the hole in it.) □ *The bicycle chain came off the sprockets.* □ *The holes in the edge of the computer paper fit onto these sprockets on the computer printer.*

sprout   a young plant. □ *I took a look at the sprouts in the garden.* □ *I put a handful of alfalfa sprouts on my sandwich.*

squeeze bottle   a flexible bottle that can be squeezed in order to move the contents out. □ *The ketchup comes in a squeeze bottle.* □ *The cyclist squirted water from a squeeze bottle into her mouth.*

stack   a vertical pipe that allows unwanted gas to escape into the outside air. □ *The soil stack vents sewer gas from the toilets.* □ *The furnace stack comes out through the roof.*

stainless (flatware) knives, forks, and spoons made of STAINLESS STEEL. □ *I got a set of stainless flatware.* □ *What pattern did you choose for your stainless?*

stainless steel a kind of steel that resists rust. □ *The stainless steel knife will last a lifetime.* □ *My kitchen pans are made of stainless steel.*

stain remover a substance that can clean a stain. (See also PREWASH.) □ *I sprayed stain remover on the dark spot in the carpet.* □ *Is this stain remover safe to use on silk?*

stairway a set of steps. □ *A narrow stairway led up to the second floor.* □ *We stumbled down the stairway in the dark.*

stairwell a vertical space containing stairs in a building. □ *The light in the stairwell went out.* □ *That door leads to the stairwell.*

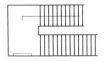

stalk a rigid, vertical part of a plant. □ *Use 3 stalks of celery, finely chopped.* □ *The hailstorm broke and battered the corn stalks.*

stall [for an engine] suddenly to stop running. □ *The car stalled in the middle of a left-hand turn.* □ *There's a car stalled on I-94. It's blocking traffic.*

standard AND **manual** [of a car transmission] having gears that must be changed by hand. (Contrasts with AUTOMATIC.) □ *Is this truck standard or automatic?* □ *I don't know how to drive a car with a manual transmission.*

standard play AND **SP** a slow speed for recording and playing videotapes. (Using SP, you will get 2 hours of material on a standard 2-hour cassette.) □ *This button allows you to choose between SP and SLP.* □ *Recording at standard play will result in the best picture quality.*

standpipe a pipe with openings on the outside of a building into which water can be pumped by firefighters for putting out fires in the building. □ *We installed a system of standpipes and sprinklers.* □ *Water is maintained in* *the standpipe under pressure, and is forced out in case of fire.*

staple **1.** a metal fastener made of a wire with a 90-degree bend at each end. □ *The papers were fastened with a staple at the top corner.* □ *I used staples to fasten the drywall onto the studs.* **2.** to fasten something using STAPLES. □ *She stapled the carpeting to the floor.* □ *Staple this document to your application form.*

staple gun a device for driving a STAPLE into a hard surface. □ *Using a staple gun, I stapled the upholstery to the chair frame.* □ *This staple gun is powerful enough to affix staples to hardwoods.*

stapler a device for driving a STAPLE into a flexible surface such as paper or cloth. □ *The stapler ran out of staples.* □ *I squared up the stack of paper and fastened it with the stapler.*

staple remover a hinged tool for pulling STAPLES out of a surface. □ *I slid the teeth of the staple remover under the staple.* □ *He clamped the staple remover shut and pulled.*

starch a powdery chemical found in foods such as potatoes, beans, and grains, and often used to stiffen cloth. □ *I'm a diabetic. I can't have much starch in my diet.* □ *She sprayed starch on the shirt before she ironed it.*

start a young plant for planting in a garden. □ *I bought a set of tomato starts.* □ *He went to the nursery and bought a variety of starts for his garden.*

starter an electric motor used to start a car engine. □ *The cable that connects the battery to the starter has come loose.* □ *I heard the starter turning, but the engine wouldn't start.*

static fuzziness in a television picture or buzzing and popping in a radio signal, caused by electric charges in the atmosphere. □ *The thunderstorm caused a lot of static on the TV.* □ *The radio music was overcome by static.*

stationery   **1.** paper and envelopes for writing letters. (Compare with LETTERHEAD.) □ *She had monogrammed stationery.* □ *I wrote a thank-you letter on formal stationery.* **2.** materials used for writing, such as paper, pencils, pens, envelopes, etc. (See also OFFICE SUPPLIES.) □ *You'll find manila envelopes in the stationery section.* □ *I bought a fountain pen at the stationery store.*

station wagon   a car with a cargo compartment behind the back seat. □ *The station wagon will have plenty of room for our luggage.* □ *The rear seats of the station wagon fold down, so that you can carry a large load in the back.*

staystitch   to stitch along the edge of a clothing pattern piece in order to help it keep its shape. □ *Staystitch around the neckline.* □ *The pattern markings show where you will need to staystitch.*

steak sauce   a spicy sauce for use on meat. □ *He poured steak sauce onto his hamburger.* □ *She dipped her forkful of steak into the steak sauce.*

steam   **1.** hot water vapor. □ *Steam poured out of the teakettle.* □ *The hot shower filled the bathroom with steam.* **2.** to cook something in hot water vapor. □ *Steam the green beans until they are just tender.* □ *Steam the onions in a saucepan.*

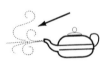

steam cleaner   a device that cleans a surface with STEAM. (See also CARPET CLEANER.) □ *I rented a steam cleaner to get the carpet clean.* □ *He cleaned the curtains with a steam cleaner.*

steamer basket   a wood or metal container for holding food above boiling water in order to STEAM it. □ *I arranged the dumplings in the bamboo steamer basket.* □ *The spaghetti pot comes with a steamer basket.*

steam heat   a system that passes STEAM through pipes and into radiators to heat a building. □ *Do these apartments have hot water or steam heat?* □ *MARY: How is the building heated? JANE: Steam heat.*

steam iron an electric iron that can spray STEAM onto cloth. □ *I used the steam iron to get the wrinkles out of the cotton blouse.* □ *I plugged in the steam iron and let it warm up.*

steel wool a material made of fine steel fibers, used to scrub things. □ *I had to use steel wool to get the grime off the oven rack.* □ *I cleaned the copper pot with steel wool.*

steep to remain in a hot liquid. □ *Allow the tea to steep for five minutes.* □ *The noodles were steeped in chicken broth.*

steeper a device that holds something in a hot liquid. (See also INFUSER.) □ *I measured loose tea into the steeper.* □ *You can make either coffee or tea in this steeper.*

steering column the cylindrical structure that supports a vehicle's STEERING WHEEL. □ *The gearshift is located on the steering column.* □ *The mechanic connected the horn to a wire in the steering column.*

steering fluid a liquid that lubricates and maintains pressure in a car's power steering system. □ *The steering is not responding well. I'd better check the level on the steering fluid.* □ *Open the reservoir and add steering fluid.*

steering wheel a circular device that controls the turning of a vehicle's wheels. □ *The driving instructor told me to keep both hands on the steering wheel.* □ *Turn the steering wheel in the direction you want the car to go.*

stem **1.** a rigid, vertical plant structure that supports a leaf, flower, or fruit. □ *I removed the stem from the apple.* □ *The weather was dry. Flowers drooped on their stems.* **2.** a rigid vertical structure. □ *I picked up the pocket watch and wound it, turning the knob at the end of the stem.* □ *The crystal wineglass had a long stem.* □ *The handlebar stem is attached to the bicycle frame.*

stemware drinking glasses with STEMS. □ *I served the guests with my best crystal stemware.* □ *Both the stemware and the china had gold rims.*

step   a platform leading from one level to another. □ *A set of steps forms a staircase.* □ *Two steps led up to the porch.*

stepladder   a ladder shaped like an upside-down V, which can be ascended like a set of STEPS. □ *I had to use a stepladder to reach the top shelf.* □ *He stood on a stepladder to paint the upper part of the wall.*

stereo   **1.** an electronic device for playing recorded sound through two SPEAKERS. □ *I put my new CD on the stereo.* □ *I like to listen to the stereo while I make dinner.* **2.** having sound recorded on two different electronic channels. □ *This is a stereo recording.* □ *My TV has stereo sound.*

Sterno™   a brand of canned cooking fuel. □ *The caterer used Sterno to heat the chafing dishes.* □ *We took a supply of Sterno along on our camping trip.*

stew   **1.** a mixture of meats and vegetables cooked in liquid in a pot. □ *We had beef stew for lunch.* □ *I'll use the potatoes in a stew.* **2.** to cook something in liquid in a pot. □ *Stew the prunes for half an hour.* □ *First brown the lamb, then stew it in a mixture of soup stock and tomato paste.*

still   a photograph. (A STILL contrasts with a motion picture or videotape.) □ *The photographer took stills of the movie actors.* □ *I took a lot of videos of the party, but no stills.*

still-frame button   a control that allows you to view or record a videotape one frame, or image, at a time. □ *I used the still-frame button on the video camera to make an animated cartoon.* □ *I pressed the still-frame button to get a better look at the building in the background.*

stir   to mix something by moving a utensil around and around through it. □ *Stir the pasta so it won't boil over.* □ *I stirred the paint until the color was uniform.*

stir fry   **1.** to cook something by moving it around and around in hot oil. □ *I stir fried the chicken with some vegetables.* □ *Stir fry the pea pods for a minute or two.* **2.** a mixture of foods cooked by STIR FRYING. □ *I had beef stir fry for lunch.* □ *Try our vegetable stir fry on rice.*

stock **1.** the broad end of a rifle or shotgun. □ *She balanced the stock against her shoulder.* □ *The shotgun had a carved wooden stock.* **2.** a liquid left over from cooking something in water. (See also BOUILLON, BROTH.) □ *The soup is made with beef stock.* □ *When you cook beans, save the stock for soup.*

stock pot a large, cylindrical pot for making or storing STOCK. □ *A stock pot simmered on the back of the stove.* □ *I drained the cooking liquid into my stock pot.*

stoop a step or set of steps just outside a door. □ *He sat down on the stoop.* □ *The paper carrier tossed the newspaper onto my front stoop.*

stop light See TRAFFIC LIGHT.

stopper a plug that stops air or liquid from flowing out. □ *I put the stopper in the sink and filled it with hot water.* □ *Is there a stopper for this bottle?*

storm door a sturdy door attached outside an outside door in order to keep out wind and rain. □ *Every October, I put up the storm doors.* □ *The cold wind came in through a crack in the storm door.*

storm window a sturdy window attached outside an ordinary window to keep out wind and rain. □ *I slid the storm window into place.* □ *He fit the storm window into the window frame.*

story a level of a building. □ *The bank building is twelve stories tall.* □ *Grandma had to sell her two-story house because she is too frail to go up and down the stairs.*

stove a device that produces heat for cooking. (See also (KITCHEN) RANGE.) □ *I forgot to turn off the stove, and the pot boiled dry.* □ *She had something cooking on every burner of the stove.*

stovepipe   a pipe that carries hot air and smoke from a wood-burning STOVE to the outside air. □ *I cut a hole in the cabin wall for the stovepipe.* □ *Don't touch the stovepipe. It's hot!*

straight 8   an engine with eight cylinders all in one line. □ *The mechanic had never seen a straight 8 before.* □ *The straight 8 gave the car plenty of accelerating power.*

straight stitch   sewing in a straight line. (Compare with ZIGZAG STITCH.) □ *Use straight stitch for the seams.* □ *This control on the sewing machine regulates the length of the straight stitch.*

strainer   a device that traps solid material and allows liquid to pass through. □ *The strainer in the bathtub drain will catch hair and large dirt particles.* □ *I poured the peas into a strainer and shook it to get all the water out.*

strapping tape   tape with strong fibers running parallel to the edges, used to hold packages shut. □ *I wound strapping tape around the carton.* □ *A wide piece of strapping tape sealed the box.*

street sweeper   a machine that uses rotating metal brushes to clean the surface of a street. □ *The street sweeper does our street every Wednesday morning.* □ *The street sweeper scoured the grime out of the gutters.*

strike plate AND **striker plate**   a metal plate with an opening where the latch on a door lock can fit. □ *Install the strike plate on the doorjamb.* □ *The latch is not properly aligned with the striker plate. That's why the door won't close.*

striker plate   See STRIKE PLATE.

strip   1. a narrow piece of something. □ *Cut a strip of cloth for the waistband.* □ *A strip of grass separated my front door from the sidewalk.* 2. to scrape off the teeth or ridges from a gear, screw, or bolt. □ *I threaded the screw in at an angle and wound up stripping it.* □ *I stripped the gears on my bicycle.*

strobe   to flash on and off. □ *Why is the monitor strobing like that?* □ *The fluorescent light strobed for a second or two before going out.*

stud   **1.** a piece of wood that supports a wall. □ *I nailed drywall onto the studs.* □ *Make sure to anchor the shelf to a stud.* **2.** a round-headed, usually metal, decoration. □ *He wore a leather bracelet with silver studs.* □ *She had garnet studs in her ears.*

stuffing   **1.** soft material used to fill something, such as a toy or a cushion. □ *The teddy bear was filled with cotton stuffing.* □ *The stuffing was leaking out of the old chair.* **2.** a mixture of foods, usually including bread crumbs or rice, cooked inside a fowl or a cut of meat. □ *We roasted a goose with chestnut stuffing.* □ *Everyone's mouth watered as Mom spooned the stuffing out of the turkey.*

stylus   a small, thin, pointed piece of metal that comes in contact with the groove on an LP record; part of a phonograph. (See also CARTRIDGE, NEEDLE.) □ *Gently lower the stylus onto the record.* □ *I cleaned the dust and hair off the stylus.*

Styrofoam™   a brand of stiff, light plastic foam. □ *The coffee was served in Styrofoam cups.* □ *I pulled the computer out from the Styrofoam packing material.*

subdirectory   a group of computer files within a larger group. □ *There are three subdirectories in the directory labeled LETTERS.* □ *Make a separate subdirectory for the budget spreadsheets.*

subfloor   a rough floor that supports a finished floor. □ *Water leaked through into the subfloor and rotted the wood.* □ *They removed the carpet, then ripped up the floor all the way down to the subfloor.*

sub(marine sandwich) AND **hero (sandwich); grinder**   a sandwich on a long bread roll. □ *The hero sandwich was piled high with lunch meats, cheeses, and vegetables.* □ *I stopped by the deli and got a hero for lunch.* □ *The restaurant* *specializes in submarine sandwiches.* □ *You can choose from four different kinds of bread for your sub.* □ *The Italian meatball grinder comes with onions and special tomato sauce.*

subscript one or more characters printed slightly below a line of type. (Compare with SUPERSCRIPT.) □ *In H_2O, the 2 is a subscript.* □ *How do I set up a subscript on this word processor?*

subsoil the layers of soil below the surface. (Compare with TOPSOIL.) □ *The subsoil here is clay.* □ *There's a nice sandy subsoil in this garden plot. It should drain well.*

subway a system of underground trains. □ *I got on the subway at 12th Avenue.* □ *The subway runs parallel to State Street.*

subway stop a place where people get on or off a SUBWAY train. □ *There's a subway stop two blocks from my house.* □ *The subway stops are marked with red signs.*

subwoofer a device for turning electronic signals into very low-pitched sounds; part of a stereo system. □ *The subwoofer really makes the walls vibrate!* □ *The bass line of the song came pounding out of the subwoofer.*

sugar bowl a bowl for serving sugar. □ *I spooned sugar out of the sugar bowl.* □ *I filled the sugar bowl before setting it on the table.*

sugar cone a sweet, brown, cone-shaped pastry in which ice cream is served. □ *CUSTOMER: I'd like two scoops of chocolate, please. ICE CREAM SALES CLERK: Would you like that in a regular cone or a sugar cone?* □ *I heaped ice cream into the sugar cone.*

sugar cube granulated sugar molded into a cube. □ *I dropped the sugar cube into my cup of tea.* □ *The sugar bowl was filled with sugar cubes.*

sugar packet a small, usually paper, package containing about a teaspoonful of sugar. □ *A basket on the restaurant* *table held a supply of sugar packets.* □ *He opened a sugar packet and poured the sugar into his coffee.*

sugar tongs a tool for moving SUGAR CUBES. □ *I picked up a couple of cubes with the sugar tongs.* □ *Joan, holding the sugar tongs, asked, "One lump or two?"*

suit coat AND **suit jacket** a tailored coat that is part of a suit, together with matching pants. □ *I took my suit coat to the dry cleaner's.* □ *Do you have a suit jacket to go with those pants?*

suit jacket See SUIT COAT.

sump pump a pump that removes unwanted water from the basement or foundation of a building. □ *The sump pump never stopped pumping throughout the rainstorm.* □ *The sump pump kept the basement from flooding.*

sun roof a car roof with panels that can be removed. □ *He opened the sun roof on his car and went for a drive.* □ *I like the sporty sun roof on this model.*

super glue a very strong glue. □ *I used super glue to put the vase back together.* □ *Will super glue work on plastics?*

super long play AND **SLP** a speed for recording and playing a videotape that allows you to fit six hours of material onto a standard two-hour tape. □ *This button lets you choose between SP and SLP.* □ *The show was recorded at super long play.*

supermarket a store that sells a large variety of foods and other items. (See also GROCERY STORE.) □ *Where's the nearest supermarket?* □ *There's a big sale on toilet paper at the supermarket.*

superscript one or more characters printed slightly above a line of type. (Compare with SUBSCRIPT.) □ *In x^2, the 2 is a superscript.* □ *The footnotes should be indicated by a superscript.*

supply duct   a pipe or passageway that takes air from a furnace or central air conditioner to the rooms of a building. □ *There doesn't seem to be any air flow in the supply duct.* □ *Is this a supply duct or a return duct?*

supply line   a pipe that carries water into a building or a fixture. □ *Shut off the water at the main supply line.* □ *Shut off the hot water supply line at the water heater.*

supply reel   a wheel that holds a supply of film or audio-tape. (Compare with TAKE UP REEL.) □ *Place the supply reel on this spindle and thread the film through the projector.* □ *As the tape played, it moved from the supply reel onto the take up reel.*

suppository   a solid medicine designed to be placed in a body opening other than the mouth. □ *Nausea made it impossible for the patient to take oral medication, so the doctor prescribed a suppository.* □ *These suppositories stop hemorrhoidal itching fast.*

suspension   a system that keeps a car body from shaking as it travels over rough roads. □ *These mountain roads really put the suspension to the test.* □ *The car's poor suspension made for a jolting ride.*

suspension bridge   a bridge that hangs from cables attached to two large supports. □ *A suspension bridge spanned the bay.* □ *Some of the suspension bridge cables snapped in the high wind.*

sustain pedal   See FORTE PEDAL.

swatch   a small piece of material. □ *The fabric company sent me a set of swatches of their various cotton prints.* □ *I took a swatch of the dress material to the store with me, to see if I could find shoes that matched the color.*

sweater   a thick, knitted shirt. □ *In the fall, I take my sweaters out of storage.* □ *Put on a sweater if you're going outside.*

sweatpants loose pants made of knit material with elastic at the ankles and waist, usually worn to keep warm while exercising. (See also SWEATS, SWEATSHIRT.) □ *I put on my sweatpants and a T-shirt and went jogging.* □ *She wore sweatpants to do the housework.*

sweats loose clothing made of knit material, usually worn to keep warm while exercising. (Slang. See also SWEATPANTS, SWEATSHIRT, WARM-UPS.) □ *I lounged around the house in my sweats.* □ *The football players wore sweats to early morning practice.*

sweatshirt a long-sleeved shirt made of thick, knit material, often worn while exercising. (See also SWEATPANTS, SWEATS.) □ *The gift shop at the zoo sold souvenir sweatshirts with pictures of zoo animals on them.* □ *The runner peeled off his sweatshirt as he warmed up.*

sweat socks thick socks, often worn to keep warm while exercising. □ *She wore a sweatshirt, sweat pants, sweat socks, and running shoes.* □ *After soccer practice, I took off my sweat socks and put them in the laundry.*

sweetbread the thymus gland of a calf. □ *I served sweetbreads in cream sauce.* □ *Roll the sweetbreads in flour and place them on the broiler.*

sweetened condensed milk milk with sugar added and much of the water removed. □ *These cookies are made with sweetened condensed milk.* □ *I stirred a spoonful of sweetened condensed milk into my coffee.*

Sweet'n Low™ a brand of ARTIFICIAL SWEETENER. □ *"Please bring me some Sweet'n Low," I said to the waitress.* □ *"Would you like some Sweet'n Low for your iced tea?" Mary offered.*

sweet pickle a cucumber pickle cured in vinegar, sugar, and spices. □ *Would you like sweet pickles or dill pickles on your hamburger?* □ *The sandwich was garnished with tiny sweet pickles.*

(swimming) pool   a structure containing water for swimming. (See also WADING POOL.) ☐ *The Smiths have a swimming pool in their backyard.* ☐ *We spent most of the summer in the pool at the park.*

switch   a lever or sliding device that controls something. (See also BUTTON, DIAL, KEY, KNOB.) ☐ *I flipped the switch and the lights came on.* ☐ *This switch turns on the modem.*

switch hook   a control on a telephone that connects and disconnects a call. ☐ *Realizing I had dialed the wrong number, I pressed the switch hook to cut off the call.* ☐ *When you put the receiver in the cradle, it presses down on the switch hook.*

switch plate AND **cover plate**   a flat piece of material that covers the wiring behind a light switch. ☐ *She unscrewed the two screws that held the switch plate in place.* ☐ *He installed a decorative porcelain cover plate.*

swivel   **1.** a structure that allows something to swing or turn. (See also HINGE, PIVOT.) ☐ *The tripod leg is attached with a swivel.* ☐ *The strap attaches to this swivel.* **2.** to swing or turn as if on a SWIVEL. ☐ *The antenna can swivel in any direction.* ☐ *The desk chair swivels back and forth.*

synthesizer   an electronic device that creates musical sounds. ☐ *All the music on this recording was produced on a synthesizer.* ☐ *I programmed the synthesizer to sound like a violin.*

system crash   the failure of a computer system. (See also CRASH.) ☐ *A computer virus invaded the system and caused a system crash.* ☐ *The technicians tried to restore the computers after the system crash.*

T

tab   **1.** a set place along a line of type. □ *I set a tab every five spaces along the line.* □ *Push shift-F3 to set a tab at the location of the cursor.* **2.** a key on a typewriter or computer keyboard that moves the carriage or cursor forward to a pre-set place. □ *Press the tab twice. That will take you to the middle of the page.* □ *Where's the tab on this keyboard?*

Tabasco™ sauce   a brand of sauce made of spicy hot peppers. (See also HOT SAUCE.) □ *"Tabasco sauce is what makes the soups so spicy," said Jill.* □ *"I like to put Tabasco sauce on popcorn," James told us.*

tab collar   a shirt collar with plain, pointed ends. (Compare with BUTTON-DOWN COLLAR.) □ *The shirt is available with a button-down or tab collar.* □ *He used a silver collar bar to keep the ends of his tab collar in place.*

(table) linen   tablecloths, napkins, or table runners. □ *She set the table with her best china and silver on her prettiest table linen.* □ *The home store stocks all the crystal, china, and linen you need for gracious entertaining.*

tablespoon   a measure equaling ½ a fluid ounce. (A TABLESPOON is also equivalent to three TEASPOONS.) □ *Add a tablespoon of soy sauce.* □ *I measured out a tablespoon of cornstarch.*

tablet   **1.** a round, solid pill. (See also CAPLET, CAPSULE, GELCAP.) □ *One tablet contains 50 milligrams of medicine.* □ *I took a couple of aspirin tablets.* **2.** a number of sheets of paper, bound at one end. □ *The children practiced their printing on special school tablets.* □ *I took notes on a tablet I keep by the phone.*

tachometer   a device that indicates how fast something is rotating. □ *The sports car had a speedometer, an odometer, and a tachometer.* □ *Watch the tachometer. When it gets to this point, change gears.*

tackless strip   a thin piece of material with small, project-ing spikes, used for fastening carpeting to a floor. □ *Nail the tackless strip around the edge of the floor.* □ *Use the knee kicker to stretch the carpeting onto the tackless strip.*

tack lifter AND **tack puller**   a tool with a notched end, used to pull out nails and tacks. □ *Remove the nail with a tack lifter.* □ *This tack puller is magnetic, giving you a better grip on the nail.*

tack puller   See TACK LIFTER.

tacky   thick and sticky. □ *Let the glue dry until it becomes tacky.* □ *Press the paper onto the tacky rubber cement.*

taillight   a red light at the rear of a vehicle. □ *I saw a car's taillights up ahead.* □ *I put a new bulb in the taillight.*

tailored   [of clothing] having simple lines, and designed to fit the body fairly closely. □ *He wore a tailored jacket.* □ *I prefer tailored dresses to frilly ones.*

tailor's chalk   chalk designed for marking cloth. □ *Use tailor's chalk to mark the darts on the pattern piece.* □ *I marked the alterations on the pants with tailor's chalk.*

tailpipe   See EXHAUST PIPE.

take up reel   a wheel that gathers up film or audiotape that has passed through a machine. (Compare with SUPPLY REEL.) □ *The leading end of the film fits into this little slot on the take up reel.* □ *Most of the tape had been played. The take up reel was nearly full.*

tampon   a piece of absorbent material inserted into the vagina to absorb menstrual blood. □ *Do you use tampons or sanitary pads?* □ *She kept a tampon in her purse in case her period started when she was away from home.*

tandem bicycle   a bicycle with seats and pedals for two people. □ *We rented a tandem bicycle and rode around the park.* □ *Have you ever steered a tandem bicycle?*

tang   the part of a knife blade that attaches to the handle. □ *This is a good, solid knife. The tang extends all the way to the end of the handle.* □ *The tang was riveted to the handle.*

tank top   a sleeveless shirt with a SCOOP NECK. □ *It was a hot day. I put on a tank top and shorts.* □ *The runners all wore tank tops.*

tap   a VALVE out of which water flows into a sink or tub. □ *Turn on the tap.* □ *I opened up the hot water tap.*

tape counter   a device that measures how much of an audiotape or videotape has passed through a machine. □ *I used the tape counter to mark the part of the video that I wanted to see.* □ *To get to the beginning of the song, fast-forward until the tape counter reads 257.*

tape head   a device that reads or records sound or images on audiotape or videotape. □ *I opened up the tape recorder and cleaned the tape head with alcohol.* □ *The picture on the VCR is looking fuzzy. The tape heads probably need cleaning.*

tape measure   a strip of metal or plastic marked with measurements, such as inches or centimeters, and held in a rigid case. □ *I ran the tape measure along the wall.* □ *I used a tape measure to mark a cutting line on the board.*

taper   **1.** to become narrower. □ *The pant legs taper down to the ankle.* □ *The knife blade tapers to a point.* **2.** a long, thin CANDLE. □ *I put white tapers into the candelabra.* □ *The store sells both tapers and pillar candles.*

tap water   water that comes out of a faucet or tap. (See also DISTILLED WATER.) □ *Is it safe to drink the tap water here?* □ *You can use tap water in this steam iron.*

tarp(aulin)   a piece of WATERPROOF material used to cover something. □ *I spread a tarpaulin over the load of firewood in the back of my pickup truck.* □ *I fastened a tarp over the tent.*

tart a PASTRY with a bottom crust containing a filling. □ *Make these individual cherry tarts in a muffin tin.* □ *I baked a custard tart.*

tassel a bundle of hanging yarn or threads, used as a decoration. □ *There was a gold tassel on each corner of the pillow.* □ *A row of tassels ornamented the curtain valance.*

Tater Tots™ a brand of processed potatoes molded into small cylinders and fried. □ *The instructions read, "Spread the Tater Tots on a greased baking sheet and bake them at 400 degrees."* □ *"Today's special is fish with a side dish of Tater Tots," said the sign in the restaurant.*

taxi **1.** [for a plane] to move on wheels along the ground. □ *The plane taxied to the runway.* □ *It took twenty minutes for the plane to taxi from the runway to the gate.* **2.** See TAXICAB.

taxicab AND **taxi** a car for hire. □ *I called a taxi to take me to the bus station.* □ *A line of taxicabs waited outside the airport.*

tea bag a paper pouch containing loose tea. □ *Use one tea bag in two cups of hot water.* □ *I put a tea bag in my cup and poured hot water over it.*

tea ball a ball-shaped container with holes in it, used for steeping tea. (Compare with INFUSER.) □ *I put a teaspoon of tea into the tea ball.* □ *I dunked the tea ball in my cup.*

tea cosy AND **tea cozy** a cloth cover for keeping a pot of tea warm. □ *My aunt crocheted this tea cosy.* □ *I fitted the tea cosy over the teapot.*

tea cozy See TEA COSY.

teakettle a metal container with a spout, used for heating water. (TEAKETTLES are often designed to whistle when the steam from boiling water passes through a cover on the spout.) □ *I hear the teakettle whistling. Now we can have tea.* □ *I filled the teakettle and put it on the stove.*

teapot a container with a spout, used for brewing and serving tea. □ *I spooned tea into the china teapot.* □ *My grandmother gave me this silver teapot.*

tea service a set of dishes for formally serving tea. (A TEA SERVICE usually includes a TEAPOT, a sugar bowl, a creamer, and sometimes a tray. See also TEA SET.) □ *What a beautiful silver tea service!* □ *The hostess brought in the tea service and began to pour tea for her guests.*

tea set a set of dishes for serving tea. (A TEA SET usually includes a TEAPOT, a sugar bowl, a creamer, cups, and saucers. See also TEA SERVICE.) □ *I served tea in an earthenware tea set.* □ *A tea set was arranged on the breakfast table.*

teaspoon **1.** a measure equal to 1/6 of a fluid ounce. □ *Add a teaspoon of vanilla.* □ *Use two teaspoons of baking soda.* **2.** a small spoon for stirring tea or coffee. □ *The flatware set includes four teaspoons and four soup spoons.* □ *I stirred sugar into my tea with a teaspoon.*

Teflon™ a brand of coating that forms a NON-STICK surface. □ *"I have a set of Teflon pans. They're very easy to clean," said Jill.* □ *"The loaf pan is coated with Teflon," said the sales clerk.*

telephoto lens a camera lens that allows you to take pictures of objects far away. □ *The photographer put a telephoto lens on her camera.* □ *The journalist used a telephoto lens to get a picture of the politician, who was standing across the street.*

telescopic sight AND **scope** a small telescope attached to a rifle, used to sight and aim at distant objects. □ *She peered through the scope at her target.* □ *I adjusted the focus on my telescopic sight.*

television AND **TV** a device that receives pictures and sounds broadcast through either the air or a cable. (See also BIG SCREEN TV, CABLE TELEVISION, PROJECTION TV. TV is informal.) □ *Anything good on television tonight?* □ *I went into the living room and turned on the TV.*

temperature probe   a device that measures the temperature of something into which it is inserted. (TEMPERATURE PROBES are often used to check the temperature of food cooking in a MICROWAVE (OVEN).) □ *Put the microwave temperature probe into the chicken.* □ *The oven will stop when the temperature probe indicates that the water is boiling.*

temple   the part of a pair of eyeglasses that passes along the side of the head, connecting the lenses with the part that hooks over the ears. □ *The plastic temples on this pair of glasses are very flexible.* □ *I adjusted the temples until the glasses fit well.*

tenderizer   a substance or a tool used to make meat more tender. □ *I sprinkled tenderizer on the steak.* □ *Pound the meat with this tenderizer for a minute or two.*

tendril   a thin part of a vine that will curl around anything it touches. □ *The tendrils of the pea plants clung to the support frame.* □ *The squash plant was putting out tendrils.*

tennies   See TENNIS SHOES.

tennis shoes AND **tennies; athletic shoes**   shoes with sturdy rubber soles, designed to be worn while playing sports. (See also SNEAKERS.) □ *I put on some tennis shoes and went jogging.* □ *The soles of my tennies are almost worn through.* □ *These athletic shoes give extra support to your foot.*

tension bar   a metal bar supporting a metal fence or gate. □ *The chain link was clipped to the tension bar.* □ *The gate swung freely on the tension bar.*

ten-speed (bicycle)   a bicycle with ten different gears. □ *She got a ten-speed bicycle for her fifteenth birthday.* □ *This ten-speed is good for getting up steep hills. You can put it in a very low gear.*

terminal   **1.** a building where buses, trains, or airplanes take on and let off passengers. □ *You can purchase tickets in the main terminal.* □ *I'll meet you at the candy shop in the bus* *terminal.* **2.** a device that allows you to communicate with a mainframe computer. □ *I sat down at the terminal and typed in my password.* □ *I hooked the terminal up to the modem.* **3.** a place where an electrical connection to a battery can be made. □ *Connect the black clip to the negative terminal.* □ *This contact should be touching the battery terminal.*

terminal emulation a computer program that allows a personal computer to be used as a TERMINAL. □ *The terminal emulation can be set to VT100 or ANSI, depending on the terminal type preferred by the mainframe.* □ *The communications program includes a terminal emulation.*

terraced having several levels that resemble steps. □ *I looked at the terraced fields on the side of the mountain.* □ *The landscaper constructed a terraced garden in front of our building.*

terrazzo a floor covering made of small pieces of stone arranged in a pattern. □ *The foyer had a black-and-white terrazzo floor.* □ *The terrazzo floor contained six different colors of marble.*

terry cloth cloth with a fuzzy surface of small loops of thread. □ *My bathrobe is made of terry cloth.* □ *The soft terry cloth of the washrag felt good against my sunburned skin.*

terry towel a towel made of TERRY CLOTH. □ *I dried off with a terry towel.* □ *You can take this terry towel to the beach with you.*

text file a computer file consisting only of written information, not instructions to the computer. □ *I downloaded a text file to my word processor.* □ *All the files with a .DOC extension are text files.*

thaw **1.** [for a frozen item] to warm beyond the freezing point. □ *I left the meat to thaw in the sink.* □ *It takes two hours for the frozen bread dough to thaw.* **2.** to allow a frozen item to warm beyond the freezing point. □ *Thaw the chicken thoroughly.* □ *I thawed some vegetables for dinner.*

thermal paper   slick paper on which heat can form an image. (THERMAL PAPER is used in some electric typewriters, calculators, and word processors.) ☐ *Over time, the printing will fade from thermal paper.* ☐ *I need a roll of thermal paper for my calculator.*

thermocouple   a device that senses temperature. ☐ *The pilot light on the gas furnace heats a thermocouple, which opens the gas supply line.* ☐ *The thermocouple on the water heater regulates the burner.*

thermos (bottle)   an insulated bottle. ☐ *I took a thermos bottle full of hot coffee along in the car.* ☐ *I put some soup in the thermos in my little boy's lunch box.*

thermostat   a device that turns on a heating or cooling system when the temperature reaches a set point. ☐ *I set the thermostat at 78 degrees.* ☐ *The thermostat turned on the furnace.*

thicken   **1.** to become thick. ☐ *Stir the sauce until it thickens.* ☐ *The pudding will thicken as it cools.* **2.** to make something thick. ☐ *Both flour and cornstarch can be used to thicken a sauce.* ☐ *Thicken the syrup by boiling it.*

thimble   a cover that protects the tip of a finger or thumb while sewing. ☐ *I put the thimble on my finger and pushed the needle through the cloth.* ☐ *The thimble kept me from getting callouses on my finger.*

thin   **1.** to make something thinner. ☐ *Thin the paint with turpentine.* ☐ *I thinned the sauce with a little water.* **2.** to remove some plants in order to let others grow better. ☐ *I thinned the rows of carrots in the garden.* ☐ *That sweet basil needs thinning.*

35 mm   **1.** [of photographic film] 35 millimeters wide. ☐ *I need some 35-mm film.* ☐ *I got a 35-mm print of the movie.* **2.** [of a camera] using film that is 35 millimeters wide. ☐ *I use a 35-mm SLR.* ☐ *I have a disc camera and a 35 mm.*

thread count the number of threads per inch in a woven cloth. □ *These luxurious sheets have a high thread count.* □ *What's the thread count on this muslin?*

threads the spiral ridges around the long part of a screw. □ *When I forced the screw into that hole, I stripped all the threads off it.* □ *The screw had very fine threads.*

three-hole punch a device that makes three-holes along one edge of a piece of paper. □ *I put the papers through the three-hole punch and then filed them in a three-ring binder.* □ *This adjustable three-hole punch allows you to make holes that will fit a variety of notebooks and binders.*

three-quarter sleeve a sleeve that comes to the middle of the forearm. □ *This T shirt has a three-quarter sleeve.* □ *The dress has a ballet neck and three-quarter sleeves.*

three-ring binder a cardboard or plastic cover that holds pages inside with three metal rings that go through holes in one side of the paper. (See also BINDER.) □ *I took a loose-leaf page out of my three-ring binder.* □ *This three-ring binder can hold up to a one-inch stack of pages.*

three-way bulb a light bulb that can give off light at three different strengths. □ *This lamp takes a three-way bulb.* □ *There's a three-way bulb in that reading lamp. Click the switch twice if you want more light.*

three-way switch an electrical switch that allows two separate switches to turn something on or off. □ *The light over the stairs was controlled by a three-way switch. You could turn it on at the top of the stairs, go downstairs, and turn it off from down there.* □ *I installed a three-way switch so that we could turn on the kitchen light from either end of the room.*

throat lozenge See COUGH DROP.

throat plate a flat piece of metal beneath the needle of a sewing machine, containing a device that moves cloth forward or backward under the needle. □ *This lever raises and* *lowers the throat plate.* □ *The needle was too far bent to pass through the hole in the throat plate.*

throttle   a device that controls how much fuel passes into an engine's cylinders. □ *Open up the throttle and see if the engine will race.* □ *The throttle appears to be stuck in one position.*

throw   a small blanket for covering the shoulders or the legs. (See also COMFORTER.) □ *The sofa was draped with colorful woven throws.* □ *He wrapped a throw around his shoulders and sat down in the rocking chair.*

throw rug   a small rug. □ *The brightly colored throw rugs gave the room a cheerful look.* □ *She took off her slippers and put them on the throw rug beside her bed.*

thumb tack   a short pin with a round, flat head, designed to be pushed in with the thumb. (See also PUSH PIN.) □ *A thumb tack held the picture to the wall.* □ *I used a thumb tack to tack the announcement to the bulletin board.*

tights   thick stockings that fit all the way from the waist to the feet. □ *The ballet dancer put on a leotard and tights.* □ *She wore blue tights with her short blue skirt.*

tiller   a device that digs up soil and works dead plant matter into it. □ *Go over the garden plot with a tiller before you plant your seeds.* □ *The tiller worked the soil to a depth of about six inches.*

timber   a large piece of wood used in construction. □ *Timbers supported the cabin roof.* □ *The timber that formed the door lintel had buckled.*

timer   a device that does something at a set time. □ *The timer will ring when forty-five minutes are up.* □ *I set the timer to turn on the lamps at 8:30 PM.*

time zone   an area in which all clocks are set to the same time. □ *Is Philadelphia in the same time zone as Atlanta?* □ *The clocks in the news room showed the time in different time zones around the world.*

tine a thin, pointed structure on a FORK. ☐ *The tines of the old pitchfork were rusted and bent.* ☐ *This fork has three tines.*

tin foil See ALUMINUM FOIL.

tin snips a heavy pair of SCISSORS for cutting sheets of metal. ☐ *I pasted the pattern to the sheet metal and then cut it out with tin snips.* ☐ *I used tin snips to cut an opening in the tin can.*

tip 1. a pointed end. ☐ *The tip of the antenna had broken off.* ☐ *He used the tip of the paintbrush to make a fine line.* 2. a piece of useful advice. (Informal.) ☐ *An article in the paper today had tips for saving money on groceries.* ☐ *Tom gave me a tip on how to beat the rush hour traffic.*

tire a flexible covering attached to a vehicle wheel and in-flated with air. ☐ *I need to put some air in my bike tires.* ☐ *The mechanic checked the tread on the tire.*

tire chain a set of chains attached to a TIRE to give it a better grip on ice and snow. ☐ *The roads were slick. I put the tire chains on the truck.* ☐ *The tire chains bit into the ice as the car crept up the hill.*

tire iron a long-handled tool for removing the nuts that hold a vehicle's wheel onto the axle. ☐ *The car had a flat tire. I jacked it up and got out the tire iron.* ☐ *I pushed down on the tire iron with all my strength, but the nut wouldn't turn.*

toast 1. to cook something near a heat source until it turns light brown. ☐ *I toasted the bagel.* ☐ *We toasted marshmal-lows over the campfire.* 2. bread that has been TOASTED. ☐ *I had eggs and toast for breakfast.* ☐ *Would you like some jelly for your toast?*

toaster a device that TOASTS bread. ☐ *I put two slices of bread in the toaster.* ☐ *The toast popped out of the toaster, hot and brown.*

toaster oven a small electric oven in which food can be TOASTED. ☐ *I put the cheese sandwiches in the toaster oven* and heated them until the cheese bubbled. □ *I warmed up the leftover lasagna in the toaster oven.*

toaster pastry   a flat pastry that can be warmed in a TOAST-ER. □ *I had a couple of toaster pastries for breakfast.* □ *The toaster pastries come in three flavors—blueberry, strawberry, and chocolate.*

toggle bolt   a screw with two metal flaps or wings that spread outward as the screw is tightened. (See also MOLLY™ BOLT.) □ *Use a toggle bolt to install a hook in the ceiling.* □ *The rack was fastened to the drywall with toggle bolts.*

toilet   a plumbing fixture designed to receive excrement. □ *I hate scrubbing the toilet.* □ *Do you need to go to the toilet?*

toilet auger   See CLOSET AUGER.

toilet bowl   the round, hollow part of a TOILET. □ *He scrubbed the toilet bowl with a stiff brush.* □ *The toilet bowl was choked with soggy toilet paper.*

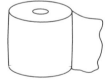

(toilet) bowl cleaner   a substance for cleaning a TOILET BOWL. (BOWL CLEANER is a euphemism.) □ *I squirted toilet bowl cleaner into the bowl.* □ *This automatic bowl cleaner freshens and cleans with every flush.*

toilet paper AND **bathroom tissue; toilet tissue**   paper used to wipe oneself after using the toilet. (BATHROOM TISSUE is a euphemism.) □ *There's no toilet paper in this bathroom stall!* □ *The blue bathroom tissue matched the blue bathroom decor.* □ *I put a new roll of toilet tissue on the spindle.*

toiletries   things or preparations used to groom oneself, such as soap, shampoo, and toothpaste. □ *I packed my toiletries in a separate bag in my suitcase.* □ *Shaving cream and other toiletries are in aisle 10.*

toilet tank   the part of a TOILET that holds the water used for flushing. □ *I took the top off the toilet tank and looked at the flush mechanism.* □ *It took several minutes for the toilet tank to refill after each flush.*

toilet tissue   See TOILET PAPER.

token   a coin-shaped piece of metal that can be exchanged for a ride on a bus or SUBWAY system. □ *I put my token in the fare box.* □ *Buy bus tokens in packages of ten.*

toll   **1.** an amount of money charged for the use of a road or bridge. □ *I stopped at the toll booth and paid my toll.* □ *The toll is 40 cents.* **2.** [of a road or bridge] charging a TOLL. □ *I-88 is a toll road.* □ *I drove two miles south to avoid the toll bridge.*

toll booth   a place where a fee or TOLL is collected from vehicles using a toll road or toll bridge. □ *I stopped at the toll booth and paid the toll.* □ *Cars were lined up for half a mile behind the toll booth.*

tone   a sound on a single pitch. □ *Please leave a message at the tone.* □ *At the tone, the time will be exactly 3:00 PM, Central standard time.*

tone arm   a metal rod hinged at one end and having a phonograph needle attached to the other. □ *Gently lower the tone arm onto the record.* □ *The tone arm will automatically lift from the record when it reaches the end.*

toner   a substance, such as an ink or powder, used to make an image in some printing devices, such as copy machines. □ *The instrument panel on the copy machine says, "Add toner."* □ *I emptied the bottle of toner into the reservoir.*

tongs   a tool made of two rods hinged in the middle, with handles at one end and flat areas at the other. (Used for gripping and lifting things.) □ *Lift the log with the fireplace tongs.* □ *She used tongs to remove the ears of corn from the boiling water.*

tongue   the part of a lace-up shoe that covers the top of the foot. □ *I pulled the tongue straight and laced up my sneaker.* □ *The stiff leather tongue on this shoe chafes against my ankle.*

tongue and groove pliers   a pair of pliers with jaws that can be firmly set at a number of different widths. □ *I gripped the metal bar with tongue and groove pliers.* □ *A pair of tongue and groove pliers is useful for gripping a hose where it connects to a pipe.*

(tooth) floss   See DENTAL FLOSS.

toothpick   a small, thin stick used to remove food from between the teeth. □ *After eating corn on the cob, I always have to use a toothpick.* □ *I got the popcorn hull out from between my teeth with a toothpick.*

top   a shirt. (Informal. Contrasts with BOTTOM.) □ *I like your new top!* □ *This classic top will go with anything.*

topiary   trees or bushes trimmed in decorative shapes. □ *The mansion's garden was full of topiary.* □ *Look at the topiary in front of that house! That bush is shaped like a horse, and that one looks like a camel!*

topo(graphic) map   a detailed map with lines connecting points with the same elevation. (TOPO MAP is informal. Compare with RELIEF MAP.) □ *We planned our mountain hike with a topographic map.* □ *The topo map shows a deep ravine in that location.*

topping   a top layer on a food item. □ *This casserole has a topping of melted cheese.* □ *I used whipped cream as a topping for the brownies.*

topsoil   the top layer of dirt. (Compare with SUBSOIL.) □ *There is a beautiful, rich topsoil in this area.* □ *I worked fertilizer and mulch into the topsoil.*

topstitch   to sew along the top of a SEAM, on the outside of a garment. □ *Topstitch the cuff in place.* □ *Topstitch with a contrasting thread for a decorative effect.*

tortilla   a flat, round bread made of wheat or corn flour. (Spanish.) □ *Would you like corn or flour tortillas with your chile rellenos?* □ *The beef burrito comes in a flour tortilla.*

tortilla chip   small, fried pieces of flat corn or wheat bread. □ *I poured the tortilla chips into a bowl.* □ *Try our new ranch flavor tortilla chips.*

tossed salad   a mixture of raw vegetables, usually including a green, leafy vegetable like lettuce or spinach. □ *The fish dinner comes with a tossed salad.* □ *I made a tossed salad with romaine lettuce, tomatoes, green peppers, and radishes.*

touch tone   [of a telephone] having numbered buttons that make an electronic tone when pressed. □ *If you are calling from a touch tone phone, press 1 now.* □ *Type in your zip code on your touch tone keypad.*

touring bicycle AND **touring bike**   a sturdy bicycle designed for long trips. □ *I installed a large basket on the rear of my touring bike.* □ *We loaded camping gear on our touring bikes and headed off for the state park.*

touring bike   See TOURING BICYCLE.

tourist (class)   See COACH (CLASS).

tow truck AND **wrecker**   a truck equipped with a device for lifting and pulling another vehicle behind it. □ *The car wouldn't start. I had to call a tow truck to take it to the garage.* □ *A wrecker hauled away the illegally parked car.*

tracing wheel   a thin, metal wheel mounted in a handle. (When you roll a TRACING WHEEL over a piece of special tracing paper, it leaves a mark on the surface underneath.) □ *Using tracing paper and a tracing wheel, mark the positions of the darts on your pattern pieces.* □ *Use tailor's chalk or a tracing wheel to mark your pattern.*

trackball   a ball-shaped device that can be spun in order to move the cursor on a computer screen. □ *The laptop has a built-in trackball.* □ *I like to use the trackball when I play computer games.*

tracking   a function of a videotape player that allows it to play a tape recorded at a slightly different speed. □ *Adjust* the tracking until the moving white lines disappear from the picture. □ This button controls the tracking.

track lighting   individual lights mounted on a track that allows you to slide them to different positions. □ *The track lighting in the room was focused to highlight the paintings on the walls.* □ *I like the modern look of track lighting.*

tractor   a vehicle for pulling farming equipment such as plows. □ *The farmer hitched the tractor up to the plow.* □ *The tractor went back and forth across the fields, seeding the new crop.*

traffic cone   a brightly colored plastic cone, used to mark an area where traffic should not go. □ *The telephone workers put traffic cones in front and in back of their truck while they worked on the telephone line.* □ *A line of traffic cones closed off the left lane.*

traffic light AND **stop light**   a light that indicates which direction of traffic may cross an intersection. □ *The traffic light turned green.* □ *Go past the third stop light, then take the first left.*

trailer   a wheeled container pulled behind a car or truck. □ *I loaded all my belongings into a trailer and bade goodbye to my old home.* □ *The pickup truck was pulling a horse trailer.*

trailer hitch   a structure that makes it possible to attach a TRAILER to the rear of a vehicle. □ *I put a trailer hitch on my car so that I could haul the camper.* □ *I rented a trailer to move my furniture and had to buy a trailer hitch to hitch it up to the car.*

training pants   absorbent underpants for a child who is learning to use the toilet. □ *My youngest is out of diapers and into training pants.* □ *Little Sally is so proud of her training pants. She didn't wet them once today.*

training wheels   a pair of wheels attached to the rear wheel of a bicycle, used to keep the bicycle stable while

someone learns to ride it. □ *Jimmy insisted that he was ready to try riding the bike without the training wheels.* □ *Mandy got too big for the tricycle, so now she's riding a bike with training wheels.*

train station a building where a train stops to let passengers on and off. □ *Is there a train station in Elmhurst?* □ *I bought a round-trip ticket at the train station.*

tranquilizer See SEDATIVE.

transceiver a radio that can both send and receive signals. □ *I contacted the distant radio operator on my transceiver.* □ *This cable connects the transceiver to the antenna.*

transmission a system that transfers energy from a vehicle's engine to its wheels. □ *This model has an automatic transmission.* □ *The car won't stay in gear. There must be something wrong with the transmission.*

transom a window above a door. □ *Someone must be in the room. I can see light coming through the transom.* □ *I opened the transom to get a breeze flowing through.*

transparency AND **view graph** a sheet of transparent material with an image printed or drawn on it. (The TRANSPARENCY can be put on a projector and the image projected on a vertical surface such as a screen. VIEW GRAPH is used mostly by scientists.) □ *The speaker illustrated his talk with transparencies showing the latest statistics.* □ *The astronomer prepared a set of view graphs for her lecture.*

trap a pipe with a bend in it, used to keep sewer gas from passing back up through a drain. □ *There's a plug at the bottom of the trap.* □ *I fit a new trap underneath the sink.*

trash bag a paper or plastic bag used to collect and carry waste material. □ *I lined the wastebasket with a trash bag.* □ *I carried the full trash bags out to the trash can.*

trash can See GARBAGE CAN.

trash compactor   See GARBAGE COMPACTOR.

traverse rod   a rod for hanging a curtain, with a mechanism that allows the curtain to be opened and shut by pulling on a cord. □ *These curtains are designed to hang on a traverse rod.* □ *We installed traverse rods over all the windows.*

tread   1. the flat, horizontal part of a step. □ *The treads on these stairs are very narrow.* □ *The step needs a new tread.* 2. the ridges on the part of a shoe or a tire that comes into contact with the ground. □ *These hiking shoes have thick treads.* □ *The tread had almost worn off the tire.*

(tree) stump   the part of a tree that remains above the ground after the tree has been cut down. □ *I had to use a tractor to pull the old tree stump out of my backyard.* □ *The city workers cut down the trees along the street, leaving a row of stumps.*

trellis   a structure of wooden slats on which climbing plants can grow. □ *I put in a trellis as a support for the pea plants.* □ *The gardener had trained roses to cover the trellis, and in the summertime, it was covered with red blossoms.*

trench   a long, narrow opening dug in the ground. □ *I dug a trench to drain the water out of the backyard.* □ *The construction workers dug a trench for the electrical lines.*

trial size   a small size, containing just enough for you to try the product inside. □ *I got this trial size shampoo in the mail.* □ *One whole row of the drugstore has bins of trial size cosmetics.*

tricycle   a three-wheeled vehicle, powered by pushing on pedals. (TRICYCLES are usually ridden by children.) □ *Billy rode around the block on his tricycle.* □ *She scraped her knee when she fell off her tricycle.*

trifle bowl   a glass bowl for serving trifle, a dessert containing layers of custard, fruit, cake, and whipped cream. □ *She carefully spooned the layers into the trifle bowl.* □ *The pudding was served in a cut-glass trifle bowl.*

trigger **1.** a lever that fires a gun when pulled. □ *She took careful aim, then pulled the trigger.* □ *He had one finger on the trigger.* **2.** a lever that forces something out of a container when pulled. □ *The window cleaner comes in a bottle with a trigger spray.* □ *This trigger on the camcorder starts recording the videotape.*

trim decorative material sewed along an edge. □ *The shirt collar has a lace trim.* □ *The blue jacket has contrasting yellow trim.*

trip [for a CIRCUIT BREAKER] to go off. □ *Check the circuit breakers. Did one of them trip?* □ *When the air conditioner went on, it overloaded the circuit, and the circuit breaker tripped.*

tripod a support with three legs. (There are special TRIPODS for supporting cameras.) □ *The photographer set up a camera tripod.* □ *The fondue pot rests on a metal tripod.*

trivet a piece of wood, metal, or ceramic that protects a surface from something hot. □ *Put down a trivet before you put that hot saucepan on the table.* □ *I put the hot teakettle on a trivet on the countertop.*

trowel **1.** a tool with a short handle and a broad, shovel-shaped, pointed metal blade, used for digging dirt. □ *I dug up the tomato plant with a trowel.* □ *Loosen the soil with a trowel, then plant the seeds.* **2.** a tool with a short handle and a flat triangular blade, used for spreading MORTAR. □ *I picked up some cement on my trowel.* □ *I smoothed the mortar with a trowel.* **3.** to use a TROWEL to spread something. □ *He troweled mortar onto the top of the wall.* □ *She troweled cement into the mold.*

trunk **1.** a large, covered compartment in the rear of a car. □ *Put your suitcase in the trunk.* □ *I keep a first-aid kit in the trunk of my car.* **2.** the rigid, vertical part of a tree. □ *The trunk of the old oak tree was three feet in diameter.* □ *A squirrel made a nest in the tree trunk.*

truss   a triangular framework that supports something, such as a roof or a bridge. □ *The construction workers raised the roof truss to the top of the building and fixed it in place.* □ *A series of steel trusses reinforced the bridge.*

T shirt   a PULLOVER shirt made of knitted material. □ *The T shirt was printed with the store's name.* □ *He wore a T shirt and jeans.*

T square   a tool shaped like the letter T, with the top bar meeting the bottom one at a perfect right angle. □ *I used a T square to draw a ninety-degree angle.* □ *With the T square, I made a line at right angles to the edge of the page.*

tumbler   **1.** a drinking glass with a flat bottom. □ *Fill the tumbler with ice water.* □ *I put a few ice cubes in the tumbler.* **2.** the part inside a lock that is turned by the key. □ *A lock with five tumblers offers better security than one with only three.* □ *One of the tumblers is not lining up properly.*

tuna salad   a mixture of tuna fish, mayonnaise, and seasonings. □ *I would like tuna salad on my sandwich.* □ *I like to put chopped green olives in my tuna salad.*

tuner   a device that adjusts a radio or television to receive a signal. □ *Connect the tuner to the amplifier so we can hear the radio.* □ *The TV picture cleared up when I adjusted the tuner.*

tune-up   the process of checking various parts of an engine, including the spark plugs, ignition system, and carburetor, and adjusting or repairing them if necessary. □ *The manufacturer recommends a tune-up every 6 months or 6,000 miles, whichever comes first.* □ *All the spark plugs were replaced the last time the car had a tune-up.*

tunic   a long shirt. □ *She wore a tunic over a pair of leggings.* □ *This tunic is long enough to wear as a dress.*

Tupperware™   a brand of plastic storage containers. □ *"Put away the leftovers in that green Tupperware bowl," Mom* *called from the living room.* □ *"This Tupperware container can go in the freezer," Jane remarked as she put it there.*

turbo [of a computer] having the capability to make calculations very fast. □ *The turbo processor makes data searching fast and easy.* □ *When the turbo light is on, the processor is working at high speed.*

tureen a large, decorative bowl for serving soup. □ *She brought the soup in a silver tureen.* □ *I ladled broth out of the tureen.*

turkey burger a patty of ground turkey meat. □ *Is there a turkey burger on the menu? I'm on a diet, and I can't have red meat.* □ *I cooked some turkey burgers on the grill.*

turn over [for an engine] to start. (Informal.) □ *The starter motor is working, but the engine won't turn over.* □ *I pumped the gas pedal a few times, and the engine finally turned over.*

turnover a food item made of a filling folded into a rich crust and baked. □ *Have one of these apple turnovers.* □ *I made cheese turnovers for an appetizer.*

(turn) signal AND **blinker** a flashing light on the front or back of a car, used to signal a turn. (BLINKER is informal.) □ *Turn on your blinker if you're going to turn here.* □ *His turn signal was flashing, but he kept driving straight ahead.* □ *Why do you have your signal on?*

turntable **1.** a round, revolving platform on which a phonograph record can be placed. □ *Place the LP gently onto the turntable.* □ *Why isn't the turntable revolving?* **2.** a device for playing phonograph records, including a TURNTABLE and a TONE ARM. □ *I connected the turntable to the stereo amplifier.* □ *I don't have a turntable, just a CD player.*

turpentine an oil made from pine sap and used to clean or dilute oil-based paint. □ *I cleaned the paintbrush with turpentine.* □ *The smell of turpentine filled the workshop.*

turtleneck   a knitted shirt with a high, tubular neck that folds over. ☐ *He wore a turtleneck and a sport coat.* ☐ *I got a blue turtleneck to match my navy blue pants.*

tutorial (program)   a computer program that teaches you how to do something. ☐ *I went through the word processor tutorial to learn the basic commands.* ☐ *This tutorial program will show you how to work with the mouse.*

TV   See TELEVISION.

TV dinner   See FROZEN DINNER.

TV listing   a schedule of television programs. ☐ *The Sunday newspaper includes a TV listing for the week.* ☐ *According to the TV listing, there's a John Wayne movie on at 8:00 PM.*

tweed   a rough, woven wool cloth. ☐ *He put on a tweed jacket for his walk in the cool morning air.* ☐ *She wore a brown tweed blazer.*

tweeter   a device that converts electronic signals to high-pitched sounds; part of a SPEAKER. (TWEETERS are measured by diameter.) ☐ *This speaker has a two-inch tweeter and a five-inch woofer.* ☐ *The tweeter on this speaker gives you nice, clear high tones.*

twill   a fabric woven with a diagonal pattern. ☐ *The pants are made of cotton twill.* ☐ *The jacket was made of a thick, woolen twill.*

twin bed   one of a matching pair of beds. (A TWIN BED is usually designed for only one person to sleep in.) ☐ *I bought twin beds for the girls' room.* ☐ *Will this mattress fit a twin bed?*

twin lens reflex   a camera with two lenses, one that allows you to see and focus the image, and one that puts the image onto the film. ☐ *This twin lens reflex uses 120 film.* ☐ *I adjusted the viewing lens of my twin lens reflex until the image came into focus.*

twist-off cap   a bottle cap that is designed to be twisted off with the hands. □ *Is this a twist-off cap, or do I need a bottle opener?* □ *The two-liter bottle has a twist-off cap.*

twist tie   a piece of wire coated with a flat layer of paper or plastic and used to hold a bag shut. □ *I shut the garbage bag with a twist tie.* □ *I undid the twist tie and opened the bag.*

two-way radio   a radio that can both receive and send a signal. (See also WALKIE TALKIE.) □ *The delivery truck was equipped with a two-way radio.* □ *We talked to headquarters via two-way radio.*

Tylenol™   a brand of ACETAMINOPHEN, a pain relieving drug. □ *"Take two Tylenol tablets every four hours," the doctor advised.* □ *"I prefer Tylenol to aspirin," said Bill. "Do you have any?"*

typeface   a style of letters and numbers. □ *This computer printer is capable of producing six different typefaces in three different sizes.* □ *I wanted a bold, attention-getting typeface for the title of my report.*

typo(graphical error)   a mistake in typing. (TYPO is informal.) □ *I noticed a typographical error in the document I was proofreading.* □ *That secretary can't seem to type a letter without a dozen typos.*

U

UHF See ULTRA HIGH FREQUENCY.

ultra high frequency AND **UHF** a high band of television signals. □ *Channel 53 is a UHF channel.* □ *Can your TV pick up ultra high frequency stations?*

underpass a place where one road or rail line passes under another. (Compare with OVERPASS.) □ *The bicyclist waited beneath the underpass for the rain to stop.* □ *There's a bridge over the railway underpass.*

underwriter's knot a special knot tied in the end of an electrical wire to keep it from being pulled out of a lamp. □ *When rewiring a lamp, make sure to tie an underwriter's knot in the wire.* □ *The wire must be split in order to tie an underwriter's knot.*

unisex intended for both men and women. □ *These unisex sweatshirts come in small, medium, and large.* □ *Unisex hair salon—everyone welcome.*

unit a manufactured item. □ *Where did you purchase the unit?* □ *Should the unit malfunction, take it to the nearest authorized service center.*

universal product code AND **UPC** a machine-readable code that gives information about a manufactured product. (See also BAR CODE.) □ *The grocery store clerk scanned the UPC on the jar of salsa.* □ *To receive your $2 rebate, send in the universal product code and receipt from your purchase of our product.*

unrefined sugar coarse sugar from which little of the molasses has been removed. □ *The health food store sells unrefined sugar.* □ *Unrefined sugar has a strong taste to it.*

UPC See UNIVERSAL PRODUCT CODE.

upgrade a new version of a computer program. □ *A new upgrade for this word processor will be available next summer.* □ *The upgrade will make it easier for you to keep track of your files.*

upholstery material covering a piece of furniture. □ *The sofa had soft velvet upholstery.* □ *The chair's worn leather upholstery needed to be replaced.*

upload to move a file from your computer to another computer. (Contrasts with DOWNLOAD.) □ *I uploaded the data I had collected onto the computer at the lab.* □ *The sales representatives uploaded their monthly sales reports.*

upper the top parts of a shoe; everything but the sole. □ *These walking shoes have leather uppers.* □ *The sandals have canvas uppers and a leather sole.*

upper case [of letters] large. (In English, UPPER CASE letters are used to begin sentences and at the beginning of proper names. Contrasts with LOWER CASE.) □ *In this sentence, the word UPPER is in upper case.* □ *When completing this form, please print in upper case letters.*

upright vacuum cleaner a VACUUM (CLEANER) with a bag attached to a long, vertical handle. □ *I used a heavy-duty upright vacuum cleaner to clean the floors in the office.* □ *This new model upright vacuum cleaner is very easy to push.*

user friendly [of a computer program] easy to use and to understand. □ *This software is menu driven and completely user friendly.* □ *The user friendly interface will prompt you before taking any action that might delete a file.*

user interface the way a computer program communicates with the person using it. □ *The user interface on this browser is easy to understand.* □ *This user interface requires you to have some knowledge of DOS commands.*

user's manual a book of instructions for using something. □ *Is there a user's manual for this spreadsheet program?* □ *The user's manual for the VCR has a very useful index.*

utensil   a tool used in cooking or eating. □ *A pancake turner is a very useful utensil.* □ *We took plastic eating utensils along on the camping trip.*

utility knife   **1.** a tool with a plastic handle containing a sharp blade. □ *I slit open the box with a utility knife.* □ *The utility knife sliced through the tape.* **2.** a small kitchen knife used for many purposes. □ *You can pare the apple with this utility knife.* □ *I used the utility knife to prick the potato.*

utility room   a room for storing useful things. □ *There's a toolbox in the utility room.* □ *The utility room has hookups for a washer and dryer.*

V

V-8   an engine with eight cylinders arranged in two rows that meet in a V-shape. □ *This cross section shows the interior of the cylinders in a typical V-8 engine.* □ *This V-8 gives you plenty of accelerating power.*

vacuum bag AND **dust bag**   a bag inside a VACUUM (CLEANER) that collects the dirt that the vacuum takes in. □ *The vacuum bag was full, so I replaced it with an empty one.* □ *I took the dust bag out to the trash and emptied it.*

vacuum (cleaner)   a device that uses suction to remove dirt from a surface and collects the dirt in a VACUUM BAG. □ *I pushed the vacuum cleaner back and forth across the floor.* □ *Uh-oh. I spilled dirt on the carpet. Better get the vacuum.*

valance   a decorative piece of cloth draped across the top of a window. □ *The satin curtains come with a matching valance.* □ *A fringed valance covered the tops of the curtains.*

valve   a device that can start or stop the flow of a liquid or gas. □ *Open this valve to let out the air in the radiator.* □ *I connected the air pump to the valve on the bicycle tire.*

valve stem   the long, thin, straight part of a VALVE. □ *The valve stem moved up and down the valve shaft.* □ *The valve stems were pitted and corroded.*

vanity   **1.** a cabinet in a bathroom, usually containing a sink. □ *I have extra toilet paper stored in the vanity.* □ *There was a lovely marble-topped vanity in the bathroom.* **2.** a small table with a mirror, used while dressing or applying make-up. □ *The top of the vanity was littered with cosmetics.* □ *She peered into the mirror on her vanity.*

vaporizer   a device that sprays water vapor into the air. (See also HUMIDIFIER.) □ *The baby had a cold, so I put a* *vaporizer in her room.* □ *Unplug the vaporizer and fill it with water.*

vapor lock   an engine shutdown caused by vapor in the fuel system. □ *Let the car cool off and then try to start it. It may just be a case of vapor lock.* □ *The engine's overheating resulted in vapor lock.*

variety store   a store that sells a large selection of inexpensive things. □ *You can get good deals on cleaning supplies at the variety store down the street.* □ *The variety store was having a special on ladies' scarves.*

varnish   a clear substance applied to a wood surface to protect it and make it look good. □ *The glossy varnish really brings out the beautiful grain in the wood.* □ *I spread a coat of varnish onto the wooden molding.*

Vaseline™   a brand of PETROLEUM JELLY. □ *"Try some Vaseline on those cold sores," Jim suggested.* □ *"Vaseline is great for dry skin," Nancy said.*

VCR   See VIDEO CASSETTE RECORDER.

vegetable brush   a brush with stiff bristles, used to scrub dirt off vegetables. □ *Scrub the potatoes with a vegetable brush.* □ *I cleaned off the mushrooms with a vegetable brush.*

Velcro™   a brand of HOOK AND LOOP FASTENER. □ *"These sneakers have a Velcro fastener, so it's easy for the kids to get them on and off," said Joe.* □ *"The wallet closes with a Velcro strip," said the description in the catalog.*

velour   a fabric resembling VELVET, with a surface of short, soft threads. □ *She wore a long-sleeved velour shirt.* □ *The chair was upholstered with velour.*

Velveeta™   a brand of processed cheese. □ *"Try melting some Velveeta in the microwave on some toast," said the helpful hints column in the newspaper.* □ *"Try this recipe for spicy dip made with Velveeta," Bill said.*

velvet a woven silk or cotton cloth with a fuzzy surface. □ *She wore a black velvet evening gown.* □ *The tuxedo had velvet lapels.*

veneer a thin layer of wood glued to the surface of a piece of furniture. □ *The bookshelves are particle board with an oak veneer.* □ *The tabletop veneer was peeling away.*

venetian blind a window covering made of horizontal strips of flexible material that can be adjusted to let in more or less light. (See also MINIBLIND.) □ *I raised the venetian blind and looked outside.* □ *This cord closes the venetian blinds.*

vent **1.** an opening that allows a gas to flow out. □ *Hot air from the dryer passes out through this vent.* □ *The furnace vent was clogged with dust and hair.* **2.** a vertical opening at the hem of a garment. □ *The jacket has side vents.* □ *The vent in the back of the skirt allows the wearer to move freely.*

veranda a roofed platform attached to the outside of a building. (See also BALCONY, GALLERY, PORCH.) □ *We sat out on the veranda, watching the fireflies.* □ *A screened-in veranda ran around two sides of the house.*

vermiculite a material consisting of light stone pellets, often mixed into soil to help plants grow. □ *I started the seeds in vermiculite, then transplanted them into soil.* □ *I worked vermiculite into the potting soil.*

very high frequency AND **VHF** a band of television signals. (Television channels 2 through 13 are VHF channels.) □ *I get very poor reception of very high frequency channels.* □ *I adjusted the VHF antenna on the TV set.*

VHF See VERY HIGH FREQUENCY.

VHS™ a videotape format. □ *"This VCR takes VHS tapes,"* said the salesperson. □ *"Is this tape VHS?" I asked the clerk at the video store.*

video cassette recorder AND **VCR**   a device for recording and playing videotape. □ *I programmed the VCR to tape the movie on Channel 12.* □ *Put the tape into the video cassette recorder.*

video(tape)   a cassette containing film on tape. (VIDEO is informal.) □ *Let's rent a video.* □ *I put a videotape into the machine.*

viewfinder   a device on a camera that shows what will be included in the picture. □ *I looked through the viewfinder to make sure everyone would be in the picture.* □ *I adjusted the camera's position until the mountain appeared in the middle of the viewfinder.*

view graph   See TRANSPARENCY.

vinegar   a sour liquid made from fermented wine or cider. □ *Add vinegar to the salad dressing.* □ *The pie crust was flavored with apple cider vinegar.*

vinyl   **1.** a kind of plastic. □ *The sofa's vinyl upholstery squeaked as I sat down on it.* □ *I installed vinyl tile on the kitchen floor.* **2.** phonograph records made of VINYL. (Slang.) □ *Jim has a vast collection of vinyl.* □ *Let's put some vinyl on the turntable.*

violation   the breaking of a law. □ *I got a ticket for a parking violation.* □ *He had a number of traffic violations on his record.*

viscose   a synthetic material. □ *This jacket is made of a polyester/viscose blend.* □ *The fabric is 40 percent cotton, 60 percent viscose.*

vise   a device with moveable jaws, used to hold something in place. □ *I clamped the wood in a vise and began to saw it.* □ *Hold the metal block steady in a vise.*

Vise-Grips™   a brand of pliers with jaws that can be locked in place. (See also LOCKING PLIERS.) □ *"Use the Vise-Grips to* *loosen that stubborn bolt," said Cathy. ☐ "I'll fix the Vise-Grips in place on the hose connection while you put the clamp in place," Jim said.*

V neck   a garment neck with a V-shaped opening in front. (See also BOAT NECK, CREW NECK, SCOOP NECK.) ☐ *She wore a button-down shirt under a sweater with a V neck. ☐ The blouse has a V neck.*

voltmeter   a device that measures a difference in electric potential. ☐ *I used a voltmeter to check the voltage of the car battery. ☐ The electrician measured the incoming voltage with a voltmeter.*

volume   **1.** the space something occupies or contains. ☐ *This package is measured by weight, not volume. ☐ This saucepan has a volume of two quarts.* **2.** the loudness of a sound. ☐ *Turn up the volume on the TV. I can hardly hear it. ☐ My neighbor likes to play her stereo at an ear-splitting volume.* **3.** a book, especially one book out of a series of books. ☐ *I consulted the D-E volume of the encyclopedia. ☐ The history text was a work in two volumes.*

volume control   a device that allows you to control the loudness of a television, radio, or stereo. ☐ *The volume control is this button here. ☐ I adjusted the volume control on the radio.*

W

wading pool a shallow structure containing water for walking and sitting in. (See also (SWIMMING) POOL.) □ *The kids played in the wading pool.* □ *I filled the plastic wading pool with water from the hose.*

wafer a small, flat, rigid object. □ *The ice cream is garnished with a sugar wafer.* □ *The technician etched a circuit onto a wafer of plastic.*

waffle cone a flat, ridged pastry folded into a cone. (WAFFLE CONES are often used to serve ice cream.) □ *I would like two scoops of chocolate on a waffle cone.* □ *The hot fudge yogurt sundae comes in a waffle cone.*

waffle iron a heated device for cooking waffles. □ *I poured batter onto the waffle iron.* □ *She opened the waffle iron and took out the fresh, hot waffles.*

wafflestompers sturdy shoes with thick, deeply ridged soles. □ *I wore my wafflestompers for hiking up the mountain.* □ *The wafflestompers gave me a good grip on the slippery trail.*

waistband a strip of cloth fitting around the waist; part of a garment. □ *The waistband on these pants is getting kind of tight on me.* □ *The skirt had a fancy embroidered waistband.*

walkie-talkie a hand-held device that can send and receive radio signals. (See also TWO-WAY RADIO.) □ *The hikers communicated via walkie-talkie.* □ *I used a walkie-talkie to radio my friend down the block.*

Walkman™ a brand of small, portable radio and cassette player with headphones, manufactured by Sony Electronics. □ *"Want to listen to my Walkman?" Mary offered.* □ *"I listen to his Walkman while I jog around the track," said Jim. "That way, I can keep up with the latest news."*

wall-mounted   solidly attached to a wall. □ *This wall-mounted electric can opener swings out of the way when not in use.* □ *The contractor gave me an estimate for putting in wall-mounted cabinets.*

wallpaper   paper for decorating walls. □ *I put up teddy bear wallpaper in the baby's room.* □ *Evenly spread the wallpaper paste on the back of the wallpaper.*

wallpaper paste   a substance used to stick WALLPAPER onto a wall. □ *Brush the back of the wallpaper with wallpaper paste.* □ *The wallpaper paste will take several hours to dry.*

wall socket   an ELECTRICAL RECEPTACLE set in a wall. □ *Please plug the vacuum cleaner into the wall socket.* □ *In our house, we have a wall socket every 6 feet along the wall.*

wall-to-wall carpet   carpeting that covers the entire floor of a room. □ *The apartment has wall-to-wall carpet.* □ *I want to install wall-to-wall carpet in the living room.*

warm-ups   loose, warm garments worn while exercising. (See also SWEATS.) □ *The dancers put on their warm-ups before dance class began.* □ *The jogger wore thick, fleecy warm-ups.*

warranty   a promise to repair or replace something if it breaks during a given time period. □ *The car comes with a 3-year warranty.* □ *We give a 90-day warranty on all our repairs.*

wash and wear   [of cloth] not needing to be ironed. □ *The store offers several lines of wash and wear clothing.* □ *These wash and wear blouses are great for travel.*

washcloth AND **washrag**   a piece of absorbent cloth used to wash the face and body. (WASHRAG is folksy.) □ *I worked soap into the washcloth.* □ *Do you have a washrag I can use?*

washer   **1.** a metal disc with a hole in the middle. (See also LOCK WASHER.) □ *Place a washer between the nut and the*

wood surface. □ *The sink faucet needs a new washer.* **2.** See
WASHING MACHINE.

washing machine AND **washer**   a machine for washing
clothes. □ *I put a load of laundry in the washing machine.*
□ *There are two washers and two dryers in the laundry
room.*

washrag   See WASHCLOTH.

waste(paper) basket   a container for garbage, especially
waste paper. □ *Where's your wastepaper basket? I need to
throw this away.* □ *I collected the trash from all the waste
baskets in the house.*

water closet   a room containing a TOILET. (British.) □
Where's the water closet? □ *The door of the water closet
was labeled "WC."*

water faucet   a tube out of which water from a plumbing
system can flow. □ *Oops! I left the water faucet running.* □
*Hook up the hose to the water faucet on the back wall of the
house.*

water glass   a glass for drinking water. □ *The waiter filled
my water glass.* □ *The set of crystal includes wineglasses
and water glasses.*

watering can   a spouted container for pouring water on
plants and the soil where they grow. □ *I watered the flowers
with a watering can.* □ *A gentle stream of water flowed from
the watering can onto the potted plant.*

water meter   a device that measures the amount of water
used in a building. □ *The water company reads our water
meter once a month.* □ *Where is the water meter located on
this house?*

Water Pik™   a brand of device that cleans the mouth with
a spray of water. □ *"The Water Pik keeps my teeth nice and
clean," said Jim.* □ *"Try using a Water Pik," the dentist
suggested.*

waterproof   not able to be damaged or dissolved by water. ☐ *I painted the deck with waterproof paint.* ☐ *This is a waterproof watch.*

water pump   a device that moves water and coolant through an engine in order to cool the cylinders. ☐ *The water pump is mounted on the engine block.* ☐ *There's a leak in the radiator hose near the water pump.*

water repellent   keeping water out. ☐ *This auto wax forms a water repellent finish.* ☐ *The raincoat is made of water repellent fabric.*

water resistant   able to keep some water out. ☐ *This watch is water resistant. You can wear it while you wash dishes, but it's not a good idea to wear it while you swim.* ☐ *Try this new water resistant make-up.*

water softener   a device that removes unwanted chemicals and particles from water. ☐ *I put a new block of salt in the water softener.* ☐ *This water softener attaches to the faucet.*

wax(ed) paper   paper coated with wax. ☐ *I wrapped the sandwich in waxed paper.* ☐ *Roll out the pastry dough on wax paper.*

weather radar   a device that uses radar to detect rain and snow. ☐ *I took a look at the weather radar on Channel 17 to see if there was any rain on the way.* ☐ *The weather radar showed tornadoes to the south.*

weather stripping   a strip of material used to seal the gap at the bottom of a door. ☐ *I fit plastic weather stripping into the groove beneath the door.* ☐ *There's a cold draft coming in under the door. We need some weather stripping.*

weather vane   a device that shows the direction of the wind. ☐ *According to the weather vane, it's a west wind out there.* ☐ *The weather vane turned gently in the faint breeze.*

webbing loosely woven or knitted material. □ *The carrying strap is made of cotton webbing.* □ *He attached the sleeping bag to his backpack with nylon webbing.*

weed **1.** an unwanted plant. □ *The vegetable garden is full of weeds.* □ *Weeds are taking over my backyard.* **2.** to remove unwanted plants. □ *Ellen's out weeding the flower bed.* □ *I weeded the garden every couple of days.*

Weed Eater™ a brand of device for trimming grass in a narrow space. (See also EDGER.) □ *"Run the Weed Eater around the edge of the lawn," I said to the young man who was mowing the lawn for me.* □ *"This Weed Eater is great for keeping grass trimmed along the sidewalk. You ought to get one," said Joe.*

weed whacker See EDGER.

weep hole a hole that allows water to pass through the bottom of a wall. □ *A length of pipe between the bricks formed a weep hole.* □ *The water was trickling out of the weep holes in the retaining wall.*

wet and dry vac See WET VAC.

wet vac AND **wet and dry vac** a device that uses suction to pick up both solids and liquids. (See also SHOP VAC.) □ *We used a wet vac to clean up the basement after the flood.* □ *The wet and dry vac will clean up that spill.*

wheat bread See (WHOLE) WHEAT BREAD.

wheat flour finely ground wheat. □ *You can use either wheat flour or rye flour in this recipe.* □ *Use two cups wheat flour and half a cup of rice flour.*

wheelbarrow a cart with a wheel in the front and two handles at the back. □ *I carried the manure out to the garden in a wheelbarrow.* □ *He pushed the wheelbarrow across the farmyard.*

wheel cover   See HUBCAP.

wheel well   the part of a car body into which a wheel fits. ☐ *The wheel well has rusted through.* ☐ *Mud from the dirt road was caked on the inside of the wheel well.*

whetstone   a smooth stone used for sharpening a blade. ☐ *I sharpened the knife with a whetstone.* ☐ *He gently rubbed the blade of his penknife on the whetstone.*

whipping cream   See HEAVY CREAM.

whipstitch   to make stitches that loop over the edge of a piece of cloth. ☐ *Whipstitch the edge of the fabric to keep it from ravelling.* ☐ *Whipstitch the arm of the sweater into the arm hole.*

whirlpool bath   a tub that can pump water through a jet, causing the water in the tub to whirl and bubble. ☐ *They had a whirlpool bath installed in their bathroom.* ☐ *There's a swimming pool and a whirlpool bath at the health club.*

whisk   to stir something with quick, energetic motions. ☐ *Whisk the eggs into the batter.* ☐ *Whisk a little cornstarch into the hot liquid.*

(white) bread   bread made from white, refined WHEAT FLOUR, which has had the wheat germ removed. ☐ *White bread is not as nutritious as whole wheat.* ☐ *What kind of bread would you like your sandwich on? White, whole wheat, rye, or sourdough?*

white glue   an opaque white adhesive that can be thinned and washed out with water. (See also ELMER'S™ GLUE.) ☐ *I bought some white glue for the kids to use for their school projects.* ☐ *You can use white glue to glue the boards together.*

white meat   meat from the breast and wings of a fowl. (Contrasts with DARK MEAT.) ☐ *MARY: What part of the bird would you like? TOM: Give me some white meat, please.* ☐ *The package of frozen chicken had pieces of both white meat and dark meat.*

white sauce   a sauce made of butter, flour, and milk. □ *White sauce is the base for many easy-to-make dishes.* □ *I added some cheese to the white sauce and poured it over the macaroni.*

whitewall   a tire with a white stripe on the edge where it meets the wheel. □ *Those whitewalls sure look sharp.* □ *I bought a set of whitewalls for my car.*

whiz   to mix something, especially a liquid, in a BLENDER. (Informal. See also BUZZ.) □ *Whiz the milk and ice cream in a blender.* □ *Pour the eggs, milk, and spices into a blender and whiz them for ten seconds or so.*

whole grain bread   bread made with flour that includes the whole grain, complete with germ and bran. □ *The bakery is famous for their whole grain bread.* □ *This whole grain bread is made with wheat, rye, oats, and corn.*

(whole) wheat bread   bread made with WHEAT FLOUR that includes the whole grain, complete with germ and bran. □ *I had a peanut-butter sandwich on whole wheat bread.* □ *Would you like your turkey sandwich on white or wheat bread?*

wick   a thick strand of absorbent material, especially one that is used to absorb and burn fuel. □ *I lit the lantern wick.* □ *The candle's wick had burned out.*

wide-angle lens   a camera lens that can fit a wide image into the picture. □ *The photographer needed a wide-angle lens to fit all the family members into the picture.* □ *I used a wide-angle lens to take a sweeping picture of the landscape.*

wiener   See FRANK(FURTER).

wild rice   an edible grass seed that resembles a long, brown grain of RICE. □ *The duck was served with a side dish of wild rice.* □ *Can I get your recipe for wild rice soup?*

winch   a device for pulling things using a rope or chain wrapped around a cylinder. □ *The winch on the back of the* *tow truck pulled the car out of the deep mud.* □ *We used a winch to pull the tree stump out of the ground.*

windbreaker   a short coat that protects the wearer from the wind. □ *I put on my windbreaker and grabbed an umbrella.* □ *You don't need a heavy coat. A windbreaker will do.*

window frame   a structure that holds window glass in a window opening. □ *The wooden window frame needed refinishing.* □ *The window frame held a sliding window, a window screen, and a storm window.*

(window)pane   a piece of flat glass set in a window. □ *I fitted a new windowpane into the sash.* □ *The window had a number of small, square panes.*

Windows™   a computer OPERATING SYSTEM from Microsoft Corporation. □ *The package says, "This word processor is designed to run under Windows."* □ *"All the machines in our office have Windows installed," the boss reported. "Now we need to train everyone on how to use it."*

window shade   a piece of material that can be pulled down to cover a window or rolled back up to uncover it. □ *The window shade in the bedroom matched the bedspread.* □ *The thick plastic window shade kept the room very dark.*

(window)sill   the horizontal structure across the bottom of a window. □ *A row of potted plants sat on the windowsill.* □ *Water was leaking in over the sill.*

window unit   an air conditioner that fits in a window. □ CHARLIE: *Do you have central air?* JANE: *No, we just have a couple of window units.* □ *I turned on the window unit and adjusted it to "High Cool."*

windshield   the front window of a car or truck. □ *Rain spattered against the windshield.* □ *I washed the dust off the windshield.*

(windshield) washer fluid   liquid for cleaning a WINDSHIELD. □ *This reservoir in the engine compartment holds* *windshield washer fluid.* □ *I pressed the button that squirted washer fluid onto the windshield.*

windshield wiper a device that wipes liquid off a WIND-SHIELD. □ *The windshield wipers swept back and forth across the windshield.* □ *It began to rain. I turned on the windshield wipers.*

wine cooler **1.** a device for keeping wine cold. (See also ICE BUCKET.) □ *He's a wine lover. He has a room-sized wine cooler in his basement.* □ *I kept the champagne in a wine cooler, waiting for the arrival of my guest.* **2.** a drink made of wine, fruit juice, and carbonated water. □ *I brought a six pack of wine coolers to the party.* □ *She sat on the porch, sipping a wine cooler.*

wing a section of a building that sticks out from the main part. □ *Modern paintings are displayed in the north wing of the museum.* □ *The executive offices are in a separate wing.*

wing nut AND **butterfly nut** a metal nut with two projecting tabs, designed to be tightened by thumb and forefinger. □ *Tighten the butterfly nut just two or three turns.* □ *The microphone stand is adjusted with a butterfly nut.*

wingtip (shoe) a shoe with a pointed decoration on the toe. □ *He wore brown wingtip shoes with his gray suit.* □ *I have a pair of wingtips for business wear.*

winter over [for a plant] to survive the winter. □ *Give the strawberry beds a good layer of mulch and they will winter over just fine.* □ *I brought the rhubarb into the greenhouse to winter over.*

wire rack See COOLING RACK.

wire stripper a tool for removing the plastic coating from wires. □ *I used the wire stripper to strip the coating off an inch at the end of the wire.* □ *The electrician stripped the wire with a wire stripper.*

wire whisk   a tool with several long loops of wire fixed in a handle; used for mixing food. □ *Beat the eggs with a wire whisk.* □ *Use a wire whisk to fold the blueberries into the batter.*

wishbone   a V-shaped bone from a fowl's breast. (According to superstition, if two people break a WISHBONE by pulling on the ends, the person who gets the larger piece will get his or her wish.) □ *I saved the wishbone from the chicken and gave it to the kids to pull.* □ *Who wants to pull the wishbone?*

Wite-Out™   a brand of CORRECTION FLUID. □ *"Do you have some Wite-Out?" Joe asked. "I just typed the wrong number." □ "Will this Wite-Out work on a photocopy?" Nancy wanted to know.*

wok   a wide-mouthed, round-bottomed cooking pan of a kind popular in China. □ *Stir fry the vegetables in a wok.* □ *Heat the wok over a high flame.*

wooden spoon   a broad spoon made of wood. □ *Blend the cookie batter with a wooden spoon.* □ *I used a wooden spoon to stir the soup in the pot.*

wood glue   glue designed to fasten wood to wood. □ *I mended the old chair with some wood glue and a few nails.* □ *Clamp the two pieces of wood together while the wood glue dries.*

wood screw   a screw designed to be fastened in wood. □ *This isn't a wood screw, it's a machine screw. It doesn't have a point at the end.* □ *I drilled a pilot hole slightly smaller than the wood screw I wanted to use.*

woofer   a device that converts electronic signals into low-pitched sounds; part of a SPEAKER. □ *This speaker has a 5-inch woofer.* □ *The bass notes from the woofer made the windows rattle.*

Woolite™   a brand of soap for washing delicate cloth. □ *"I wash my wool sweaters in Woolite," said Nancy. "I wouldn't* *use anything else." □ The label on these stockings says, "Rinse in warm water and Woolite."*

worcestershire sauce a dark brown sauce containing soy sauce, vinegar, anchovies, and other seasonings. (Pronounced WOOS-te-sheer sauce.) □ *I put a dash of worcestershire sauce in the tomato soup. □ Bill likes worcestershire sauce on steak.*

word processor a device or a computer program that allows you to correct and change written material before printing it on paper. □ *This computer program includes both a word processor and a database. □ The secretary is familiar with several different word processors.*

workbench a structure with a horizontal surface for working with tools. □ *The workbench has a vise attached. □ I keep my woodworking tools organized on a rack above the workbench.*

work gloves gloves worn to protect the hands while working. □ *The construction workers wore leather work gloves. □ I put on work gloves when I use machine tools.*

wrapping paper decorative paper used to wrap a gift. (See also GIFT WRAP.) □ *The wrapping paper had "Happy Birthday!" written on it in big, bright letters. □ I cut a piece of wrapping paper big enough to cover the box.*

wrecker See TOW TRUCK.

wrench a device with jaws for gripping and turning things. (See also ALLEN™ WRENCH, BOX-END WRENCH, COMBINATION WRENCH, HEX WRENCH, MONKEY WRENCH, OPEN-END WRENCH.) □ *I have a set of metric wrenches for working on my car. □ I found a wrench that would fit the nut.*

write protect tab a device on a computer disk that, when engaged, makes it impossible to make changes to the information on the disk. □ *Slide the write protect tab up to protect the files on the disk. □ I see why I can't save changes to the file. The write protect tab on the disk is engaged.*

wrought iron   iron bent into decorative shapes. □ A *wrought iron fence surrounded the yard.* □ *Just look at the wrought iron railing along the balcony.*

X

X-Acto™ knife   a brand of knife with thin, interchange-able blades, used for delicate work. □ *"Try an X-Acto knife for cutting out the pieces of the model airplane," Mom ad-vised.* □ *"Use an X-Acto knife to trim away the rough edges on the plastic," the directions said.*

Xerox™ machine   a brand of PHOTOCOPIER made by Xerox Corporation. (You may hear this word used as a verb.) □ *"I'll put the papers into the feed tray on the Xerox machine," Jim volunteered.* □ *"The Xerox machine is out of toner," he said a few minutes later.*

Y

yard　**1.** an area around a house. □ *She has a rock garden in her front yard.* □ *The kids are playing in the yard.* **2.** three feet. □ *I bought two yards of fabric.* □ *The window was about a yard wide.*

yardage　a quantity of something, given in YARDS. □ *The pattern lists the yardage of fabric necessary to make the outfit.* □ *You will need a substantial yardage of yarn to knit this sweater.*

yardstick　a flat stick three feet long, with inches and feet marked on it. □ *I measured the door with a yardstick.* □ *I lined up the yardstick against the top edge of the window.*

yogurt　a food made of milk with bacteria cultures added. □ *I had cherry yogurt for breakfast.* □ *You can substitute low-fat yogurt for sour cream in this recipe.*

yoke　part of a garment to which a gathered piece is attached. □ *The Western shirt had a satin yoke.* □ *This skirt has a close-fitting yoke and elegant, flared gores.*

Z

zest   the outer layer of the peel of a citrus fruit, such as a lemon or lime. ☐ *Add a teaspoon of lemon zest to the custard.* ☐ *The drink was flavored with the zest of a lime.*

zigzag stitch   a form of sewing in which the stitches meet in V-shapes. (Compare with STRAIGHT STITCH.) ☐ *This sewing machine can do a zigzag stitch in several different widths.* ☐ *I hemmed the knitted shirt with a zigzag stitch.*

Ziploc™   a brand of plastic bags that seal with a device like a ZIPPER. ☐ *"The leftovers are in the freezer in a Ziploc bag,"* Dad said. ☐ *"Ziploc bags are great for storing craft supplies," said the clerk at the craft store.*

zipper   a fastener that works by joining or separating two rows of small metal or plastic teeth. ☐ *Could you do up the zipper on my dress, please?* ☐ *The sleeping bag closes with a zipper.*

zipper foot   a device that holds a ZIPPER in place underneath a sewing machine needle; part of a sewing machine. ☐ *You'll need the zipper foot to sew the zipper onto those pants.* ☐ *Take off the regular presser foot and put on the zipper foot.*

zipper slide   the part of a ZIPPER that is grasped and pulled in order to join or separate the rows of teeth. ☐ *Rats! The zipper slide came off the zipper!* ☐ *My cold fingers fumbled for the zipper slide on my coat.*

zoom lens   a lens that allows you to keep an image in focus while you make it larger or smaller. ☐ *The filmmaker used a zoom lens to give the feeling of gradually moving closer to the house.* ☐ *I adjusted the zoom lens until the man's face filled my viewfinder.*

Topical Index

TOPICAL INDEX

APPLIANCE

A/C
agitator
alarm clock
appliance
basket
bathroom fixtures
beater
blade
blender
blow
bread machine
broiler
burner
coffee grinder
coffee maker
coffeepot
coffee urn
condenser coil
control
convection oven
crisper
Crockpot™
crumb tray
Cuisinart™
curling iron
cycle selector
dairy compartment
deep fryer
dehumidifier
dial
digital
dishwasher
display panel
Disposall™
drip coffee maker
drum
dryer
electric blanket
electric fan
electric knife
electric mixer
electric skillet
electric toothbrush
electric typewriter

electrical tape
espresso maker
exhaust fan
fan
food dehydrator
food processor
food warmer
freezer
frost free
garbage disposer
gas grill
hair dryer
hibachi
hot plate
hot tub
humidifier
ice cream freezer
ice maker
icebox
infusion coffeepot
iron
kitchen range
knife sharpener
lint trap
magnetron
microwave cart
microwave oven
microwave safe
Mixmaster™
outdoor grill
oven rack
oven thermometer
panel
pilot light
popcorn popper
preheat
rotisserie
selector
self-cleaning oven
self-defrosting
shop vac
soleplate
specifications
spin cycle
steam cleaner

steam iron
stove
toaster
trash compactor
upright vacuum cleaner
vacuum cleaner
vaporizer
wall socket
washer
Water Pik™
water softener
wet and dry vac
whiz
window unit

AUTOMOTIVE

A/C
accelerator pedal
access road
adapter
aerial
air filter
airbag
align
alternator
ambulance
antifreeze
auto reverse
automatic shut-off
axle
backup light
bench seat
bleed valve
blinker
brake caliper
brake fluid
brake light
brake line
brake pad
brake pedal
brake shoe
bucket seat
bumper
bus stop

snow plow
snow tire
snowmobile
solenoid
spare tire
spark plug
speedometer
splash guard
spoiler
sports car
stall
starter
station wagon
steering column
steering fluid
steering wheel
stop light
straight 8
street sweeper
sun roof
suspension
tachometer
taillight
tailpipe
taxi
throttle
tire
toll
traffic cone
trailer
transmission
tread
trunk
tune-up
turn over
V-8
valve stem
vapor lock
violation
water pump
wheel cover
wheel well
whitewall
windshield
wrecker

BATHROOM

absorbent

automatic
baby oil
basin
bath mat
bath towel
bathroom fixtures
bathroom tissue
bathtub
caulk
cleanser
clog
closet bend
clothes chute
deposits
detergent
disinfectant
diverter valve
drain
Drano™
electric toothbrush
faucet
finger towel
float
grout
guest towel
hand towel
laundry hamper
mop
paper towel
petroleum jelly
plumber's friend
plumber's helper
plumber's snake
polish
potty
rinse
safety rail
scouring pad
scrub brush
scrubber
seal
septic system
septic tank
sewage
shower curtain
shower head
shower rod
silicone
sink

sponge
spout
stack
steam
stopper
strainer
tap
toilet
toilet tissue
trap
vanity
washrag
waste paper basket
water closet
water faucet
Water Pik™
whirlpool bath

BICYCLE

air pump
axle
bicycle chain
brake caliper
brake pad
brake pedal
brake shoe
chain guard
changer
coaster brakes
derailleur
fender
flat tire
fork
gear stick
hand brake
handgrip
handlebar
headlight
inner tube
kickstand
mountain bike
odometer
open-end wrench
panier
pedal
pivot
racing bike
reflector

rim
rust remover
saddle
sidewall
spanner
spoke
sprocket
stem
strip
tandem bicycle
ten-speed bicycle
tire
touring bicycle
training wheels
tricycle
valve

CAMERA

auto focus
black and white
cable release
cartridge
color
diaphragm
disc camera
exploded view
exposure
eye cup
F-stop
film advance
fisheye lens
flash bulb
focus
hot shoe
Instamatic™
leader
lens
light meter
negative
photocell
point and shoot
Polaroid™
rangefinder
sensor
shutter
slide
SLR
spindle

still
swivel
35 mm
telephoto lens
tripod
twin lens reflex
viewfinder
wide-angle lens
zoom lens

CHEMICAL

acetaminophen
acetate
acetone
acid
additive
aerosol
alkaline
ammonia
antacid
antibiotic
antifreeze
antihistamine
antioxidant
antiseptic
aspirin
baking soda
battery
beeswax
bicarbonate of soda
bug spray
caplet
capsule
CO_2 extinguisher
CO detector
coolant
corrosion
de-icer
decongestant
disinfectant
distilled water
drain opener
Drano™
drugstore
dry cell
dry-clean
electrode
emission

enamel
ExLax™
eye drops
fertilizer
fixative
Formica™
Freon™
fungicide
gas
gelcap
hard water
herbicide
ibuprofen
insecticide
laminate
latex paint
laxative
lighter
Mace™
melt
Mercurochrome™
milk of magnesia
mouthwash
Mylar™
Naugahyde™
Nicad™ battery
nylon
octane
oil finish
ointment
OTC
pain killer
pain reliever
paint remover
paint thinner
Pepto-Bismol™
pesticide
pestle
petroleum jelly
pH
plant food
Plastic Wood™
Plexiglas™
polyester
polyurethane
porous
preservative
propane torch
Raid™

blower
boiler
BTU
C/A
central heating
circulating pump
compressor
condenser coil
convector
coolant
cooling coil
dehumidifier
dew point
electric blanket
electric fan
exhaust fan
fan
forced air heat
Freon™
furnace
gas
hardy plant
heat exchanger
heat pump
hot water heat
hot water pipe
humidifier
hygrometer
main
radiator
refrigerant
return duct
safety valve
shut-off valve
solar panel
steam heat
supply duct
thermocouple
thermostat
vaporizer
window unit

CLOTHING

accessory
acetate
appliqué
apron
athletic shoes

backpack
bias
blazer
blouse
bluing
boat neck
bodice
bottom
brassiere
briefs
broadcloth
bureau
burlap
button
button-down collar
cambric
camisole
cap
cardigan
cheesecloth
chinos
cleat
clog
clothes chute
clothesline
clothespin
crew neck
crimp
cuff
culottes
dart
denim
dolman sleeve
drawstring
dry-clean
dryer
drying rack
ease
eyelet
fabric softener
facing
fanny pack
fastener
flannel
flat-felled seam
flats
fly
French curve
fringe

fusible interfacing
fusible web
gather
gingham
gore
gusset
hem
high heels
hook and eye
hook and loop fastener
hosiery
insulation
interfacing
iron
Jams™
jersey
jumper
kick pleat
lapel
launder
laundry bag
laundry basket
laundry detergent
laundry hamper
laundry room
leggings
Levi's™
lingerie
lint
machine washable
mandarin collar
manufacturer
maternity clothes
mercerized
mitten
muffler
muslin
nap
Naugahyde™
neutral
nylon
one size fits all
outerwear
Oxford cloth
pantyhose
patch pocket
penny loafers
Perma-Prest™
permanent press

Peter Pan collar
pile
placket
pleat
plus size
polo shirt
polyester
pre-shrunk
press
prewash
pullover
pumps
quilted
raglan sleeve
ravel
rayon
ruffle
sash
scarf
scoop neck
Scotchgard™
seam
separates
set-in sleeve
shawl collar
sheath
sheer
shell
shirt cardboard
shirt tail
sideseam pocket
slash pocket
sleeve
slip
snap
sneakers
snow pants
sports jacket
starch
staystitch
steam iron
stud
suit jacket
swatch
sweat socks
sweater
sweatpants
sweats
T shirt

tab collar
tailor's chalk
tailored
tank top
taper
tennies
terry cloth
three-quarter sleeve
tights
tongue
top
tread
trim
tunic
turtleneck
tweed
twill
unisex
upper
V neck
Velcro™
velour
velvet
vent
viscose
wafflestompers
waistband
warm-ups
wash and wear
washer
water repellent
water resistant
waterproof
webbing
windbreaker
wingtip shoe
Woolite™
work gloves
yoke
zipper

**COMMUNICA-
TIONS**

AM
answering machine
antenna
band
baud rate

beacon
beeper
big screen TV
bullhorn
cable ready
cable television
caller ID
camcorder
CATV
CB radio
cellular phone
channel
coaxial cable
cordless telephone
cradle
dial tone
digital
e-mail
800 number
earphones
earpiece
EBB
encrypt
exploded view
fax
hailer
ham radio
handset
headphones
headset
hold button
hookup
ID
interactive
intercom
interference
internet
LAN
magazine
mail box
mail drop
mail merge
mail slot
mailer
mailing label
manual
modem
modular jack
mouthpiece

multimedia
900 number
on line
online
operating system
owner's manual
PA
PC
periodical
phone card
political map
projection TV
redial
relief map
Rolodex™
rotary dial
shortwave radio
speaker
speed dial
static
switch hook
tone
touch tone
transceiver
TV
two-way radio
user interface
walkie-talkie

COMPUTER

accessory
adapter
arrow key
ASCII
automatic feed
backspace key
backup
baud rate
bit
boldface
boot up
bus wire
byte
CAD
CAM
carriage return
CD-ROM
Centronics™ cable

character
click on something
coaxial cable
compatible
computer paper
contrast
crash
CRT
Ctrl
cursor
cut
daisy wheel
digital
database
dedicated
desktop computer
desktop publishing
dialog box
directory
disk drive
document
DOS™
dot matrix printer
double click on something
download
driver
dumb terminal
e-mail
EBB
edit
eject
encrypt
enter
environment
error message
escape key
Excel™
expansion slot
extension
faulty
fax modem
feature
FF
file
floppy disk
folder
font
footer
form letter

function key
glitch
global
graphics
hard disk
hard drive
hardware
header
highlight
hookup
IBM™
icon
inkjet printer
install
interactive
internet
italic
key
kilobyte
LAN
laptop computer
laser paper
laser printer
LCD
letter-quality
LF
Macintosh™
macro
mail merge
margin
math coprocessor
megabyte
menu
microprocessor
mode
monitor
mouse
multimedia
notebook computer
num lock key
on line
on/off switch
online
operating system
OS/2™
overload
palmtop
paper bail
parallel port

parity
password
paste
PC
peripheral
plain text
print head
printer
printout
prong
protocol
pull-down menu
RAM
reboot
reset
resolution
RGB
ribbon
ROM
root directory
scanner
scroll
serial cable
serial port
service
shell
shift key
software
sound card
space bar
spell checker
spool
spreadsheet
sprocket
subdirectory
subscript
superscript
system crash
tab
terminal
text file
trackball
turbo
tutorial
typeface
upgrade
upload
upper case
user's manual

user friendly
user interface
Windows™
word processor
write protect tab

CONSTRUCTION

abutment
apron
armature
awning
backhoe
baffle
balcony
balustrade
barbed wire
base coat
baseboard
basement
berm
bevel
Bobcat™
bow window
breezeway
broom closet
built-in
bulldozer
C/A
carpenter's level
carpenter's square
casement window
catwalk
caulk
central heating
cesspool
chain link fence
chain saw
chimney
chipboard
chisel
coping
cornice
cramp
crawl space
Cyclone™ fence
dado
dam
deck

dike
ditch
doorjamb
doorstep
dormer window
double-hung window
dowel
downspout
drain
drawbridge
drywall
duct
eaves
elevator
end grain
entryway
faceplate
fanlight
fascia
fatigue
fence post
firebrick
fireplace
flier
flights of stairs
floor joist
footbridge
Formica™
foundation
foyer
freight elevator
French door
front porch
furnace
gallery
garage door opener
garbage chute
gate
girder
glazing
grain
grout
gutter
hammer
handrail
hardwood floor
infill
install
insulation

DISHES

dish soap
dish towel
dishwasher safe
drying rack
egg cup
finger bowl
flan ring
flask
gravy boat
ice tongs
liqueur glass
microwave safe
microwaveable
muffin stand
muffin tin
mug
napkin holder
napkin ring
oven rack
ovenproof
paper cup
paper plate
pie plate
pie shell
pie tin
pitcher
platter
ramekin
ring mold
roaster
saucepan
saucer
sauté pan
shotglass
side dish
silver plate
springform mold
squeeze bottle
stemware
sugar bowl
tea service
tea set
teapot
thermos bottle
trifle bowl
tumbler
Tupperware™
tureen
water glass

ELECTRICAL

a/b switch
adapter
alkaline battery
alternator
baseboard heat
battery
blow
bus wire
ceiling fan
cell
chandelier
circuit
compressor
condenser coil
continuity tester
control
cooling coil
cover plate
current
DC
diaphragm
diode
distributor
dry cell
electric blanket
electric fan
electric knife
electric meter
electric razor
electric receptacle
electric skillet
electric toothbrush
electric typewriter
electrical outlet
electrical tape
electrode
extension cord
fan
filament
fluorescent bulb
fuse
fusible element
glass insulator
gooseneck lamp
ground
heating element
heating pad
hookup

hot slot
hot wire
housing
incandescent bulb
junction box
light rail
lineman's pliers
long-life bulb
Mixmaster™
multimeter
Nicad™ battery
on/off switch
overload
portable generator
potentiometer
power cord
power drill
power saw
power tool
rechargeable battery
ribbon cable
safety valve
self-timer
service panel
short circuit
socket
solenoid
spark plug
steam iron
switch
terminal
three-way bulb
three-way switch
timer
track lighting
trip
underwriter's knot
voltmeter
wire stripper

ELECTRONICS

a/b switch
accessory
adapter
aerial
amp
analog
answering machine

tuner
turbo
turntable
TV
tweeter
two-way radio
UHF
UPC
user's manual
VCR
VHF
VHS™
videotape
vinyl
volume
walkie-talkie
Walkman™
woofer

FOOD

à la mode
additive
alligator pear
allspice
angel food cake
appetizer
apple corer
artificial sweetener
aspic
baby bottle
baby food
baby formula
bacon bits
bagel
Baggies™
bake
baking mix
baking pan
baking powder
baking soda
bar cookie
barbecue
baste
batter
beat
beverage
bicarbonate of soda
biscuit

bisque
Bisquick™
blanch
blend
boil
bouillon
braise
bran
bread
breast
brine
bring something to a boil
brisket
broil
broth
brown
brunch
buckwheat
buffet
bulb baster
bulk
Bundt™ pan
bushel
butter
buzz
Caesar salad
cake
calorie
canapé
carving fork
carving knife
casserole
cereal
chafing dish
cheese board
cheese plane
cheese slicer
cheesecloth
cherry stoner
cherry tomato
Chicago-style
chili
chopper
chowder
chuck roast
cleaver
clove
cobbler
cocoa

coffee cake
coffee can
coffee cone
coffee filter
coffee grinder
coffee grounds
coffee maker
coffeepot
coffee scoop
coffee urn
cola
cold cut
cole slaw
concentrate
condensed milk
condiment
confectioner's sugar
convenience store
cookie cutter
cookie gun
cookie press
cookie sheet
cookware
cooler
core
corn syrup
corned beef
Corning Ware™
cottage cheese
coupon
cream
crepe
Crisco™
crisp
Crockpot™
croquette
crouton
crumb
crust
Cuisinart™
cupcake
custard
cut in
cutlery
cutting board
dairy compartment
dark meat
dash
decorating bag

spoon
spork
spread
sprig
springform mold
sprout
squeeze bottle
stalk
starch
steak sauce
steam
steep
stem
Sterno™
stew
stir
stock
stove
strainer
stuffing
sugar cone
sugar cube
sugar packet
sugar tongs
supermarket
Sweet'n Low™
sweet pickle
sweetbread
sweetened condensed milk
Tabasco™ sauce
tart
Tater Tots™
tea bag
tea ball
tea cozy
teakettle
Teflon™
temperature probe
tenderizer
thaw
thicken
thin
tin foil
toast
tongs
topping
tortilla
tossed salad

trivet
tuna salad
turkey burger
turnover
TV dinner
unrefined sugar
utensil
utility knife
vegetable brush
Velveeta™
vinegar
wafer
waffle cone
waffle iron
waxed paper
wheat flour
whipping cream
whisk
white bread
white meat
white sauce
whiz
whole grain bread
whole wheat bread
wiener
wild rice
wine cooler
wire rack
wire whisk
wishbone
wok
wooden spoon
worcestershire sauce
yogurt
zest
Ziploc™

FURNITURE

area rug
ashtray
bedpost
bedstead
booster seat
box spring
breakfast nook
breakfront
buffet
bureau

butcher block
café curtains
café rod
caning
card table
carpet cleaner
caster
ceiling fan
chaise longue
chest of drawers
china cabinet
counter
crib
cushion
damper pedal
deck chair
decor
draperies
drawer
drop leaf table
dust ruffle
easy chair
faux finish
finial
folding chair
footboard
footstool
Formica™
fringe
full bed
furniture polish
gate leg table
gooseneck lamp
grandfather clock
hammock
harp
headboard
high chair
Hollywood bed
hutch
indoor/outdoor carpeting
king-size bed
kitchen cabinet
kitchen table
lampshade
lawn chair
linseed oil
love seat
mattress

microwave cart
miniblind
Murphy bed
Naugahyde™
oil finish
ottoman
padding
parquetry
piano bench
Portacrib™
pull-out sofa
queen-size bed
recliner chair
reupholster
runner
rush bottomed
Scotchgard™
shelf paper
shellac
side rail
sideboard
single pedestal table
sleeper sofa
slipcover
stuffing
sustain pedal
twin bed
upholstery
valance
vanity
velour
veneer

GARDEN

acid
alkaline
annual
AstroTurf™
bulb
bushel
cold frame
compost
cover crop
ditch
dwarf variety
espalier
fertilizer
flat

flowerpot
garden clippers
garden hose
hardy plant
hedge
herb
hoe
houseplant
John Deere™
lawn mower
loam
manure
mulch
organic
peat
perennial
pesticide
pH
pitchfork
plant food
planter
porous
prune
pruning shears
push mower
raised bed
rake
riding mower
runner
seeder
self-seeding
shrub
slip
slug
sod
spade
spading fork
sprig
sprinkle
sprout
stalk
start
stem
subsoil
tendril
thin
tiller
topiary
topsoil

tractor
tree stump
trellis
trowel
trunk
vermiculite
watering can
weed
wheelbarrow
winter over
yard

HAIR CARE

barrette
bluing
bobby pin
bristle
clip
curling iron
hair clip
hair coloring
hair conditioner
hair dryer
hair net
hair pin
hair roller
hair spray
hot rollers
knot
ribbon
shampoo

HARDWARE

aerator
air pump
Aquastat
awl
axe
ballpeen hammer
beater
belt sander
binder
blade
bleed valve
bolt
box-end wrench
brace and bit

HEALTH

bifocals
bran
breath mint
bug spray
cake
caplet
capsule
castor oil
Chap Stick™
cleanser
contraceptive
cotton swab
daily wear contact lens
decongestant
deodorant
dietary fiber
disinfectant
drugstore
electric toothbrush
enamel
ExLax™
eyedrops
feminine hygiene
feminine napkin
fungicide
gelcap
health food
heating pad
ibuprofen
Kleenex™
laxative
lens
lotion
Mercurochrome™
milk of magnesia
mouthwash
nail clipper
nail scissors
ointment
organic
OTC
pain killer
pain reliever
paramedic
Pepto-Bismol™
petroleum jelly
pharmacy
probe
Q-Tip™

rinse
rubbing alcohol
sanitary pad
sauna
seal
sliver
sponge
suppository
tablet
tampon
temple
throat lozenge
tooth floss
toothpick
tranquilizer
twist-off cap
Tylenol™
unrefined sugar
Vaseline™
Water Pik™
whirlpool bath

HOME

a/b switch
A/C
à la mode
absorbent
accessory
acid
adapter
additive
adhesive
aerator
aerial
aerosol
afghan
aftershave
agitator
air duct
air ionizer
air pump
alarm clock
alkaline
alligator pear
allspice
amp
andiron
angel food cake

annual
answering machine
antenna
appetizer
apple corer
appliance
apron
Aquastat
area rug
armature
artificial sweetener
ashtray
aspic
attic
automatic
awning
baby bottle
baby food
baby oil
baby powder
bacon bits
bagel
Baggies™
bake
baking mix
baking pan
baking powder
baking soda
balcony
balustrade
bar cookie
barbecue
barbed wire
base coat
baseboard
basement
basin
basket
baste
bath mat
bath towel
bathroom fixtures
bathroom tissue
bathtub
batter
beat
bed linen
bedclothes
bedpost

egg topper
egg white
egg yolk
eggbeater drill
electric blanket
electric fan
electric knife
electric mixer
electric razor
electric skillet
electric toothbrush
electrical outlet
electrical tape
Elmer's™ glue
enamel
end grain
English muffin
entertainment system
entryway
environment
escutcheon plate
espalier
espresso
ethnic food
evaporated milk
exhaust fan
extract
eye
fabric softener
faceplate
fan
farina
fascia
fastener
fatigue
faucet
faulty
faux finish
feather duster
feature
fence post
fertilizer
fillet
filling
finger bowl
finger food
finger towel
finial
fire extinguisher

fire iron
firebrick
fireplace
fish burger
fish poacher
fish scaler
fish stick
fitted sheet
fitting
fixings
flan ring
flange
flask
flat sheet
flatware
flier
flights of stairs
float
floor joist
flour
flowerpot
flue
fluorescent bulb
flush
fold
fondue
food coloring
food dehydrator
food mill
food processor
food warmer
footboard
footstool
forced air heat
Formica™
foundation
foyer
freezer
French door
French fries
Freon™
fricassee
fringe
fritter
front porch
frost free
frosting
fruit leather
fry

full bed
funnel
furnace
furniture polish
fuse
fusible element
gadget
gallery
garage
garbage chute
garbage disposer
garbage pail
garden clippers
garden hose
garlic press
garnish
gas
gate
giblets
girder
gizzard
glaze
glazing
glue stick
go off
gooseneck lamp
graham cracker
graham flour
grain
grandfather clock
granny fork
granola
granulated sugar
grate
gravy
grease
Greek salad
griddle
grill
grinder
grits
grout
guest towel
gutter
hair roller
half-and-half
hamburger
hammer
hammock

protective goggles
prune
pruning shears
pudding
pull-out sofa
pulley
pulp
pumpernickel
pumpkin pie spice
punch
push mower
putty
PVC pipe
quarter
queen-size bed
quick bread
quilt
quoin
rabbit ears
rack of lamb
radiator
rafter
Raid™
raised bed
rake
ramekin
ranch dressing
rancid
range hood
raw sugar
razor
recliner chair
recycle
recycling bin
red meat
refinish
refrigerant
refrigerator cookie
relish
reservoir
return duct
reupholster
rice
riding mower
rind
ring mold
rinse
riser
roast

roll
rotary beater
rotary cutter
rotisserie
round
rubber lid grip
rubber spatula
ruffle
rump roast
run
rush bottomed
rust remover
rye bread
safety rail
safety valve
salad dressing
salad spinner
salsa
salt shaker
salt substitute
saltine cracker
sander
sandpaper
Sanka™
sash
satin finish
saucepan
saucer
sauna
sauté
sauté pan
sawhorse
scald
scant
scissors
scoop
scorch
Scotch™ tape
Scotchgard™
scouring pad
scrambled eggs
scratching post
scrub brush
scrubber
seal
sear
season
sediment
seeder

selector
self-cleaning oven
self-defrosting
self-healing
self-rising flour
self-seeding
self-timer
semisweet chocolate
sensor
septic system
septic tank
serial number
serrated
service
serving
sewage
shakes
shampoo
sharpener
shaving cream
shears
sheer
Sheetrock™
shelf paper
shell
shingle
shop vac
short circuit
short ribs
shortening
shortwave radio
shotglass
shovel
shower curtain
shower head
shred
shrub
shuck
shut-off valve
shutter
side dish
side panel
side rail
sideboard
siding
sieve
silicone
silver
simmer

KITCHEN

water glass
waxed paper
wheat flour
whipping cream
whisk
white bread
white meat
white sauce
whiz
whole grain bread
whole wheat bread
wiener
wild rice
wine cooler
wire rack
wire whisk
wishbone
wok
wooden spoon
worcestershire sauce
yogurt
zest
Ziploc™

LINENS
afghan
bath towel
beach towel
bed linen
bedclothes
bedspread
candlewick
canopy
comforter
counterpane
dish towel
draperies
dust ruffle
duvet
electric blanket
finger towel
fitted sheet
flat sheet
guest towel
hand towel
kitchen towel
linen closet
mattress pad

napkin
paper napkin
paper towel
pile
pillow sham
press cloth
quilt
ruffle
runner
sheer
shower curtain
table linen
tea cozy
terry cloth
terry towel
thread count
throw
washrag

MACHINERY
backhoe
Bobcat™
bulldozer
compressor
furnace
garage door opener
incinerator
John Deere™
manual
mulching mower
overhaul
owner's manual
push mower
riding mower
rotor
snowblower
snowplow
street sweeper
valve
winch

MAIL
aerogram
commemorative stamp
e-mail
fax
mail box

mail drop
mail merge
mail order
mail slot
mailer
mailing label
manila envelope
manila folder
packing material
postage meter
postage scale
return address
roll
self-stick

MATERIALS
adhesive
armature
barbed wire
baseboard
caulk
chain link fence
chipboard
coaxial cable
Cyclone™ fence
dowel
drywall
Elmer's™ glue
firebrick
flash
floor joist
foundation
girder
glazing
glue stick
grout
hardwood floor
infill
insulation
knot
laminate
latex paint
linseed oil
louvers
lumber
masonry
matte
miter

molding
mortar
mortise and tenon
Naugahyde™
nylon
oil finish
panel
parquetry
partition wall
peg
picket fence
pipe
plank
Plastic Wood™
Plexiglas™
pliable
plywood
polyester
polyurethane
popsicle stick
porous
post-consumer
potpourri
pulp
putty
quoin
recycle
recycling bin
refinish
sealant
season
set
shakes
Sheetrock™
shim
shingle
siding
silicone
sizing
slat
solder
spackling
sponge
steel wool
stud
Styrofoam™
timber
white glue
wood glue

wrought iron

MEASURE

alarm clock
align
anemometer
ascending order
automatic
barometer
baud rate
bevel
BTU
bulk
bushel
byte
calculator
calorie
carpenter's level
carpenter's square
clock radio
coffee scoop
continuity tester
cross section
crosswise
CST
current
Daylight savings time
descending order
dew point
dial
digital display
digital watch
dipstick
dispenser
dollop
dry measure
economy size
egg timer
electric meter
EST
flush
gas gauge
gas meter
grandfather clock
gross
hp
hygrometer
in season

ISBN
jigger
kilobyte
knot
lengthwise
level
light meter
liquid measure
lukewarm
math coprocessor
measuring tape
meat thermometer
megabyte
metronome
micrometer
MST
multimeter
odometer
oven thermometer
Pacific standard time
parity
parking meter
peck
pH
pinch
plumb
postage meter
postage scale
potentiometer
preheat
quarter
scant
score
self-timer
serving
sewing gauge
shotglass
snooze button
speedometer
tablespoon
tachometer
tape counter
tape measure
teaspoon
temperature probe
thermostat
time zone
timer
voltmeter

volume
water meter
yard

MUSIC

amp
cartridge
cassette
CD
changer
clock radio
counterweight
crank
cueing
damper pedal
Dolby™
dub
elevator music
entertainment system
EP
equalizer
45
fast-forward
head cleaner
interference
jack
line in jack
loudness control
LP
metronome
microcassette
mike
multimedia
Muzak™
needle
phonograph
piano bench
piano hammer
piano key
piano string
piped music
playback
record
rewind
78
scan
selector
sleeve

SLP
sound card
SP
static
stereo
stylus
subwoofer
supply reel
sustain pedal
synthesizer
take up reel
tape counter
tape head
tone
turntable
tweeter
vinyl
woofer

OFFICE

adhesive
appliance
automatic feed
ballpoint pen
barrel
binder
boldface
carriage
cartridge
copy machine
correction fluid
desktop publishing
electric typewriter
Elmer's™ glue
fax
flap
folder
form letter
fountain pen
graphics
hanging file
highlighter pen
holepunch
ink cartridge
key
laminate
laser paper
letterhead

Liquid Paper™
lobby
logo
looseleaf paper
mail merge
mailer
mailing label
manila envelope
manila folder
manual typewriter
margin
masking tape
mechanical pencil
modem
modular jack
office paper
office supplies
on line
on off switch
online
overhaul
paper bail
paper clip
paste
PC
pencil sharpener
Pendaflex™
perforated
personal organizer
platen
portable generator
punch
push pin
redrope
return address
ribbon
Rolodex™
rubber cement
Scotch™ tape
sharpener
shift key
signature block
space bar
spreadsheet
staple
stationery
swivel
tab
thermal paper

three-hole punch
three-ring binder
thumb tack
toner
typographical error
view graph
white glue
Windows™
wing
Wite-Out™
word processor
X-Acto knife™
Xerox™ machine

PERSONAL CARE

Ace™ bandage
acetaminophen
aftershave
antacid
antibiotic
antihistamine
antioxidant
antiperspirant
antiseptic
aspirin
baby oil
baby powder
baking soda
Band Aid™
barrette
bathroom tissue
bathtub
bicarbonate of soda
bifocals
bobby pin
breath mint
bug spray
cake
caplet
capsule
castor oil
Chap Stick™
contact lens
contraceptive
cosmetics
cotton swab
curling iron
daily wear contact lens

decongestant
deodorant
depilatory
drugstore
electric razor
emery board
enamel
ExLax™
eyedrops
feminine hygiene
feminine napkin
(finger)nail file
fungicide
gelcap
hair clip
hair coloring
hair conditioner
hair dryer
hair net
hair pin
hair roller
hair spray
heating pad
hot rollers
ibuprofen
Kleenex™
laxative
lens
lotion
make-up
matte
Mercurochrome™
milk of magnesia
mouthwash
nail clipper
nail scissors
ointment
OTC
pain killer
pain reliever
paramedic
Pepto-Bismol™
petroleum jelly
pharmacy
polish
Q-Tip™
razor
ribbon
rinse

rubbing alcohol
sanitary pad
sauna
shampoo
shaving cream
stud
suppository
tablet
tampon
temple
throat lozenge
toiletries
tooth floss
toothpick
tranquilizer
Tylenol™
Vaseline™
Water Pik™
whirlpool bath

PETS

flea collar
kitty litter
scratching post

PLUMBING

basin
bathtub
bleed valve
cesspool
clog
closet bend
cold water pipe
coupling
crawl space
diverter valve
drain
Drano™
escutcheon plate
faucet
faulty
fitting
flange
float
gasket
hard water
hot tub

hot water heater
hot water pipe
lock washer
main
O-ring
P-trap
pipe
plumber's friend
plumber's helper
plumber's snake
potty
prime a pump
PVC pipe
safety valve
seal
septic system
septic tank
sewage
shower head
shut-off valve
sink
soft water
spout
stack
standpipe
stopper
sump pump
supply line
tap
thermocouple
toilet
trap
washer
water closet
water faucet
water meter
water softener
whirlpool bath

PRINTING

accessory
adapter
automatic feed
boldface
Centronics™ cable
computer paper
daisy wheel
desktop publishing

dot matrix printer
driver
fax
FF
font
ink cartridge
inkjet printer
ISBN
italic
laser paper
laser printer
letter-quality
LF
logo
lower case
magazine
mailing label
manual
margin
office paper
office supplies
on line
on/off switch
online
owner's manual
paper bail
parallel port
PC
periodical
peripheral
print head
printer
printout
resolution
ribbon
scanner
serial cable
serial port
signature block
spine
subscript
superscript
toner
typeface
typographical error
upper case
user's manual
volume
Xerox™ machine

RECREATION

AstroTurf™
athletic shoes
cleat
elevator music
entertainment system
fishhook
hot tub
inboard motor
inner tube
mountain bike
Muzak™
pedal
piped music
projection TV
racing bike
remote control
sneakers
snowmobile
sports car
swimming pool
tandem bicycle
ten-speed bicycle
tennies
touring bicycle
training wheels
tricycle
wading pool
warm-ups

SAFETY

airbag
beacon
bumper
burglar alarm
CO_2 extinguisher
CO detector
dead bolt
dishwasher safe
fire alarm
fire extinguisher
fire plug
flare
four ways
go off
guard rail
hair net
hand brake

hasp
hot pad
keyless lock
latch
lock
microwave safe
oven mitt
ovenproof
padlock
parking brake
password
peekhole
Plexiglas™
protective goggles
railroad crossing
reflector
safety
seat belt
smoke detector
sprinkler
standpipe
water repellent
water resistant
waterproof

SECURITY

burglar alarm
dead bolt
encrypt
key
latch
lock
padlock
password
peekhole
PIN
safety
seat belt
serial number
ski rack
smoke detector
tumbler

SEWING

appliqué
backstitch
baste

bias
bobbin
broadcloth
burlap
button
cambric
chalk
clip
crimp
dart
ease
eye
facing
flannel
flat-felled seam
French curve
fusible interfacing
fusible web
gather
gingham
gore
gusset
hem
interfacing
jersey
measuring tape
mercerized
muslin
nap
needle
notions
patch pocket
pattern
pedal
pin cushion
pink
pleat
presser foot
quilt
raglan sleeve
ravel
ribbon
rotary cutter
scissors
seam
self-healing
selvage
set-in sleeve
sewing gauge

shank button
shears
sideseam pocket
sleeve cap
spool
staystitch
straight stitch
stuffing
swatch
tailor's chalk
thimble
thread count
throat plate
topstitch
tracing wheel
whipstitch
yard
yoke
zigzag stitch
zipper foot

SHOPPING

accessory
bar code
blister pack
brand
bulk
card reader
cash register
check-out line
check cashing card
cold storage
comparison shop
consumer electronics
convenience store
coupon
courtesy booth
curb service
deli-style
delicatessen
department store
deposit
dime store
discount store
disposable
drive-in
drugstore
economy size

fast-food
feature
five and ten cent store
flat
full-service
generic
gift box
gift wrap
grocery store
guarantee
health food
hosiery
housewares
lingerie
mail order
manufacturer
model
OTC
outerwear
packing material
pharmacy
plus size
poultry
produce
proof of purchase
rebate
receipt
scanner
self-serve
separates
service
shrinkwrap
side panel
six pack
supermarket
swatch
trial size
twist tie
unisex
unit
UPC
variety store
warranty
wrapping paper

SPORTS

AstroTurf™
athletic shoes

cleat
fishhook
inboard motor
inner tube
pedal
racing bike
sneakers
snowmobile
swimming pool
ten-speed bicycle
tennies
touring bicycle
wading pool
warm-ups

STATIONERY

aerogram
ballpoint pen
barrel
binder
brad
cash register tape
computer paper
correction fluid
flap
folder
fountain pen
highlighter pen
ink cartridge
letterhead
Liquid Paper™
logo
looseleaf paper
mailer
mailing label
manila envelope
manila folder
manual typewriter
masking tape
mechanical pencil
mucilage
office paper
office supplies
packing tape
paper clip
personal organizer
redrope
self-stick

stationery
tablet
three-ring binder

STRUCTURE

abutment
air duct
armature
attic
awning
balcony
balustrade
bow window
bracket
breezeway
built-in
bumper
casement window
catwalk
chain link fence
chimney
chipboard
clothesline
coping
cornice
counter
cramp
crawl space
dam
deck
dike
doorjamb
dormer window
double-hung window
downspout
drainpipe
drawbridge
drywall
duct
eaves
elevator
entryway
fireplace
flier
flights of stairs
floor joist
flue
footboard